MIGRANT HEARTS AND
THE ATLANTIC RETURN

MIGRANT HEARTS AND THE ATLANTIC RETURN

Transnationalism and the Roman Catholic Church

Valentina Napolitano

Fordham University Press

New York   2016

Frontispiece: Virgen Dolorosa, Church of Santa Maria Della Luce. Photo by the author.

Fordham University Press has no responsibility for the persistence or accuracy of URLs for external or third-party Internet websites referred to in this publication and does not guarantee that any content on such websites is, or will remain, accurate or appropriate.

Fordham University Press also publishes its books in a variety of electronic formats. Some content that appears in print may not be available in electronic books.

Visit us online at www.fordhampress.com.

Library of Congress Cataloging-in-Publication Data

Napolitano, Valentina.
    Migrant hearts and the Atlantic return : transnationalism and the Roman Catholic Church / Valentina Napolitano. — 1st ed.
       pages   cm
    Includes bibliographical references and index.
    ISBN 978-0-8232-6748-4 (cloth : alk. paper) —
ISBN 978-0-8232-6749-1 (pbk. : alk. paper)
    1. Emigration and immigration—Religious aspects—Catholic Church.   2. Transnationalism—History.   3. Latin Americans—Migrations—History.   4. Church and state—Catholic Church.
5. Catholic Church—History.   I. Title.
    BX1795.E44N37   2015
    282.086'912—dc23

                                    2015002945

Printed in the United States of America

18 17 16 5 4 3 2 1

First edition

to Kamau, il Guerriero Silenzioso

To Dan,
as we are
all fellow
in growth

[signature]

Contents

Acknowledgments

Single authorship of a book is a myth. Many voices, people, ideas, and stories percolate through writings. I cannot see this book only as *farina del mio sacco* (lit., a sack of flour, meaning "my own work"). Ideas are co-created. They emerge in small and big talks, through shared silences, in front of midmorning and late-night coffees. They come through us, more than they are by us.

I am indebted in this journey to all the formidable people I met in Rome, in the Latin American mission and beyond, including Ada, Ana Maria, Angel, Carlos(es) (one Costa Rican and one Ecuadorian), Cena, Conchis, Elizabeth, Elvezio, Frida, Gloria, Griselda, Lina, Lorena, Maria Rosa, Maricela, Marina, Marisol, Myriam, Rosa, Ricardo, Rudy, Ruth, Sandra, Teo, Vincenzo, and many, many more whom I cannot mention here. A deeply felt thank-you to the religious fathers Alfredo, Antonio, Helkyn, Jesús, Jorge, José, Juan Carlos, Oscar, and Pancho, who let me wander around the Latin American mission churches or met me at the Colégio Mexicano in Monte Mario or talked about their life in Rome, asking from time to time if the book had come out. I know it took much more time than I hoped for, but thank you for your infinite patience.

In Rome I am in debt to Mario Brunello, the brilliant librarian of ARSI, the Jesuit archives, and to the wonderful new and old friends in Rome: dear Isabel Cruz and Mattia Chiusano, who opened so many doors with their warmth and friendship, and Jesús Colina, who, with his friend-ship and great insights into the organization of the Catholic Church, gave me many contacts and ideas to consider. Eloisa Stella and Angelo Marano, with their gregariousness and witty discussions of Italian politics, kept me sane in moments of fieldwork impasse and made me realize that the "return" I write about is also a personal one. I am grateful to my dear uncle and aunt Luigi and Loredana Napolitano, who with their hospitality and warmth made my life in Rome so much easier and familiar, and to my cousins Daniele, Matteo, and Nicolò and their families, who engage more than I do with the Catholic faith. Thanks also to my joyful, warm sister, Antonella, with witty and insightful Barry; Anna with my beloved father, Picchio; and my wonderful nephew and niece, Noah and Sarah, who remind me that being brought up in mixed-faith homes can seed wonders.

I am especially indebted to my colleagues in Toronto and elsewhere who gave me so much food for thought and heartfelt intellectual blood to make this project reach its conclusion: among them Joshua Barker, Janice Boddy, Kevin Coleman, Simon Coleman, Jane Cowan, Hillary Cunningham, Girish Daswani, Naisarge Dave, Andrew Gilbert, Paul Kingston, Rebecca Kingston, Chris Krupa, Ashley Lebner, Tania Li, Nimrod Luz, Maya Mayblin, Carlota McAlister, Ken Mills, Andrea Muehlebach, Alejandro Paz, Xotchil Ruiz, Rosa Sarabia, Gavin Smith, Nurit Stadler, Edward Swenson, and Donna Young. At the University of Toronto my students, among them Norangie Carballo-Garcia, Connie Goyliardi, Alejandra Gonzalez Jimenez, Mac Graham, Daniella Jofre, Peter Skrivanic, and Daniel Spotswood, have also been a great source of inspiration and helped refine my thinking. In addition, I thank many other passionate students, whom I cannot all name here, who have put up with my less-than-clear and often too-experimental ideas. And I would have never completed this without the administrative and intelligent support of Annette Chan and Berenice Villagomez. Thanks also to colleagues at the Università della Sapienza in Rome, Alessandro Lupo and Pino Scirripa, who gracefully reminded me of the depth of Italian anthropology. Thanks also to the late and visionary Helen Tartar at Fordham University Press, who cannot see this book in press; she is sorely missed. I also thank Thomas Lay, with whom I have worked in the final production of this book, as well as Teresa Jesionowski and Justin Sully, who carefully edited the book manuscript (and were patient in unraveling some of my Italian-sounding, too convoluted sentences) and to the anonymous readers who have vastly improved this final version (if one could one ever say final) of the book.

This research was supported by grants from the Social Science and Humanities Research Council of Canada and the Connaught Foundation. I would never have been able to finish this book without a productive year spent in the Anthropology Department at the University of California, Berkeley, in 2011–12. I thank in particular Mariane Ferme. I also thank Stanley Brandes, Charles Briggs, Lawrence Cohen, Rosemary Joyce, Saba Mahomood, and Donald Moore. A special thanks to Charles Hirschkind, who, beyond generous ideas, kept me jolly, while writing, through wonderful (and competitive!) tennis matches; Cristiana Giordano, who read part of this work and made profound comments; and Chris Kiefer, Amal and Charles Debbas, and the life-enhancing and graceful Margarita Loinaz. I am grateful to other dear friends and colleagues who in different corners of the world have insightfully commented on this work and kept me joyful in the last ten years: Cristina Bandiera, James Durkerley, Chris Garces, Eva-Lynn Jagoe, Dalia Kandiyoti, Michael Lambek, David Lehmann, Yael Navaro-Yashin, Emanuela Nordio, Kristin Norget, Filippo Osella, Mariella Pandolfi, Sarah Radcliffe, Fiona Samuels, Ann Varley, and Alberto Zaffaroni, and Ato Quayson, who with all the ups and downs is still a heartfelt friend. Last but not least, I am thankful for, and together with, my beloved son, Kamau Mattia, who gives me more joy and wisdom than I can ever imagine and who reminds me that humanity is never given, but always lived for.

May you all be free from suffering and live at ease.

Rome, July 2014

Some sections of chapter 3 appeared in "Phantomatic Presences and Bioreligiosity—On the Legionaries of Christ and the Jesuits," *Postscripts: The Journal of Sacred Texts and Contemporary Worlds* 5, no. 3 (2011): 293–317.

Some sections of chapter 4 appeared in "Of Migrant Revelations and Anthropological Awakenings," *Social Anthropology* 15, no. 1 (2007): 75–93.

Some sections of chapter 5 appeared in "The Virgin of Guadalupe, a Nexus of Affects," *Journal of the Royal Anthropological Institute* 15, no. 1 (2009): 96–112.

MIGRANT HEARTS AND THE ATLANTIC RETURN

Introduction

Catholic *Humanitas*

> It was he, old and tired. Four popes had died, eternal Rome was showing the first signs of decrepitude, and still he waited. "I've waited so long it can't be much longer now," he told me as he said good-bye after almost four hours of nostalgia. "It may be a matter of months." He shuffled down the middle of the street, wearing the combat boots and faded cap of an old Roman, ignoring the puddles of rain where the light was beginning to decay. Then I had no doubts, if I ever had any at all, that the Saint was Margarito. Without realizing it, by means of his daughter's incorruptible body and while he was still alive, he had spent twenty-two years fighting for the legitimate cause of his own canonization.
> —Gabriel García Márquez, "The Saint," in *Strange Pilgrims*

On a Thursday afternoon, the view from Ponte Garibaldi is stunning. On one side the tall synagogue of Rome is in shining light and in the distance, on the left, is another well-known dome, the cupola of St. Peter's. In front lies the neighborhood of Trastevere, which, with a buzzing entertainment life and charming little winding streets, has become a fancy and expensive place to live. Tourists are on the streets but also many people going about their errands and chores. I am walking with Eloisa, a very smart, soft-spoken Peruvian migrant—raven hair, bright smile, hands unaltered by repetitive use of cleaning products. She moves with slow, poised, and graceful movements—nothing seems to agitate her in the few years we have known each other. At least not on the outside. We are talking about the parish we are heading to, the headquarters of the Misión Latino Americana in Rome (Latin American Mission, henceforth MLA) for the weekly celebration of El Santísimo.[1] The sixteenth-century church is Santa Maria della Luce—a rather ordinary one by Roman aesthetic standards; it is located in a hidden street of Trastevere. This church, dedicated to the Latin American migrants in Rome, is in Eloisa's words a "world of its own" (*mundo a parte*). I agree that it is—and that it is not.

The Roman Catholic Church is increasingly a key political subject in matters of governmentality over migration around the world, even if locally it is often imagined as a mundo a parte. The Catholic Church unfolds its care for migrants locally and at the same time globally. On 5 December 2011 the Holy See became an official member of the Organization for International Migration (OIM) in Geneva, gaining strength as a moral subject in defense of a *humanitas* based on the "belief of the unique dignity and common belonging to the same human family of every human person, that is antecedent to any cultural, religious, social, political, or other consideration."[2]

This book is about being both Catholic and a Latin American transnational migrant in the context of the Catholic Church's entrenched anxiety about the never-ending project of the full conversion of the Americas. It is about a "local" migration, yet a continental and historical anxiety. Margarito's story is that of a Colombian in Rome, advocating for the canonization of his dead daughter, who lies buried across the Atlantic. The daughter has not been canonized and perhaps never will be. Márquez's story not only narrates a not-yet-achieved canonization; it also evokes parallel and never-ending processes of mastery. Moreover, it contains histories of hopes, suffering, carnalities, and the sanctification of ordinary lives. All these elements of what it means to be Catholic in such contexts are the subject of this book.

In conversation with Eloisa, the juxtaposition of the two words *Catholic* and *migrant* can appear rather innocent. Though once we articulate them together, they open up important questions about being "human" and the tensions between the *homely* (in the sense of being at home) and the *unhomely*. To address these questions, this book became a search for a new perspective, a new language to shed light on what can be articulated about the Catholic Church and processes of transnational migration. To address the connections between the Catholic Church and transnational migration, I propose the idea of an Atlantic Return. By this I mean the return of people of the Catholic faith from the Americas to Rome, and the Catholic Church is fortified and strengthened by this return. But the Return is more than this. The book also explores it through the affective histories and labor of the migrants from the Americas to the "center" of Catholic Western civilization and the ideas, hopes, and fantasies about what the

Catholic Church and being Catholic was, is, and will be. The return is for a future, not only of a past. The Catholic clergy see the migrants as new blood for the church that has the potential to feed, as they see it, a much-needed revitalization of the Catholic heart of Europe. Pope Francis, who was elected well after I finished the ethnographic work for this book, is a symbolic tip of this Return. The Return is not just about the past; it is very much for a present and a future of an imagined humanity by Catholics and non-Catholics around the globe.

Many may not know that when you enter the Vatican State in Rome from Porta Saint Anna you are welcomed by Swiss guards, that you must have your shoulders covered, and that you need to stop at a side office to show your passport. You are in a "foreign" state in Rome. Hence to study how Catholic migrant subjectivity is constructed we also need to understand the parallel and intersecting discourses on migration that are produced by the Italian nation-state and the Vatican. These processes are not separate. The Roman Catholic Church is a religion, a faith, but the Vatican is a state in all effects and purposes. It is, as I explain in the following chapters, *a passionate machine*. Thus I want to foreground the Catholic Church as a producer of passions and affects that are important both in the singularity of people's experiences and in the directions that different publics and politics take. The Holy See, as the Vatican state and as the Catholic Church, is a global, multifaceted political subject that shapes global assemblages on transnational migration. It is a part of, not outside, the political, intimate, and economic dynamics and frictions that constitute transnational migrant labor.[3]

The ethnographic work that is the door into these local and global, intimate and public assemblages emerges out of my fieldwork in Rome. Conducted over periods of varying length between 2004 and 2011,[4] it has been an intimate and distant affair that at times worked and at times did not. Born and bred in Catholic northeast Italy, formed as a British social anthropologist, and with acquired kinship ties with West Africa, I have had a long-time love for the elsewhere—yet for me this has been strangely a "return home." It was just after engagements with liberation theology in Mexico, Mexican day laborers in San Francisco, and Jesuits in Guadalajara that I turned to the thread of one of these fieldwork interests, which took me to the Gregorian University in Rome. From there I went to the Comunidad Católica Mexicana—a small group that had begun to meet regularly in the early 2000s in a parish on the outskirts of Rome through a joint initiative with the MLA—and then to the Church of the Virgin of

Guadalupe entrusted to priests of the Legionaries of Christ order. Different field trips to Rome allowed some important friendships to develop, but working on transnational migration and being myself in the thick of it between England and later Canada, I also found the "return" at times disappointing. Some of the people I had known were not there; priests had moved away from Rome; seminarians had finished their period of training; and mobile phone numbers were no longer in service.[5]

The transitoriness of life, which appears only more acutely through a transnational paradigm, had to become more of a friend than an enemy. So when I could, I moved to cultivate an intimacy of friendship that also brought me to explore the puzzling domains, moments, and narratives that I have sought to unravel in this book. They have been unnerving in some instances, not just because they often appeared after the tape recorder was turned off. A sense of writing as poaching[6] has been very much with me while writing parts of this book: Writing can be a loss and a mistemporality. Closures are not only epistemological affairs, but embodied chances in life.

I have chosen in some parts of this book to "reveal" stories, rather than to recount them, not so much for their unsayable nature, or the violence of their public secret,[7] but in order to open up the field of being Catholic and migrant as a living, nuanced, and sometime difficult itinerary to be lived. Without judgment, I am also placing myself within these stories of ("wrong") desires, sexual and sensual attractions, longing, and doubts. Having assumed in the unfolding of this research the role of both confidante and confider, I am also part of these stories, not apart from them. I hope that these moments, stories, and intimacies can be understood as a larger narrative of the complexities of migrant life, religious callings, and the experience of being incarnated in a gendered body.

But intimate puzzlements and impasses are also institutional, and so they belong to the church too. Hence the aim of this book, as an ethnography, is to bridge the long-standing and unhelpful divide between popular and institutional Catholicism, between devotional, embodied passions and the Catholic Church's long history of anxieties about and hopes for the conversion of Latin America. Throughout the fifteen to eighteen centuries the project of conversion to Catholicism in the New World gravitated toward a purification of indigenous souls and the control of eroticism, especially of women's bodies, and paralleled by the appropriation of labor and resources. In the eyes of some missionaries, such as Vasco de Quiroga in sixteenth-century Michoacán, conversion raised the possibility of a

New Church in the New World, a rejuvenation of the corrupted church in Europe. Most important, the theological hinge of Catholic conversion was ultimately to transform Otherness into Sameness. But conversions often were not successful, could not last, or were partial. In this sense the presence of Latin American Catholics in Rome subtly stirs a long-time fear of the never fully achieved conversion from Otherness into Sameness. This tension is foundational in ethnographic practice and the anthropological discipline. Explorations of an anthropology beyond the subject that have begun to emerge in the twenty-first century are also in response to the limitations imposed by the concepts of Sameness and Otherness. Thus this book is also a contribution to a larger debate that has to do with the Catholic underpinnings of a genealogy of anthropological theory and its limitations, not yet fully explored.

Ethnographically speaking, the subject of this research is the Misión Latino Americana (MLA) in Rome, which is a Catholic umbrella organization, formed in 2003, to organize pastoral care for a plethora of national Latin American parishes. The MLA headquarters are located in the neighborhood of Trastevere and attended mainly by women from countries such as Colombia, Ecuador, Peru, Brazil, and Bolivia. They come into the church to participate in the Catholic celebrations but also to seek jobs in the caring sector through an office in the parish that connects care workers, or *badanti*,[8] and Italians seeking domestic laborers and caregivers. In this sense the MLA is a small job center. Father Alfonso, an Italian chaplain and Scalabrinian priest, who had previously lived for a long time in Argentina, coordinated the MLA from 2003 to 2012. He was assisted by Latin American vice-chaplains—mainly from Mexico, Chile, and Brazil.

The Comunidad Católica Mexicana (CCM) was a prominent member of the MLA network, but in 2005 it decided to break away from its Latin American counterparts to operate independently and to celebrate Mexican national events under the rubric of the Catholic Church. This group, composed mainly of Italo-Mexican mixed couples (often the wife is Mexican and the husband Italian) and of Mexican nuns and priests who are currently training or residing in Rome, is in a way a microcosm of some of the strengths and the tensions involved in the return of migration to the heart of Catholicism and to the Italian capital. Although my fieldwork sought to grasp the nature and practices consistent throughout this network of migrant religious communities—for example, the material importance of work in the caregiving sector and the prevalence of mixed marriages with Italians—the ethnography presented in this book is structured around

Catholic devotions such as the devotion to the Virgin of Guadalupe and the Corazón de Jesus, or Sacred Heart of Jesus, as well as the Peruvian Brotherhood de El Señor de los Milagros and the Mexican celebrations of El Día de las Madres (Mother's Day) and El Día de la Independencia (Independence Day).

In Rome, Mexican nation-state memories and affective returns of religious histories are, on one hand, harvested by conservative streams of the Catholic Church, such as the Legionaries of Christ, producing narratives of martyrdoms and a church under attack.[9] On the other hand, these memories engender new possibilities of migrant Catholic presence. The CCM, for example, has distanced itself from the MLA precisely because of criticisms that the chaplains of MLA moved toward the community for its celebration of nation-state commemorations and the relatively little interest it has shown in promoting an apostolic path to Catholic pan-American identity. For the CCM, the church is more an Iglesia Morena (literally a "brown church," meaning a racially composite church) than it is an aspiration for an elite church, which is what characterizes the sociality of the Legionaries of Christ (which I analyze in chapter 3), who have privileged a whiter, economically powerful, and less indigenously rooted church. This tension renews, within the relatively small Mexican presence in Italy, an old colonial racial cleavage.

However, many Latin American migrants in Rome do not take part in the MLA or CCM and do not think of themselves as particularly Catholic; they may belong to other denominations. My intention is not to describe a representative Latin American migrant community in Rome but to focus on migrant itineraries, by which I mean an analytical attention to how threads of gendered lay and religious labor, family, and national histories, as well as devotional affects, intersect and recraft particular pedagogies and materialities of Catholicism. By making this analytical move, I can address first wider and important tensions of centrality and periphery that characterize the (re)production of the Roman Catholic Church from within. Second, I can break away from such problematic notions of migration as the sociological imagination of transnational migrant communities as formed by the push and pull of resistance and agency, social participation and absence of representation, assimilation and lack of social mobility, and instead I can move toward an open-ended inquiry of historically and materially crafted struggles for desires and the homely in the process of migration.

Ethnographically, what emerges from this are two points. First, the migrant itineraries in this book often show a longing for the nation, which interrupts the Catholic Church's desire to forge a "common" Catholic identity of pan-Americanism. Second, and at the same time, histories of betrayal of kinship, families, and nations are often the unspoken affective matrix out of which those migrant itineraries unfold. Pedagogies of family reunification, so much championed by the Catholic Church, fall short of capturing and responding to the complexity of these betrayals. I use here and throughout the book the term *pedagogies* to signal that the relation between the Catholic Church and migrants is a relation of orientation, guidance, and "walking together." In this sense the word *pedagogy* captures a developmental path (from childhood to adulthood) that frames the pastoral church's relationship with transnational migrants.[10]

Moreover, the idea of the Atlantic Return helps in exploring the articulation between migrant itineraries and the histories of being Catholic. These histories include colonial encounters, labor, and imagination. A return of the missions, part of an Atlantic Return, then raises a debate about the remainders of coloniality in present-day postcolonial and post-Fordist formations.[11] Anibal Quijano rightly notes that coloniality is a lens through which we understand the present existence of ideologies, materialities, and dispositions in race and labor relations. These were shaped in colonial encounters but have survived the end of colonial empires in new postcolonial formations. He argues that Otherness and Sameness have been, and still are, central to the reproduction of inequalities in Atlantic terrains from the conquest of America onward, especially as a hegemonic form of knowing.

This persistence of coloniality is partly about knowledge but also, I would argue beyond Quijano's position, about subtle returns of affective histories and their carnalities as modes of being and living. In this book they are connected to the anxieties of a never-ending project of full conversion to, and continuous apostolic expansion of, Catholicism. Taken together, they are then historically informed ontologies that migrants need to become the living blood for the New Evangelization—the new missionaries, so to speak.[12] In Benedict XVI's words, the same Virgin of Guadalupe in America and in Rome drives this *afán apostólico* (apostolic longing).[13] So this migration is a reinforcement of a traditionalist wing of the church at the heart of Rome at the same time that it is a decentering of the Catholic heart of Europe. Hence this migration as an expression of the Atlantic return is profoundly ambiguous.

Such ambiguity embraces postcolonial trajectories that result in the destabilization of old imperial binaries and with them Western notions of sameness and subjectivity,[14] mobilizing uncharted processes of space-making and subject formation where metropolitan Europe is itself reshaped by this return of migration. Central to a modality of postcolonial powers has been an anxiety about hybridity and the location of "civilized humans," as well as forms of mimicry of, complicity with, and subversion of power relations. Indeed, the actions of the MLA, the Legionaries of Christ, and the CCM in Rome show traces of both the reproduction *and* the destabilization of hierarchies.

Both the reproduction and destabilization of hierarchies quiver around the central node of Catholic humanitas. Since the Renaissance, a racial distribution of knowledge made belonging to the category of "fully human," humanitas, an apparently inclusive, but actually exclusive, attribute of sameness.[15] More than ever now it is relevant to ask how a (Catholic) faith, based on such a notion of sameness, can still be both inclusive and exclusionary when it comes to transnational migration.

Thus with such ontological and epistemological tensions in mind, this book is also a contribution to an anthropology of Catholicism and a wider debate of critical Catholic studies. I have discussed elsewhere how an anthropology of Catholicism takes inspiration from, but also takes issue with, current developments in the anthropology of Christianity.[16] Rather than add to the work on the cultures of Christianity, we need to develop an ethnographic focus on the Roman Catholic Church's governmentality (its guidance and regulation of Catholic bodies/souls in tandem with a constant remaking of its internal clerical structure). This is particularly so today, with the current revisions of Vatican II and the old/new terrains of Catholic subject formation.[17] This emergent form of the church's governmentality, as imagination, control, and action on life, bodies, and people, is shaped by emerging forms of translocalism where flows and interruptions of "symbols, images, ideas, people, and power constitute trans-border communities structured by forces other than—but not outside of—the social, political and economic exigencies of bounded nation-states."[18] This focus is important for an anthropology of Catholicism to blur the unhelpful analytical distinction between popular religiosity and the politics of institutional reproduction of the Catholic Church.

One of the kernels of an anthropology of Catholicism is the study of *carnality*. As Fenella Cannell rightly pointed out, the ambiguity in Christianity is that the "flesh is an essential part of redemption."[19] The focus is not only on a state of worldliness, or on incarnation as potentially antithetic to spiritual pursuits; carnality is the quality and state of being flesh, or as

Elizabeth Povinelli suggested, the politically and "socially built space between flesh and the environment."[20] Carnality and its dimension of incarnation of spirit into matter is a constitutive conundrum of Catholicism, as the divine, in the form of Jesus, is present in matter and yet is beyond or transcending matter. Divinity is expressed in a Trinity, but that Trinity (God, Jesus, and the Holy Spirit) needs laboring and an enfleshment to exist; it needs an oekonomia.[21] And the Labor of Mary (to give a material form to the spirit of Christ) is also what has sanctified her and the Catholic Church as an institution.

In evangelical Christianity preaching the word is a form of converting by listening, but for Catholicism the nature of the being of the flesh, its powers and limitations, and the divine laboring of matter are paramount.[22] The incarnation of Christ in a human body, of the divine presence in a fleshy vessel, is one of the theological kernels of Catholicism. This is why an anthropology of Catholicism needs more than ever to explore the boundaries of the flesh, what affectively gets stuck to it, how eroticism is mediated or unmediated in Catholic practices, and how incarnation becomes a vessel, not just a vehicle, of the (un)homely.

From the study of the Sacred Heart as well as the Virgin of Guadalupe, in migration, in this book it becomes clear that they are not only of a materiality that signifies a vehicle of the sacred; they are also about a bundle of affective and sometime repressed histories. These religious materialities can become vessels that contain, breathe, sweat the divine, and animate the homely or unhomely in migrant itineraries. As Catholic vessels, they have a particular metonymical, more than metaphorical, relation to the divine—vessels point to a communion (a coming together of that which is familiar but also estranged) and metonymical places of encounter (between divine and human). The carnality of the divine for Catholicism is also a practice of presence, as it is of place-making.[23]

Studies in anthropology of Christianity have informed important debates on the nature of mediation, presence, absence of the divine, and the nature of the material processes of Christian semiosis. This literature has also dwelled specifically on tropes of cultural ruptures to understand the inception of conversions. Concepts such as "thingification"—the process of divesting objects of their immateriality—have shown the paradoxical and ambiguous struggle of making the presence of the divine tangible, through the world and embodied actions—with the perennial doubt of becoming too worldly and wordy and less divine.[24] Ethnographies of Catholicism instead see this conundrum less as a question of mediation but more as an issue of containment. In fact, the Sacred Heart, for example, is not imagined as medium, or vehicle, of the divine, but rather as corporeal container/vessel. To explore the nature of carnality and containment in Catholicism I study in this book ethnographic encounters and histories of excesses of signification that emerge through ritual celebrations and affective devotions. Those point to the imbrication of histories in the present (to be in the place of the other), an importance of the long durée and the lingering histories,[25] rather than to ruptures of temporalities of conversion, as it has been the focus of important work in the anthropology of Christianity.

To study *forms of containment* and in a way continuity, rather than rupture, an anthropology of Catholicism needs to engage with the articulation of the church's governmentality in different terrains: studies of the affective and embodied domains that emerge in ongoing processes of enculturation, devotion, canonization, and sanctification; of the multiple ethical horizons that arise in the awareness of social suffering and physical death and in light of multiple and conflictive ethical domains;[26] and of the underpinning of Catholicization in different welfare states and labor relations.[27] A focus on emerging forms of governmentality requires that we understand how different local fragments of histories are not peripheral to the "center" of the Roman Catholic Church, but that they can be both destabilizing to center/periphery binaries and reinforcing an imagination of the Catholic roots and "blood" of Western Europe.

However, to engage anthropologically with the ethical horizons of Roman Catholicism we also need to consider the Catholic underpinning of new post-Fordist economies. Andrea Muehlebach has insightfully argued, following Carl Schmitt's notion of *complexio oppositorum,* that Catholicism in northern Italy has the capacity to effectively produce forms of moral voluntarism that give rise to productive, neoliberal moral subjects in post-Fordist societies where state welfare is receding.[28] The complexio oppositorum of the Catholic Church, unlike in a "secular" nation-state, is the institutional, ideological, and managerial capacity to foreground a politics of collective authority that defies multiple and antithetical voices within, so that there appears "to be no antithesis it does not embrace."[29] Be this a democratic or an autocratic form of government, or a theologically gendered foundation that rests on a Father God and a Mother Church, the Catholic Church has expressed this oppositorum in particular ways. One way, central to this book and much rehearsed by Benedict XVI, is by embracing a representation of the Catholic Church based on transcendence, truth, and morality, which establishes its "formal superiority over the matter of human life."[30]

The Roman Catholic Church has had a particular interest in the normative "guidance of human life." However, this human life, as a historical event, is often strategically evacuated or belittled by a history of providence, as the human is considered to be ruled by the weak nature of being an incarnated creature. From this perspective I argue that *Catholic humanitas* (as a notion of being human) is short-circuited into a *civitas humana* (as a notion of a common way of being related, a common civilization). This shift seems to be accompanied by the ambiguously related emergence of *homo relatus* within church practices—of "personalized" clerical attention and care. Hence some affective practices promoted by orders such as the Legionaries of Christ, which have paid much attention to the care of wealthy elite, show how Catholic faith can promote a homo relatus that is not in opposition but in support of an exclusive ethics of personalized attention and capitalist wealth accumulation.

Clearly a word on affect is due now. A calibrated examination of the contemporary face of Catholicism demands attention to the affective domains of gendered and transnational labor in the care of the Catholic Church. Affects have been a surging area of interest in recent anthropological exploration and critical theory. With affect we have come to understand the domain that resides at the interface between prediscursive and discursive practices: that which animates social and psychic life, without being fully articulated and enclosed in a socially shared language. The notion that affects are shared and circulated through bodies and fantasies is central to this book.[31] But fantasies of those same shared affects—through collective investments such as upward mobility, social equality, and durable intimacy—are increasingly becoming more remote from embodied, affective rhythms of survival,[32] especially in processes of migration.

Although affects can disrupt such investments, they can also reinforce a desire for normativity. The ambiguity of the reemergence of an "integralist" (or traditionalist) church and a progressive understanding of the relation between the Catholic Church and migration in the current revision of Vatican II sum up the powerful affective ambivalence toward migration as being both historical (in the sense of being part of a divine history and being a phenomenon with very old roots) and living in a singular, unpredictable moment.[33] But how might a consideration of Catholicism in particular contribute to the "affective turn" in theory and ethnography in general? I see three points that stand out.

First, Spinoza, whose *Ethics* has been rightly taken as a key formulation anticipating the turn to affect theory, foregrounds the existence of substance as that which contains all. The so-called metaphysics (the eternal, the infinite, or the divine) are there, but only present in substance. The unsettling of binaries, including the divisions between ontology and epistemology and immanence and transcendence, is at the core of Spinoza's *Ethics.* Then following from this interpretation affects are neither fully in the domain of representations (epistemological) nor fully in the domain of being (ontological); they cut across both. If affects are transmitted through matter and substances, and not only between humans but also through and across space and the environment,[34] carnality becomes particularly poignant to studies of Catholicism. The study of substance, in Spinoza's sense, is helpful in shedding light on the articulation of carnalities and Catholicism.

Second, Catholicism is a complex of Judeo, Roman, Byzantine, and Greek histories, and it is also very much part of multiple medieval traditions. Given this lineage, it is surprising how extensively research in the anthropology of Christianity has focused on conversion and the Reformation period as the generative landscape of new forms of material ideologies. Faced with this tendency in existing research, we must wonder if we are missing important strands of the history of Catholicism. One such strand of research, crucial to the interests of this book, is to follow the way in which carnality, metamorphosis, and transformation have been present throughout medieval Catholicism and Christianity into the present.[35] Uncovering some of these neglected strands is to recognize the numerous ways in which an anthropology of Catholicism needs to consider affective matter and affective histories that emerge well before the Reformation, not only as a recrafting of an anthropology of Catholicism, but possibly and more broadly, as a contribution to an archaeology of the anthropological discipline. The engagement with this archaeology is a project I can only signal here as being in need of further elaboration.[36]

Third, affective histories are also explored in this work as force fields that extend through particular types of caring labor, as well as through specific spatial landscapes and architectures (such as the churches themselves), which animate aesthetic presences (the Virgin of Guadalupe, the Sacred Heart, and El Señor de los Milagros). Thus I challenge theories of affects that engage with only the relation between affect and materialities/space and I encourage an exploration of the relations of affects and histories. Specifically I am intrigued by the potency that Catholic materialities and affective histories can have in their unfolding within different political imaginaries.

A focus on affects also complements existing approaches on studies of Catholicism and migration. Well-established North American analyses of migrant diaspora and religiosity have stressed the importance of kinship, intimate dialogue, and the emplacement and the embodiment of Catholic devotions.[37] Devotions, especially to the Virgin Mary, but also to particular saints, such as Saint Jude, are open channels for the imagination of united diasporic moral communities and often act as platforms for meaningful engagement for migrant social justice.[38] In this body of work on migration, religion is the primary vehicle for understanding mobility and the confluence of "flows" that organically intensify the experience of human suffering and happiness, and help produce the homely. Urban devotions have often been read in this literature primarily as phenomenologies of self and community making, but I add here that they also have to be studied as contested political spaces of abjection—abjection understood not always as that which stands completely outside the symbolic order, but often as marginal to it, while still gendered.

Hence a study of Catholicism, as in this book, that focuses on the symptoms, returns, and remainders of affective histories and migrant itineraries, follows but also challenges these existing analytical traditions. Building on feminist critiques that pay tribute to the psychic life of power and histories, it moves a critique to a "lived" religion approach in its analysis of Catholicism and migration. Important studies of the intersection of Catholicism and migration based on the study of "lived religion" run the risk of a certain Western/North American–centeredness. By adopting the guiding concept of an Atlantic return instead, I argue that we need to challenge an assumption of the "free-flowing" of Catholicism, since it is based on a problematized understanding of a common humanitas.

The fieldwork on which this book is based offers concrete cases that contest these types of approach by exposing the ways in which the common humanitas is hijacked in multiple directions within the Roman Catholic Church, and projected in different forms of political imaginaries and consequently different forms of governmentality of (migrant) bodies within different transnational terrains. To problematize a common humanitas in the practices of Catholic (and migrant) faith helps calibrate a political understanding of the Catholic Church as a passionate machine. And it deprovincializes the notion of humanity embedded in studies of Catholicism.

North American scholarship has engaged with Roman Catholicism as a minority immigrant religion and part of a public sphere where the presence of Catholic migrants has been ethnicized and made an object of resistance to different forms of social exclusion. Sociologically oriented studies, such as the work of Pierrette Hondagneu-Sotelo, have shown that U.S. anti-immigrant legislation and an "embedded restrictionism" (according to which migrants may have acquired rights that can be potentially lost) have bred an active and complex form of resistance and labor organizations. Especially in the southern border states, Catholic and labor movements have often come together to mobilize for social justice and inclusion under the umbrella of the Catholic faith. In a North American context, studies of Catholicism have emphasized a structure/agency tension through, for instance, a focus on "civic social capital" and new forms of leadership in migrant Catholic terrains in the United States.[39] Other studies have informed our understanding of the changing nature of the relation between Catholicism and transnational migration as the problematic encounters between Catholic clergy and (new and old) believers, as well as through the tensions between unity and integrity. The old saying that in the American Catholic Church one must "pay, pray, obey" seems not enough in the current politics of identity of immigrant Catholics in the United States—and more active social mobilization is perceived as needed, at least in quarters that have seen the growing of an "immigrant church."[40]

However, as I explain in chapter 2, in an Italian context and from a Vatican perspective, Catholicism can engender both inclusionary and dismissive postures toward migration. The latter are generated by the defense of a powerful marriage between Christian and Roman civitas. If in some U.S. cases "civility" comes from participation, civitas also emerges from an exclusionary heritage. But if a personal, empathic, and open relationship to the divine that Catholic believers engender in everyday life requires an egalitarian and serious engagement rather than a folklorization of beliefs,[41] we likewise ought to see how Catholicism, in its intersection with migration, also creates painful and unequal forms of difference, even if official discourses hinge on representations to the contrary.

Catholic Latin American migrant itineraries in Rome speak to centers and peripheries, to inclusions and exclusions. The Latin American migrant itineraries explored in this book allow me to frame the relation between migration and Catholicism differently from the way it is framed in existing North American studies: through returns of histories, the contested nature of affects for the nation, and the tension between the homely and the unhomely in the materiality of devotions and in the enfleshment of migrants' desires.

Finally zooming into the present and imagining possible futures in Catholic (missionary) terrains in Rome, this books argues that the relation between Catholicism and migration reveals neither a clear-cut process of subjugation of migrants to received doctrines nor a conflict-free "humanitarian" embrace. Focusing on the interface of migration and the return of the missions shows that this is an ongoing process of embodied negotiations and pedagogical fantasies, both shaping and being shaped by the circulatory forces of histories. Catholicism and migration are, of course, constantly in the making; so the expression, weight, and form of a Catholic humanitas—and more than ever the gendering of this humanitas—force us to query the unsettling nature of given moral representations.[42]

It is probably clear to the reader at this point that circulations and interruptions of affective histories are analytical tools derived from a feminist and psychoanalytical tradition that has focused on alterity, Lacanian gaps, and Freudian symptoms in religious imagination, including the embodiment of experience and the limitations of official histories and language.[43] From these historical, anthropological, and psychoanalytical perspectives have emerged a focus on marginality, mysticism, and the repression of the often racialized and gendered Other within multiple Catholic traditions.[44] If migration is also lived on, between, and underneath gendered skins, I hope this book is a contribution to this tradition of the study of Catholicism.

A Road Map

We all need road maps, and different road maps lead to different terrains. The road map of this book points out different aspects of an Atlantic Return in articulation with official Catholic Church postures and on-the-ground practices (the combination of which I call Catholic pedagogies) vis-à-vis migration. My biographical road map has included multiple spells of fieldwork in Rome between 2003 and 2011, living with uncles, aunts, and friends—and for a time in a convent. The fieldwork narrative I have decided to use is not only dictated by the nature of multiple visits rather than a single prolonged period of fieldwork, it was also an analytical choice.

Instead of comparing and contrasting different fieldwork sites, I foreground the relation between Catholic Church policy on migration, its

theology, and the complexity of the New Evangelization and the varia-
tion in missions by different religious orders through different ethnographic encounters, historical threads, and Catholic theological material.
My use of the ethnographic pen puts in conversation different registers of
knowledge and contributes to a field of interdisciplinary studies on the
present and future of the Catholic Church, what I call here Critical Catholic Studies. Such an approach is required because the Catholic Church is
such a tremendously important political subject in the dynamics of migration and mobility worldwide. With the papacy of Pope Francis, the role
of the Catholic Church in matters of migration has become important in
the media, but of course it has to be analyzed within a longer history and
some of its lingering in the present. My point is that an ethnographic
method, in a classic, comparative, and community-bound sense is important, but it is not enough to understand the dialogical relation between
the Catholic Church and transnational migration.

I have participated in many celebrations in the churches of Santa Maria
della Luce and Santa Lucia for Easter week, Days of the Dead, celebrations
of the Virgin of Guadalupe, and Señor de los Milagros, and I have assisted
at many Masses and meetings of the Comunidad Católica Mexicana, as
well as attended many parties, baptisms, and weddings of migrants. I have
also lived in a Mexican nuns' convent in the heart of Rome. Nonetheless,
despite these experiences, I have not privileged life histories or a sustained
comparative methodology between different church sites. I may have
"wasted time" on long bus trips accompanying migrants back from work,
or from their Thursday and Sunday gatherings, looking for Latin American restaurants open in peripheral areas of the city after Sunday masses.
Yet in many of those eclectic moments there have been startling illumina-
tions of the anxieties, hopes, and difficulties that permeate migrant itineraries at the heart of this Atlantic Return of Catholicism. The familiarity
engendered by hanging around for many years with a changing group of
migrants, clergy, nuns, and members of Catholic organizations has inspired
me to think through migrants' itineraries and to thread together multiple
ways of being Catholic. These itineraries are the weaving together of ordinary lives (rather than extraordinary encounters), threads of histories,
papal teachings, missionaries present and past, religious iconographies, as
well erotic longings, family failures, hopes, and fears. Thus my use of the
ethno-graphos, as writing about the Other, wishes to inspire a way to "do
anthropology" through traces and itineraries, together with, but also
beyond, a comparative method of the study of migrant communities.

A road map is needed for the writer as much as it is for the reader. In chapter 1, I explore changes in the Italian legislative system in relation to local municipal policies on migration during the tenures of the last two mayors of Rome, Walter Veltroni and Gianni Alemanno, and how the Latin American presence in Rome ignites tensions, fears, and nostalgia for a clear center/periphery division of "civilization." These tensions are then read through revisionist interpretations of Vatican II, which tend to leave unacknowledged potential conflicts over different cultural embodiments of the Catholic Church. Chapter 2 looks at how Latin American transnational migration in Rome stirs an old conflict within the Catholic Church: the paradox of Catholic conversion and the tension of Sameness and Otherness, which have been present at least since the "Encounter with the New World." I read closely twentieth-century Catholic pedagogies on migration that contribute to forging a Catholic humanitas that undergirds national sentiments and highlights a culture of life as the cradle of a specific universal and given notion of personhood. In chapter 3 I compare the Legionaries of Christ, an important twentieth-century Mexican order that was strong under the papacy of John Paul II, with the Jesuits. I connect it here to the study of the Catholic Church as a passionate machine that produces gendered and affective passions within this order, but also between orders, and I explore the return of the missions not only in the lived experience of religion and history, but also on what never was or was partly abjected. Through a focus on what I call the psychic glue of histories, and especially the mimetic drives of *imitatio Christi*,[45] which exist between these two religious orders at the particular conjuncture of the revision of Vatican II, I point to the force that a Catholic integralist church is acquiring in Europe—with blood (as the Mexican clergy) that is, in part, of an Atlantic return.

Chapter 4 looks at how, in twenty-first-century Rome, Catholic migrants' out-of-wedlock sexuality and eroticism, their uncanny senses of the homely and the unhomely through the Sacred Heart and the Señor de los Milagros, disturb and unsettle the completeness of the fantasy of conversion and of turning natives into new apostles—especially in the present debates of the *Nueva Evangelización*.[46] Through the analyses of ritual celebrations as well as devotional practices, Latin American migrant itineraries reveal the circulation of deep-seated anxieties about the pollution of a migrant Other. I show how those itineraries also subtly destabilize official pedagogies of migrant evangelization that wish for a shared pan-Americanism. Tropes of "migrant communities," while promoting the abode of the normative family and family reunification as the unique and most viable way for the redemption of migrants' bodies and souls, frame the experience of labor migration and immigration as a heroic spiritual journey.

Chapter 5 focuses on Mexican transnational returns of histories and the affective politics of celebrating the Virgin of Guadalupe in Rome, arguing that these transnational Catholic devotions may contain or exceed the affect of the nation. The analytical interplay between a fantasy of the nation and its political reenactment gives us important insights into how racialized transnational religious histories are intimately connected to national and political affect. So if Marian religious devotions are about presence, relationships, and lived religion, I show in this chapter how they should also be studied as a constellation of fragments that reemerge in histories that have been partially forgotten or have been abjected.

Finally, chapter 6 explores intimate affective domains of the return of the missions that emerge in the experiences of gendered migration situated at different socioeconomic conjunctures—with continuity between religious and secular domains. Looking at lay migrant women's labor and that of Mexican Catholic nuns within the convent's walls, I explore gendered spatial affectivity and its relationship to labor, histories, marriage, and memories. I show that if an ideal form of lay Latin American transnational caring labor is professed by the church missionary pedagogies as a female heroic journey in Rome, it is constantly interrupted by ambiguities, by "lying," and by stretching of different ways of experiencing time and labor between the convent's walls.

Now, having been given a road map, let's continue the journey.

1. Migrant Terrains in Italy and Rome

> Here is the entity [Rome], which has suffered so many drastic
> changes in the course of two thousand years, yet is still the
> same soil, the same hill, often even the same column or the
> same wall, and in its people one finds traces of their ancient
> character. Contemplating this, the observer becomes, as it
> were, a contemporary of the great decrees of destiny.
> —Johann Wolfgang von Goethe, *Italian Journey*, 1815/17

Goethe was as fond of Rome as he was anticlerical. The history of Rome's
"ancient character" and its pontifical powers is a complex one. In this
light, I situate broad changes in Italian legislation on migration that will
set the context for the next chapter, in which I discuss the positions on
migration of the Holy See and of particular religious orders within the
Catholic Church. Understanding the practices of religious orders in relation to migrants is fundamental to grasping the church's dual positions on
immigration. I argue that an understanding of the contemporary church
requires a multilayered, differentiated, and multipolar study of competing
positions, faces, and "souls."

Italian migrant legislation has become increasingly restrictive and based
on jus sanguinis (right of blood, or birth descent) rather than jus soli (right
of the soil, or place of birth). I read here changes in the Italian legislative
system in relation to local municipal policies on migration of the two
mayors of Rome in the period of study of this book, Walter Veltroni and
Gianni Alemanno.[1] I discuss how these two mayors have held, broadly
speaking, two different political stances toward Roman heritage as it
relates to the Catholic Church and to migration. I then illustrate, through
a particular ethnographic encounter on Piazza Mancini, how the presence
of migrants in Roman public spaces ignites tensions and fears, along with

nostalgia for a clear demarcation of a center and the periphery of "civiliza-tion." Finally, I dwell on current revisions to Vatican II and begin to map the different souls of the church toward migration that have been marked by these current revisions.

The politics of immigration in Italy has been murky since the early 1990s; since the early 2000s, this political landscape has become more regimented over the course of two distinct periods of municipal gover-nance: first, the municipal government of Mayor Walter Veltroni (2001–8), a left-leaning liberal associated with the Democratic Party, and, second, that of Mayor Gianni Alemanno (2008–13), a member of Alleanza Nazio-nale, a right-wing party that has deep, populist roots in the Roman social landscape.

During the portion of the Veltroni period that coincided with the sec-ond national mandate for Berlusconi as prime minister of Italy (2001–5), there was a schism between the national outlook on migration and the more liberal outlook of the municipality of Rome. Veltroni's vision was more in tune with the government of Romano Prodi, head of the left-center coalition of L'Ulivo (now the PD, Democratic Party), which ruled the country in 2006–7. Berlusconi's fourth mandate (2008–11) coincided with Alemanno's term, and these two governments have shared a similar outlook on migration, with no major open clashes between them.[2]

Before 2011 there were four major phases of national immigration policy in Italy: the Martelli Law (1990–98), the Turco-Napolitano Law (1998–2002), the Bossi-Fini Law (2002–8), and the Decreto Sicurezza (Security Decree, from 2009). These phases have marked important shifts in the ways in which migrant subjectivity is legally constructed in Italy, signaling a trend toward an increasingly restrictive immigration policy. The Martelli Law first marked clearer boundaries between asylum seekers, legal migrants, and undocumented migrants, and introduced a language of expulsion from the country, if undocumented migration was at stake. The Turco-Napolitano Law instituted the figure of the (legal) migrant as the bearer of rights to family reconciliation, health, and education; yet it was also the first law that introduced the Centri di Permanenza Temporanea (Centers of Temporary Permanence, CTP) more recently called Centri di Identificazione ed Espulsione. These are state-regulated and enclosed structures dedicated to the identification of migrants for purposes of either possible expulsion from the country or their right to appeal for asylum.

The Turco-Napolitano legislation framed the expulsion of undocu-mented migrants within a civil code rather than the penal code. But with the Bossi-Fini legislation the figure of the (undocumented) migrant became increasingly criminalized, and expulsion became a matter of the penal code rather than a civic code. In the process, the rules for asylum seekers were made more difficult, and what was essentially a two-tiered system was put into place that favored migrants arriving under the umbrella of binational agreements and penalized as "illegal" those who did not have already in place a *permesso di soggiorno* (permit of staying). This permit is granted or renewed only if the bearer holds a work contract, as a guarantee of their capacity to provide for their basic livelihood.

The twist of this law, however, was and remains that a work contract is required to obtain a residence permit, which makes it difficult for migrants to invite other migrants into the country. Those same conditions apply for the renewal of the permit of residency within the country—even if the migrant has been living in Italy—with a grace period of only six months. In constructing this framework, the Bossi-Fini legislation enabled the creation of paternalist and exploitative relations between employers and migrant employees. The murkiness and exploitative potential of this law is especially evident in the labor relations structuring live-in care, a niche heavily filled by migrants attending the Latin American Mission (MLA).

But it is with the Decreto Sicurezza (security decree), promoted in 2008 and ratified in 2009, that the criminalization of migration comes into full public force, moved by internal politics within Berlusconi's government that led it to concede the Northern League's anti-immigration sentiments in exchange for their support in passing the *ad personam* laws that allowed Berlusconi to avoid prosecution on different fraud and corruption charges while serving in government.[3]

The main restrictive points introduced by the Decreto Sicurezza left migrants in a more precarious condition than ever.[4] For instance, the law introduced a formal obligation for public employees to denounce anyone suspected of not possessing a legal residence permit. This civil policing initially targeted health care providers in public institutions, but as withdrawn before the law was officially passed because of the outcry from the medical community. This legislation also establishes hefty penalties—including fines and seizure of property—for landlords who rent out to migrants not in possession of legal documents. Undocumented migration itself becomes a criminal act, punishable with a large fine, expulsion, or detention in CTP. Moreover, this law legalized the formation of civil night watches (particularly active prior to the fall of the last Berlusconi government) to patrol urban areas against organized crime, a development bearing, especially in the northeast of Italy, a disturbingly anti-migrant tone. For many Italians not inclined to Northern League thinking, this is reminiscent of the not-too-distant past of Italian fascist rule.

This legislative move to an increased criminalization of undocumented immigration has prompted a degree of resistance and criticism from Catholic associations in Italy. Many Catholics have contested the detrimental effect that these laws have had on the sacredness of the family, by de facto precluding even civil marriage to undocumented migrants. Catholic media have defended individual migrant rights and the rights of children born even in civil unions, and they have criticized the idea that there is a connection between an increase in immigration and an increase in crime. The CEMi (Commissione Episcopale per le Migrazioni) has voiced that in Rome and in the Lazio region the functional connection between increased immigration and increased petty criminality is statistically inaccurate.[5] In 2012, in order to comply with EU mandates, Italy created two separate tiers of migrant labor. A new "Blue Card" was approved, enacting a 2009 EU law that gives priority to "highly qualified" immigrant populations coming to Italy from non-EU countries. The recognition of a special identity card for highly qualified workers creates a new differentiation of migrant identities in Italian labor legislation.

Capi Mundi, Kaputt Mundi

In November 2005, I accepted the invitation of a Peruvian friend to attend a public meeting about the troubles that are taking place at Piazza Mancini.[6] This piazza has been a place of contention since a highly publicized "peaceful" meeting of Filipino migrants. Since the early and mid-2000s, noisier and "undisciplined" Latin American migrants have made it their place to meet, particularly on Thursday afternoons and evenings, and all day Sundays.

We arrive with a friend, Toño, originally from Cuzco, on a rainy late afternoon in the oratory of a Catholic education college just off the piazza. Within the oratory, I turn to see whether there are any familiar faces. Father Manuel, the Scalabrinian priest in charge at the time of the Mexican and Brazilian communities in the MLA, is on the right up near the front, and in the middle rows on the right a group of Latin Americans is sitting quietly in somewhat hunched positions.[7] On the left side, opposite the long table where representatives of institutions, a group of vociferous Italians, mostly middle-aged or pensioners, are itching to take up the microphone. The right of first word is with a representative of the carabinieri[8] of the Questura of Rome, lodged in the barrack of Maurizio Giglio (around the corner), who is sitting next to Madisson Godoy Sánchez, then president of a Latin American Ecuadorian organization called Simon Bolivar.[9] The representative of the carabinieri makes a small introduction and then leaves the floor to the public. Father Manuel nervously touches his umbrella while the crowd of Italians begins to pour out stories in heavy Romanesque accents about the troubles that the Latin American migrants have brought to the piazza.

Earlier, Filipinos were using it, and that was good. They were proper and did not make much noise. But now, one old man in a jittery, pitched voice states, the piazza has turned into a bivouac, a degradation of the urban space. Not only male, but even female migrants are urinating publicly at a place where Italian mothers take their children to play. An Ecuadorian woman will complain later that the 50 cents paid for access to a public toilet is wasted, as those are kept in horrible conditions. The man carries on, spelling out that Rome used to be *capi mundi*, the center or leader of the world, but is now *kaputt mundi*, the broken down of the world:

> These gardens have been transformed into a bivouac; those people
> [pointing to the brown-skinned Latin American migrants sitting in a
> corner] don't know that we cannot piss here in public; they shit, urinate,
> I would call them *anthropomorphic*. . . . Man has dignity; those [the
> migrants] do not have it; on top of this they are our guests, and they
> should adapt to our own manner. . . . Roma is *capi mundi*, it was the
> center of an empire, and there were people here from all over the place,
> but now it is *kaputt mundi*. . . . If nothing is done, the last resort [*ultima
> spiaggia*] is to call Toto Rina [a key Sicilian mafia leader now in prison,
> but still rather powerful]. (My emphasis)

An Italian woman in her late forties grabs the microphone and states:

> The gardens are made for us, and we cannot use them. If you visit
> Germany and Austria, the police there are much stricter, and you can
> use the parks and the squares, not like here. There is no control over
> territory [*controllo sul territorio*]. . . . We are not racist, but one thing is
> certain, they have to go. . . . If D'Alema and Veltroni [a former prime
> minister of Italy and a former mayor of Rome, respectively, both of
> the Democratic Party in Rome] lived here, something would be done.
> We are class-B citizens.

The public conversation gets even more animated, and the Italian neighbors begin to direct their complaints to the Forze dell'ordine, which are on the other side of the table, and who keep on insisting that they have a limited mandate and cannot really fine people to prevent them from using the public space in a particular way, until they really breach a law. Then a neighbor proposes that all the migrants should be permitted to hang around only under the bridge, on the one side of the piazza, but a carabineer replies that this is not possible as there are no barriers on the bank, and people, even migrant children, could fall in the river Tiber. The voices are getting louder and louder; one older neighbor fidgets with the tape that holds together the stems of his broken glasses. Retired Italian people are seeing their purchasing power shrinking because of the economic recession.

The African representative of the municipality of Rome, himself a Nigerian migrant, keeps on trying to get the microphone. In the end he is given a chance to speak, and he calmly and repeatedly pictures migration as "an opening of the heart," an opening to the novelty that migration represents. His pitch feels out of place in the very tense room. It reminds me of the charitable empathy of the civilizing new Italian nation of the book *Cuore*—still utopic in twenty-first-century Italy.[10]

Finally, Madisson Godoy intervenes and proposes that a newly founded migrant association be tasked with forming a migrant patrol (wearing the recognizable association T-shirt) that could ensure that noise and littering are kept at bay, especially on Thursdays and Sunday nights. So, in the end, although this is not the first choice for the neighbors, the meeting is adjourned with this decision taken. I head back to the bus terminal with Toño, an old-time Peruvian friend, and he shakes his head as he does not think this is going to work. These newly created migrant associations, he argues, are often tied to the interests of a few. More than a few have street businesses in the piazza selling homemade food and beer. If they tackle *that,* they would go to the heart of the problem, he adds. But "Italian people do not know that." Parallel economies are at the heart of this contested public space.

This ethnographic encounter illustrates some aspects of multicultural Rome and the production of contested publics. One element of this is a nostalgia for a strong, fascist, strong-state model, the countermodel to the municipal policies of the then–mayor Veltroni. Veltroni, who had center-left impulses geared toward an "Italian" multicultural agenda, was strongly criticized by rivals for not foregrounding public security, and his party lost the 2008 mayoral election in part over this issue. Another element in this encounter is the unacknowledged proliferation of small migrant businesses that create particular strongholds on specific public spaces, just as they also renew forms of ghettoization. The neighbors' reaction to the conflict over Piazza Mancini signals what has been called a "fortress effect," shelled on the skin and in the heart of social interaction.

The emergence of an affective politics of alterity in migrant terrains, as Sara Ahmed suggests, sticks to people's skin and bodies.[11] The fortress effect revives a mythological, historical, and politically loaded nationalist identity, in this case transposing it onto an ideology of Italianness as a shared civic value and common culture.[12] So transnational migration, while provoking some neighbors to fidget and declaim vociferously against it, undermines from the interstices this colonial idea of the unity of the nation, and makes of Italy and the Roman landscape a case of postcoloniality occurring without the loss of territories.[13]

Antonio Gramsci warned that the Catholic Church, since medieval times but also explicitly in the worlds of post-Concordato, sees civil society as belonging to the secular state and its politics in counterposition to a society based on the family and the church.[14] For those who may not be aware of it, the Concordato, or Patti Lateranensi, is a legal accord signed between the Holy See and the Italian government (of Mussolini) in 1929. That accord formally regulated the relations between the two states in matter of freedom of cult on the Italian soil, but also established financial exemptions for the Catholic Church from Italian taxes. In 1984, there was a revision to this Concordato, which de-linked Catholicism from being the state religion of Italy.

This operational disjuncture between the Catholic Church and Italian civil society that Gramsci highlighted is still at the heart of the multilayered pedagogies that the current Roman Catholic Church implements in the field of transnational migration. These pedagogies operate with an implicit dimension of "saving" civil society from its own demise, rather than allowing for the Catholic Church itself to be changed through its dialectic interaction with it. To paraphrase *Divini Illius Magistri*, Pius XI's 1939 encyclical, a natural perfection of civil society helps the development of family, but it is subordinated to the spiritual order of the Catholic Church.[15]

Multicultural Rome

Rome is an interesting migrant landscape because, as with a few other cities in Italy, it has been the cradle for the encounter of different immigrants since the Roman Empire. It has undergone different waves of expansion and contraction in trade and labor, and the changing topography of the urban landscape has reflected the consolidation of different migrant waves at different historical conjunctures.[16] In the 1920s and 1930s, during the development of the Fascist regime, Rome reached a population of just over a million. Nowadays more than 194 groups of different ethnic and national origins are present in Rome; they constitute cosmopolitan, migrant, and diasporic communities as well as minority religious groups. Migrant demographics in Rome show an overall increase of immigration since the late 1980s. Interestingly enough, the same Catholic Church in Rome has been both a producer of analyses of migrant labor conditions and the active coordinator of some of that migrant labor. Catholic "field observatories" have produced statistical analyses that are then used by the state and local governments to understand changing migration patterns.[17] From these statistics (which give the number of documented migrants), Peruvians and Ecuadorians—who make up the largest part of the Latin American Mission—are the most consistent presence; the Mexican numbers are lower, but growing.[18]

In a 2000 renewal of a municipal Roman statute, four Consiglieri Aggiunti (lit., added councillors) were introduced to the municipal council, each representing a different immigrant population (although these institutional figures were not renewed at the end of their last mandate in 2013). They participate in the activity of the council, but they have neither the right to vote nor the right to veto—they are in a way an absent presence in the municipal council. So although the city has a long history as an immigrant city, government structures at the municipal level have registered this only in a symbolic way, at best.

Broadly speaking, up to 2013 the two municipal governments of Rome led by Walter Veltroni and Gianni Alemanno were marked by a shift in the city's political relation to the Holy See. The Veltroni government had an interest in promoting an image of Rome as possessing a dynamic cultural heritage that is partly shared, yet identified within a wider Christian umbrella and the Roman Catholic Church. Under Alemanno, however, the city emphasized the fundamentally Catholic heritage of Roman civil society as the cradle of Western civilization. Key initiatives introduced by the Veltroni municipal government pivoted around a vision of Rome as a multicultural city, distinguished, since the inception of the Roman Empire, by its welcoming and engaged attitude toward migrant and diasporic communities. Many of the initiatives, at least on paper, fostered the construction of a collective citizens' memory and the development of a sense of shared multi-ethnic civic identity. Piazza Mancini shows, however, how these multicultural policies and representations of a multi-ethnic civitas are, in practice, intersected by affects of fear and shame.

From the late 1990s until the mid-2000s, several multicultural and intercultural initiatives in Rome were media-based and for political ends.[19] Part of municipal funding for migration-related services was directed to online information provision and multi-ethnic local guides to events and associations with the direct editorial contribution of migrants and linked to Servizio Intercultura—a municipally funded initiative through local libraries to enhance the cultural presence of migrant and diasporic communities.[20] Many of these initiatives, however, were filtered through a fundamentally conservative conception of cultural heritage—that is to say a conception of Roman culture rooted in the city's classical art and architecture (housed, for instance, in museums such as the Musei Capitolini) and promoted to *extracomunitari*[21] migrants with the implied intention of furthering their cultural integration through exposure to the wealth of Roman and Italian culture.[22] Integration (*integrazione*) has also been at the forefront of Roman Catholic policies on immigration in Rome, and often in tandem with, or covering for, a lack of municipal and national long-term policies. An example is the Forum per l'intercultura founded in 1991 by CARITAS Roma for the organization and promotion of intercultural education, which has aimed for a "positive" integration of migrants into Italian communities, while appreciating their cultural roots.

A principal shortcoming of Veltroni's municipal initiatives vis-à-vis migrants was that they lacked institutional support for fostering and maintaining existing social and linguistic networks *within* Rome's migrant communities.[23] Forms of pan-ethnic identities, which were often the default mechanisms of municipal interventions, did not take hold on the ground, especially for categories such as Latin Americans. Such categories and modes of governmental address failed to recognize the many racial and class divides within these "pan" and ethnic identities and the way that ethnic migrant groups are themselves internally percolated by forms of racialization and class distinction.

These tensions are partly captured in the conflicts that arose around Piazza Mancini, one of several public spaces of contention in the Roman landscape. Piazza Mancini is also a space where migrants' economic differentiation takes place, which is something that both categories of pan–Latin American migrant communities and the Catholic image of the suffering migrant on a Christic (Jesus-like) path of redemption fall short of capturing (which I discuss in the following chapters). Migrants are, of course, laboring subjects, but also different laboring subjects.

With Alemanno's municipal government, Programma Integra replaced culture-centered initiatives, emphasizing instead the "integration" of migrants and refugees, not only in the labor market but also in "Italian" culture, foregrounding the command of the Italian language. Municipal resources for fostering cultural diversity and celebrations of migrant culture were curtailed or redirected to programs geared to increasing the skills of migrant laborers and to improving the legally sanctioned trait d'union between employees and employers. The cultural aspects, as well as in some cases the folklorization of migrant cultural celebrations, became confined more than ever to private artistic initiatives and to the Catholic Church. Within this period of Alemanno's leadership, media attention contributed to a criminalization of the figure of the migrant, and there was also a surge in acts of violence against unprotected migrant labor, and a strong stand against nonsedentary communities.[24] In a clear conjuncture of economic downturn, Othering had become (as it continues to be today) a political leverage informing a patterned anti-immigration reaction as well as an eruption of what the media have often defined as "apparently meaningless" violence.

The conjuncture of economic downturn in Italy is as much about labor restructuring as it is about changing family demographics and orientations. Much literature has discussed and engaged with transnational migrant labor in the caring industry as a labor of love and Latin American migration, especially from the Andean countries, finds its insertion in this labor market.[25] Compared with Eastern European migration, Latin Americans have a higher number of family reunifications, even while often little family network and welfare support is available to these female migrants. Moreover the rule of jus sanguinis rather than jus soli has clear consequences for children's care, their behavior, and integration into Italian way of life. Members of the youth section of the Latin American Mission, themselves second generation migrants, complain that either one is left alone at home or one grows up in enclosed and straitjacketing Catholic colleges in Rome, where one may be in a class with Italians from very different social backgrounds. In other parts of Italy the presence of Latin American youth has been studied in relation to the increase in youth street gangs.[26] Targeted and attentive care to Latin American youth has increasingly become a key concern for Peruvian and Ecuadorian migrant networks and associations, as well as to therapeutically oriented social services available to migrants.[27]

Indications of a critical attitude toward homogenizing definitions of migrants have begun to emerge in the analysis of current immigration in Italy. Interesting analytical tools such as "internal frontiers" productively challenge collective metaphors of migration. In ethnographically engaged studies of badanti in Tuscany, for example, this tool has provided an understanding of life cycle phases within existing local traditional caring models to open up how the dynamic of badanti becomes a "bottom-up process of experience of multiculturalism, which may erode the cultural frontier gap in the context of routine everyday life."[28] In this sense, from the perspective of affective labor, the intersections between migration and the Catholic Church are multiple. One dominant perspective engendered by both the Scalabrinian order and CARITAS,[29] begins with reenvisioning the church in terms of a voluntary-based openness to a marginalized and pauperized migrant presence in Rome. Thus, "being the Church" implies a "listening center, the path of accompaniment for a defense of human rights, the construction of relationships for people who live in solitude and marginalization."[30] So the Catholic Church's position is both to connect migrant labor to Italian families (especially for the care of the elderly living on their own) where isolation is a growing problem, and it is to help migrants themselves to come out of the isolation they experience in the path of migration. Through this perspective both documented and undocumented migrants seem to share an affective terrain of isolation with a local aging and ailing population.

But the Catholic Church holds multiple views on migration. In the 2009 annual papal visit to the municipality of Rome, Benedict XVI responded to the mayor's proposal for a new "Observatory for Religious Freedom" by emphasizing the "ancient law" and the Christian faith as the best roots the city has for peaceful civil cohabitation. He also reiterated the connection between migration and individual rights, stressing how the Roman Catholic community remains central and essential for the "respect of the fundamental rights of the person in the respect of legality."[31]

Based in Rome, the "Observatory for Religious Freedom" is a new official partnership between the municipal Roman government and the Italian Ministry of Foreign Affairs, which was ratified at the beginning of 2012. The observatory, among other things, was to compile an annual report of national indexes for religious freedom. At the inauguration of the observatory, then-mayor Alemanno recalled attacks suffered by the church, "such as the one suffered in Nigeria by the Christians, that in the world are the first to suffer attacks to their personal religious freedom, with physical threats, killings and massacres."[32] The then Italian foreign minister counterpart, Giulio Terzi di Sant' Agata, emphasized: "The promotion of the freedom of worship and the peaceful cohabitation of faiths will continue to be a qualifying trait of the ethical dimension of foreigner-related Italian policy."[33]

Mayor Alemanno strongly supported the observatory as an instrument of partnership between the Roman local government and the pontifical state, based on a common root in Catholic evangelization—once again demonstrating the strong relationship of the Catholic Church and the Italian state. This interface between municipal and Catholic action on the Roman territory shows some "openness" to the process of migration, but it also has its subtle counterpart of closure, clearly diverging from the conception of a partnership based on the common defense of a tangible Roman cultural heritage promoted by his predecessor.[34] A documented ambivalence by the Roman municipal government and the Italian state over processes of transnational migration,[35] I argue, is paralleled by a similar ambivalence within the Vatican.

Migration is intrinsically connected to the foundational act of delimiting the modern state. As Adelmalek Sayad beautifully argues in his work on the suffering of migrants of Algerian origins to France, this state of openness and closure also animates a recurrent representation of emancipation in the process of migration, when migrants are confronted with the violence of the realization of migration's fantasy and impossibility.[36] This paradox between the fantasy and the reality of migration is grasped (or not) in multiple ways within the Catholic Church itself. Moreover, different political imaginaries around migration are mutually shaped across the relation between the church and municipal and state governments in Italy; none of the multiple positions can be understood in isolation from the others.

Different bodies within the church have conceptualized and operationalized work with migrants differently. There are, broadly speaking, three different approaches toward transnational migration—different souls, to use an emblematic metaphor—within the Roman Catholic Church. A first broad approach to migration within the church is represented by a contingent within the Roman Curia associated with cardinals such as Giacomo Biffi, who understands migration to Italy through a prism of illegality, with limited interest in improving conditions of social plurality. Cardinal Biffi, in early 2000, sparked a major debate in the press, coalescing major conservative voices around the spirit of European civilization. Together with Cardinal Angelo Sodano, Cardinal Biffi has been a strong ally of the Legionaries of Christ (at least prior to the demise of its founder, which I will address in the next chapter), stressing a particular understanding of "humanism" as the root of Italian/European culture.[37] What is even more complex is that this point of view has also been partially shared (around the sanctity of the baptized family) by more liberal voices within the Italian church, such as in the case of the late Cardinal of Milan and Jesuit Carlo Maria Martini.[38]

The second approach is most closely associated with one key organization in Rome and across Italy: Migrantes, a Catholic foundation dedicated to the care of human mobility.[39] Since 1992, Migrantes, along with other groups in the city including the Community of Sant'Egidio and the ACLI (Italian Catholic Labor Association), started a process of reflection on the dynamics of migration. Members of this association even commented on drafts of the Bossi-Fini law, though largely without the hoped-for effect. In May 2008 Father Bruno Mioli, a Scalabrinian father from Vicenza, who was the head of the organization at the time, complained in a personal interview that the changes within the church had not been fast enough to respond to legislative restrictions on immigration in Italy. Father Mioli insisted that part of the church is not in favor of the criminalization of migration but rather sees the need to impose some sort of restriction, a form of "regulatory rationale." For him, the divisions within the church are more a matter of degrees of restriction of migration and whether to make the issue of migration a priority in the everyday practices of the church and its public interventions.

As processes of political subjectivities, migrant itineraries are deeply entangled in embodied and mediatic productions of publics.[40] However, these migrant itineraries are often validated and nested within forms of Catholic pious and voluntary labor and still circumscribed in their production by subtle forms of exclusion. Some of these forms of exclusion are sharply visible in the third key formation shaping the contemporary politics of migration in the church. A more entrepreneurial side of the Catholic priest body has seen migration as not a priority issue for the church. The willingness of this segment of the clergy to dismiss migration as a distinct priority for the church is consonant with the church's historical failure to adopt positions critical of the social and economical structures that have produced the type of migration associated with poverty world-wide. I am not arguing here that Pope Francis's 2013 statements concerning the "culture of waste" of capitalism and the need for the church to pay attention to poverty and transnational migration in the world did not exist prior to his papacy. I am here interested in the different compositions of and the multiple responses to transnational migration that have been present and are still present within the Catholic Church and, to certain extent, regardless of current indications by Pope Francis.

The complexity of Pope Francis's papacy is beyond the purview of this book. Nonetheless, it is important to understand that the church is not just the pope; the pope is one of its faces, more or less courted by the global media, but still only one among many. The long history of the interface between the Catholic Church and transnational migration enlightens the present. The Catholic Church is composed of many dynamic and ever-changing souls that make the analytic of "conservative" versus "progressive" rather inadequate for understanding its many local and global expressions. In fact, a part of the church and the clergy in Rome that could be described as "conservative" because it is not particularly critical of the global economic conjunctures that have created increasing wealth for a few and poverty for many is also "modern," competent, and innovative in creating the ZENIT Catholic web news service, although this was founded by the "conservative" Legionaries of Christ. The web news service has become, since the early 2000s, a key player in online Catholic news distribution. As I describe in the following chapters, the Mexican-based Legionaries of Christ is a neoliberal order in that it courts capital markets and the wealthy elites, but it is considered innovative in its use of the media and, although traditional in its liturgical posture, modern in its evangelical horizons.

The coexistence and the conflict of the different souls of the church are also reflected in concrete, although often minor, examples of migrant presence in the media in Rome. That is the case of the radio program *Hola mi Gente (Ciao Amici)*. This program was promoted by the CICS (Interdisciplinary Center for Social Communication) at the Gregorian University under the guidance of a motivated Venezuelan Jesuit priest, with a small source of funding from the EU (which ran out in 2008—since then the broadcasting has been funded on a shoe string by the Vatican Radio), and in synergy with a CARITAS network of local radio stations in Western Europe and South America. The program has aimed to disclose some of the myths of Spanish-speaking migration to Italy and opens up a forum to give voice to the lives of ordinary migrants, while providing information on how to improve the lives migrants and their integration into Italian society. The program has addressed many themes, including the condition of children of migrants in Italy, the conundrum of labor de-skilling especially for Andean origin women (but also others), and the distribution of information about education opportunities in Italy.

The program was run for many years out of the Gregorian University. Since the funding from the EU ran out, the program has been broadcast from Radio Vaticana, and the organizers work on a voluntary basis (with only travel expenses reimbursed). Two of the highly skilled women (Ecuadorian and Mexican) who have run the program think critically about migration and provide a small but growing Spanish/Italian forum to create bridges, especially for Latin American migrant laborers who are too often stuck behind walls going about their daily cleaning chores. Until 2007 the program was coordinated by an Italian radio producer, who was the only one paid a salary from the EU/Gregorian University sponsorship. However, Maria Luisa, an articulate, bright Ecuadorian woman married to an Italian, who was one of the organizers of the program, was puzzled by the division of labor within the organization of the program and that the Italians were still officially leading, although the organizational work of the program was really the fruit of the migrant women. The Jesuit priest organizer often asked her to be patient and not to voice her concerns.

Maria Luisa found herself in a conundrum: She realized that her labor was not valued enough, and that Italian laborers always have the upper hand. She felt that the Italians thought of themselves as knowing best, as "having more culture"—and seeing migrants as coming from "uncivilized places." It was clear in her mind that even in the context of this program, where we find the church embracing a progressive discourse on migration and cultural pluralism, the status quo of material inequality was reproduced to a certain degree by the Jesuit priest/organization behind the program. Migrant labor, she mentioned, is often seen as voluntary labor, whereas the Italian laborer (even if not so skilled as the migrant one) gets preferential treatment in a condition of scarcity of resources.

Once the EU funding ran out, the Italian radio producer shifted to other programs, and *Hola mi Gente* continued to be broadcast from Vatican radio facilities, but a sense of uneasiness stayed with Maria Luisa for a while. She is now an Italian citizen and active in different migrant networks and labor organizations; she balances these commitments with much dedication, but she is also juggling with housework, her husband,

and two young daughters. For her it was clear that subtle forms of exclusion were still active even among more liberal factions of the Catholic Church, in the name of Italian culture and civilization. Toño, the Peruvian man who first brought me to Piazza Mancini and an organizer of the radio program for a time, said that, behind the lack of "society integration," there was a lack of labor integration, based in turn on much ignorance. Too many Italians, both he and Maria Luisa argued, know little about migrants' worlds; nonetheless, they keep an upper hand on labor relations. Although Maria Luisa may no longer be bothered by the conflict at the radio program, it is still an episode deeply expressive of the ways in which even embryonic forms of migrant female labor mobility face challenges within the world of the lay Catholic voluntary sector. Even if the Second Vatican Council has named the lay sector as a priority for the church's apostolic renewal and attention, labor relations between lay people and clerics in their affective, gendered, and productive regimes are still a terrain of contestation. This aspect of the Second Vatican Council's recommendations has still not been fulfilled.

Migration and the Second Vatican Council

A main focus of Vatican II has been on the church's relation to "liberation" and "inculturation" and the role of lay Catholics in the promotion of the church. The current conjuncture of revisions of and rethinking about what Vatican II is and has meant for the church is having subtle effects on different fields. The implications of this revisionism are not limited to the internal politics regarding the promotion of a canonical liturgy and the reassertion of a centralist and hierarchical decision-making structure. This revisionism has also had concrete effects on the politics of migration.

A major development of Vatican II has been of inculturation as a movement inspired by the *aggiornamento*—the process of revision of the church's canon law that has come to see local cultural expressions as possible proclamations of Catholicism. Inculturation refers to a relative willingness of the church to adapt Catholic doctrine to local social systems and cultural traditions and to be renewed by these encounters. This approach sees native and non-Western societies as already potentially embedded within expressions of Catholicism, in different forms and fashions. Catholic inculturation is not a new concept, and it has been a bone of contention since the beginnings of modern missionary life. It was in the middle of the seventeenth century that the Jesuit order successfully promoted Catholic missions in China by allowing the translation of the Bible into local languages and interpreting it through local understandings of the cult of the ancestors. Later, because of the demise of the Jesuits' fortune in Rome and Europe, their missionary policy was effectively undermined in China, beginning with the prohibition of the use of translated texts and the imposition of Vatican political presence within the Chinese empire.[41] The church's anxieties about its lack of control over its powerful orders translated to an increased suppression of local expressions of Catholicism.

Since the 1960s a debate on inculturation has also engendered important discussions, at least in Latin America, about the relation between evangelization and culture and the inculturation of the gospel. Through these debates, the Catholic Church began to wrestle with the historicity of its own message and the centrality of popular and local religiosity to its own theological reproduction. With this came the recognition that hybridity and syncretism offer points of departure for understanding the everyday phenomenology of Catholicism. All of this has been a radical challenge for the church from within, but potentially also that which has engendered its own backlash.

Interpretations of Vatican II have been numerous and increasingly contentious. Here I highlight two.[42] On one hand, early interpretations of Vatican II saw it as an event that reinscribed and opened up the roots of the liturgy and the standing of the church. Vatican II, although not endorsed unanimously within the church in 1965, has reformulated a relation between scriptures and tradition, allowing for a profound inculturation of the sacred word. In this respect, Vatican II signaled a shift to a praxeology and the inculturation of theology within the humanmade world, away from the divine heritage of the scriptures. This implied a theological challenge to Thomist interpretations and a renewed opening to national episcopal conferences for the interpretation and implementation of those guidelines.

On the other hand, Vatican II has been read by Benedict XVI in continuity with previous church traditions, rather than as an event that has broken away from them. Especially for Benedict XVI this rereading of the Second Vatican Council focuses on the immutability of the liturgy, the institution of the church, and its ultimate authority over the recent multiplication of biblical and liturgical movements within. Moreover, this revisionist school argues that the tension of modernists vis-à-vis antimodernists (themselves) is a false one. However, modernists, especially within the Dominican and Jesuit ranks, have privileged instead a reading of immanence, a focus on the "religion of the heart" as the one lived and experienced by the human subject, and they have held an ecumenical view of the church as extending the heart of the "mystical body" to other Christian churches. A lay counterpart of this reading was fostered by the Bologna school championed by Giuseppe Alberigo, whose position is now refuted by some.[43]

John Paul II was key to this revisionist debate of Vatican II. For John Paul II, this was a debate about the "transformation of the heart" away from the encompassing limits of civil society. He also emphasized the subjective dimension of dominion in the practice of faith, as the ethical capacity to "dominate" the world through work as "free" subjects.[44] Part of John Paul II's position in this debate is a focus on the revivification of Marian cultures, which represented a rift with the Jesuits from the beginning of his papal mandate. This rift was in part about conceiving culture connected to the principles of liberation theology in the Americas as the product of social *and* divine transformations. So both John Paul II and Benedict XVI, although in different ways, championed a revisionist reading of Vatican II, a recalibrating of the church as a passionate machine. The former did so via a particular faith on a freely chosen embrace of Marian love; the latter through an undefeated faith on the transcendental truth of Catholic liturgy.

These competing interpretations of the meaning and legacy of Vatican II intersect with the problem of migration within the church in at least two ways. First, as in the theology of Benedict XVI the backtracking over the importance of "culture" as the location of the gospel reclaims a precultural space as the location of the key sacredness of Catholicism. These revisionist interpretations of Vatican II tend to leave unacknowledged the sorts of potential conflicts over different cultural embodiments of the Catholic Church that have emerged in Rome over the course of the 2000s. Fueled by right-wing mayoralties such as that of Gianni Alemanno, the tendencies within the church that privilege a notion of Roman civic heritage that is intertwined with that of the Catholic Church tend to conflate an attack on civitas (in the singular) with an attack on Catholic humanitas.

Second, this revisionism is empowering more conservative and neotraditionalist wings of the church in Rome that promote an understanding of "the" Catholicism as the cradle of Europe. These orientations have long flourished as part of a Romanization of Catholicism in Rome itself (but also conspicuously in North America).[45] By *Romanization* I refer here to the ways in which a direct contact with the Vatican has been weighed in the professionalization of clergy worldwide. It is a long-standing practice that the "cream" of the national clergy is sent by bishops from different dioceses in Latin America to study in one of the many pontifical universities in Rome (such as the Gregorian and the Urbaniana). By being physically and historically immersed in the *romanità* of the church, priests and seminarians not only absorb a sense of Catholic civitas and humanitas but also become, through their shared connection to the Vatican, strategic players in supporting local bishops within national church's politics.

Since Pius IX in the nineteenth century, national seminaries in Rome have hosted select clergy during a period of formation and specialization, strengthening both a sense of civitas romana and an allegiance to the pope. Making future Latin American clergy "Roman at heart"[46] was both cause and effect of the creation of the Colegio Pío Latino Americano, founded by José Ignacio Víctor Eyzaguirre, a Chilean priest, in 1856. The establishment of that pedagogical hub as a formative space for young Latin American priests was also to combat "the anti-Catholic spirit, indifferentism and the corruption of habits" widely condemned by the church at the time.[47]

This historical push toward a Romanization of the Catholic Church often assumes a paradoxical appearance when it comes to immigration in Italy. Thus, one side of the clergy sees Catholic migrants as "new blood" that might renew and defend a Catholic Church that is in decline across Europe and actively under attack at the borderlands of Christianity—for example, in Palestine and Israel, or in Nigeria. Yet at the same time transnational migration is seen as destabilizing the foundational core of Europe. Transnational Catholic migration from the Americas to Rome thus carries a paradoxical symbolic weight. The indigenous migrants from the Americas form a stream of new apostolic blood revitalizing both the clergy and the popular perception of the church—Pope Francis clearly stands as the emblematic case; at the same time, as I explain in the following chapter, for the same clergy, the "return" of Latin American Catholics to Rome constitutes an unnerving reminder of its incomplete dominion over the affective and sexualized nature of migrant itineraries.

2. The "Culture of Life" and Migrant Pedagogies

> I hope that a balanced management of migratory flows and of
> human mobility in general will soon be achieved so as to ben-
> efit the entire human family, starting with practical measures
> that encourage legal emigration and the reunion of families,
> and paying special attention to women and minors. Indeed,
> the human person must always be the focal point in the vast
> field of international migration. . . . Moreover, the *migrant fam-
> ily* is in a special way a resource as long as it is respected as such;
> it must not suffer irreparable damage but must be able to stay
> united or to be reunited and carry out its mission as the *cradle
> of life* and the primary context where the human person is wel-
> comed and educated.
> —Benedict XVI, Angelus, 14 January 2007,
> World Day of Migrants and Refugees

The relation between migration and Catholicism is complex and requires
an understanding of the changing nature of Catholicism, as well as the
resilient endurance of its past in the present.[1] The present that I interrogate
in the following pages shows a tension between a part of the church that
privileges a historicized approach to migration and one shaped by a conservative revision of the meaning and legacy of Vatican II. The former,
endorsed by orders such as the Scalabrinians who run the Latin American
Mission (MLA), frames migration as an aspect of contemporary human
experience and advocates a positive response to this condition defined by
the active engagement and adaptation of church structures, pedagogy, and
practice. The latter position sees transnational migration to Rome, the
figurative heart of Catholicism, as a potential threat to an allegedly authentic and avowedly European Catholic heritage. This perspective actively
obscures issues of difference and distribution while foregrounding a uni-

versal notion of the "Culture of Life" and a Catholic humanitas. Its advocates fuel and support political expressions in Italian society that amplify discourses of the illegality and of the need for a tight control over transnational migration.

The argument here is that both of these approaches in different ways and with different accents have to grapple, first, with migrants' affective relation to their nation of origin within an imagined pan-American Catholicism and, second, with the heterogeneous practices that escape the tropes of migrant suffering and an idealized Catholic notion of migrant family and unity of the sort so apparent in the epigraphic quotation from Benedict XVI above. I use the phrase migrant pedagogies here to describe the projects championed by different religious actors in the church that aim to encourage and educate migrants to be good apostolic agents of what I have emphasized in the introduction of this book is a central, Christocentric mandate of the Catholic Church: the New Evangelization. *Pedagogy* (from the Greek *paidos*) refers to teaching children and similar types of instruction. In the case of migrant pedagogies the term foregrounds a paternalistic relation between those who are in authority in the church and the laity. Finally, I argue that this conservative tendency positions the Catholic Church as an active agent involved in shaping migrants into being "good" laborers, especially in the care industry, where the majority of Latin American female migrants to Rome are employed.

As I outlined in the introduction, Latin American transnational migration in Rome ignites an old conflict within the Catholic Church and a lasting paradox within a Catholic humanitas: the paradox of Catholic conversion as the tension between Sameness and Otherness, which has been present at least since the Encounter with the New World. This tension between Sameness and Otherness emerges from the historic debate about the nature of the human person since the Valladolid's dispute between Ginés Sepúlveda and Fray Bartolomé de Las Casas. In this chapter, I read echoes of this sedimented tension of totalizing Sameness versus Otherness as implicitly haunting the Roman Catholic Church's postures on twenty-first-century migration.

Different pontifical guidelines since *Exsul Familia* (1952)[2] have stressed migration as a "sign of the times" but current rereadings of this sign awaken conflicts within the church about it own form of governmentality.[3] These debates reflect long-sedimented tensions between territorially based parishes and their diocesan clergy and religious orders (such as the Scalabrinians and the Jesuits) working in those same territories. These tensions have a direct bearing on how migration is dealt with and managed at the level of local constituencies such at the MLA. The Scalabrinian order's strategies of engagement in Rome highlight a particular approach to migrants that emphasizes their suffering, their vulnerable position, and Jesus/Mary-like paths to redemption. That which exceeds this imagining of migrant's subjectivity creates areas of contention within the church itself.

La Vergine del Carmelo *and* El Señor de los Milagros

It is July 2009 and the migrants in the Latin American Mission in Trastevere are getting ready to celebrate the Vergine del Carmelo. This is the first time the celebration has been held in the neighborhood. The Latin American Mission is participating, and Father Alfonso, the Italian Scalabrinian priest at the head of the mission at the time, has been involved in making this happen. The Virgin will be taken around in procession through the streets of Trastevere, and will stop at Santa Maria della Luce. She is taken out of the Church of Santa Agata, among a flock of Italian devotees, some of whom have come from the provinces; others are from Trastevere itself. Gianni Alemanno, the mayor of Rome at the time and a member of the right-wing Alleanza Nazionale party, addresses the public after this short introduction by the head of the community of Sant'Egidio:[4]

> It is said that Trastevere is the heart of Rome, and we want the heart of Rome to be full of sentiments, sentiments of love, hospitality, mercy, and of meeting and dialogue. This is what Mary teaches us, and it is what we want from this celebration, from this neighborhood, which from the heart of Rome can reach all the city, so thank you, Mayor, also for the work in this direction.

A reply from Mayor Alemanno follows shortly afterward:

> Thank you. I see Trastevere as one of the most profound and old roots [of our city], but this procession and this devotion to Mary is also the soul of Trastevere, the air of our neighborhoods. In these moments we find ourselves to be stronger, more convinced to construct our future, so I am really pleased to be among you all. Let's honor Mary, since this procession will give us much strength.

The heart of Rome is a terrain of dispute. The procession, headed by an Italian cardinal and followed by the Italian Marian confraternity of the Carmele, proceeds straight for Via Lungaretta, where beyond a narrow bend the Church of Santa Maria della Luce stands. Migrant women at the church have been preparing the altar all afternoon, with flowers, *empanadas,* and fruits. When the Virgin arrives in front of the Latin American Mission's parish, a group of members of the brotherhood of the Señor de los Milagros joins the procession and helps carry her the final distance. When the Virgin arrives, Father Alfonso addresses the crowd and the institutional representatives, which include different *forze dell'ordine* (police forces) and Mayor Alemanno. Father Alfonso gives thanks for the "wonderful visit of the Virgin" to this church and community, and then becomes increasingly energetic. The vein on his neck starts to pulse visibly. Leticia, a Peruvian migrant, will describe later how he "looked enraged," and spoke as "never before." Father Alfonso's words are very direct. The core of his speech is about the oneness and power of the heart of Jesus. If you are in his heart, you are open, and as such you are open to those who come and knock at your door and ask for dignity, a life, and work. If you are not open to that, if your heart is not open to the call of these migrants, you are not in the heart of Jesus; you cannot be called a Catholic. Either you are with these migrants and with *the* church (stressed in his words), or you are outside it; you are against the real foundation of the church, the love of Jesus.

These are very strong words; I have never heard Padre Alfonso talking about these issues in front of such a "respectable crowd," and his words take on a particular resonance in front of Mayor Alemanno and just a few days after the ratification of the security decree, which has promoted harsher measures against undocumented migrants. Then the Hermanos de Los Señor de los Milagros help carry the Virgin out of the church toward the final leg of her procession. There is a startling moment. They walk with a steady, rhythmic step—something they have supposedly learned since the time they enter the brotherhood. But the Italian carriers adopt an equally well-practiced, but very different step: much faster, nearly rushing. The Virgin sways dangerously for a few meters. Some fear she may topple, but in the end it is the Italian carriers that take the lead, the pace is still fast, although not that rhythmic. This year, the Hermandad del Señor de los Milagros have to *adapt*. Maybe next year will be different.

Second encounter, two years earlier: Father R. is a diocesan chaplain of a much bigger church than Santa Maria in Trastevere, Santa Maria degli Angeli, a basilica where the Peruvian Church, part of the Latin American Mission, has had its base for a few years. The group has the spiritual guidance of a Scalabrinian priest younger than Father Alfonso, but he could not do much aside from asking the migrants to be calm and endure some of the "misunderstandings." In the words of Rosa, a Peruvian migrant who has resided in Italy for more than fifteen years, Father R. is "racist." I can see why she is saying that, as I have myself been bewildered by the manner of this priest. Perhaps an index of my partially anticlerical family upbringing in northern Italy, I share Rosa's distrust for the patronizing tone, which I have also encountered with other priests.

Father R. arrives one day in the back of the church, the oratory, where migrant women were celebrating the Virgin of the Chapi with Peruvian food and songs. He openly expressed his aversion to the look and smell of what had been cooked and shared. For sometime he has complained about how the Peruvian group makes too much clatter with its music, and he always asks them to be quiet, to make no noise. The infantilization of migrants is not new in this church, nor is it in Italy in general. Father R. repeats that this basilica is a "national" one, where "official burials take place" and official national events are held. The smell of Peruvian food can dangerously penetrate the walls of the basilica, often empty of devotees, and only full of tourists.

The tension between Father R. and the Latin American migrants meeting at the Basilica had already reached some heights. In fact in the months following the encounter in 2007 he ordered them to put the large painting of the Señor de Los Milagros in the basement, directing them to expose it only just before their Sunday Spanish mass, and to remove it immediately afterward. This leaves no way for the devoted Peruvians to pray to this much-beloved image at their own leisure. A plan to move the painting to Santa Maria della Luce is put in action in 2007. One side of the group does not want this to happen though, preferring that it be taken to another church, Santa Lucia. The painting is snatched away the day before it should have been transferred to Santa Maria in Trastevere. "Happily," the painting turns up safely the day after in the MLA in Trastevere, heralding the permanent demise of the "hijacker" group.

This story is also an index of clerical relations within parishes. There are more than a few diocesan priests who think like Father R. As a diocesan priest, he upholds the territorial government of his diocese. The Scalabrinians have to adapt to what the diocesan priests decide, although a few of them were the ones who suggested moving the painting of the Señor de Los Milagros elsewhere, away from the basilica in the first place. This is not an isolated case, nor is it a "pathology" of an individual priest, who was brought up in a heavily Catholic, provincial northern Italian small town in the 1950s. These tensions in a given dioceses, between religious orders operating in that territory and diocesan priests, have a long history in the functioning of the church—they are not an exception. Although what is a nearly xenophobic tint in Father R.'s response may be of more recent appearance in Italy; for a very long time religious orders have had, in principle and in practice, to coordinate their efforts within and under- neath the authority of the local bishop. More than ever, these relations of authority and obedience are important in Rome whose bishop is the pope.

Third encounter: In spring 2008 we are celebrating the Día de las Madres with the Comunidad Católica Mexicana (CCM) in Parco Gel- somino, a lovely, park that feels like a countryside farm, tucked away in the middle of the city, just off the Villa Aurelia. The mass in Spanish is celebrated by Father Hector, a Mexican diocesan priest from Veracruz, who has studied at the Gregorian University and later at the European University, championed by the Legionaries of Christ. Around two hun- dred people are enjoying barbequed meat and quesadilla, with Corona beer, while we mingle with religious nuns and priests: There are many Mexican women married to Italian men present, with children running around. Market stalls are set up, selling Mexican arts and crafts. I am sit- ting down with Lorinda, Damiana, and Iris, who have all been living in Italy for a while and who are married (or once married) to Italians. The security decree has just been passed, and Damiana and Lorinda agree that they have found it really uncomfortable speaking Spanish to their children in public or on the bus, for instance. Both have turned to speaking Italian to their children in public spaces, at least for the time being. Lorinda cor- rects Iris, saying that Italian people are not the children of the fascists, but are fascist themselves. Rome is becoming different and there is a sense that xenophobia has arrived for them too.

They carry on, remarking that the day of the mother is celebrated in the absence of their own mothers. There is a sense of loss and absence, Iris adds, and Damiana, who is well educated and now runs a web service for Spanish-speaking children's activities, intervenes, saying that the power of motherhood is being able to protect your children; if things turn nasty here, Damiana continues, she will pick up and leave Italy—though how could she do it, she cannot say. Then they remember the blessing of Father Hector, who earlier in the mass symbolically showered the congregation with water and mentioned the power of all mothers, and of the Virgin of Guadalupe especially. He prayed that even the mother of Felipe Calderón (the president of Mexico at the time) could inspire him to address the difficulties of the country back home. Mother's love is in the nation too.

Lorinda adds that it is great here, in Rome, to be part of something that it is "so Mexican." One of the reasons she had been initially skeptical about joining the CCM was that she thought it was Catholic; she has a past in the PRI (Partido Revolucionario Institucional) in Mexico, so the nation and national celebrations are important for her, as it is having her child take part in them.[5] I then recall, together with them, that in 2005 the issue of contention with the MLA and CCM was that the CCM was celebrating too many national celebrations and did not do enough evangelization. Odette then says that the CCM is different because the women who come here are different. The majority of them do not, and would not, do the same work that other Latin American women migrants do (as badanti, or housecleaners); nonetheless there are no jobs for them in Rome. Some of these Mexican women face a very difficult transition into the Italian labor market. Employed or jobless, they are nonetheless all Catholics, "Mexican Catholics."

A group of Mexican sisters of an order dedicated to the Immaculate Heart of Mary comes and joins us on the lawn. The music picks up before the mariachis play; some salsa and Latin music is put on a stereo. Couples are dancing, a few rather close to each other. One couple I recognize is a Mexican seminarian, who is dancing sensuously with a Mexican woman. He is not a Legionary of Christ, but he belongs to the diocese of a central Mexican state. The sisters and I look at each other in the eyes, and we kind of giggle. Love is probably not in the air, but something is there for sure. Martha, the president of the CCM, as a good *norteña* (from Monterrey) often jokes about the sexuality of the priests, and some are very good at bouncing back her jokes, while others shy away. Maybe love is not in the air, but a few boundaries are being crossed on this Día de las Madres. One sister actually stops looking and turns her sight away. We come back to the subject of speaking Spanish in public and the anti-immigrant sentiments in Rome. In other contexts, Mexican nuns too have expressed to me that they feel insecure because of their accent when they are not wearing religious habits in Rome. If a nun wears a habit, she won't be stopped by the police and asked for her papers. Clerical uniforms in Rome still give those who wear them a positive aura that overcomes, most of the time but not always, anti-immigrant sentiments.

Rogelio is a gay man who is part of the Mexican folkloric dance group Ramatitlán. Rogelio has a stand in the market, where he sells Mexican arts and crafts. For a few years, he has rented a little atelier just off the Aurelia Antica road. It took him a while to be able to afford it. Rogelio was one of the founding members of the CCM. He arrived in Italy in the middle of the 1990s, when his brother was working as a chef in Rome, but he was not warned that it would be hard, physically as well as spiritually. For years after his arrival in Italy he worked as whitewasher, after more than ten years as an insurance broker in Mexico City:

> When I arrived, I thought that in Italy there was no racism. But when I arrived here, I felt like *un indio* or *una Maria*,[6] as if I was always going around dirty. And you know there was another Mexican group here. But they were different from what the CCM is now; they just wanted Mexicans to be part of it, somehow elitists. It was like we were the indios . . . but for me it does not matter if you have a name which is Chinese or Jewish, for me you are still very much Mexican. This is also why we are now more independent [from the MLA], but we are still called Comunidad Católica Mexicana. For us this is a place for all types of people; this is the true spirit of a Catholic Mexican.

Rogelio also came to Italy because he was gay. When he was in Mexico he became really tired of having to ask a good female friend to act as his girlfriend when he had to go to work-related parties. In Rome he has a stable boyfriend, and he is not hiding his relationship. Life is not always easy, but that initial sense of betrayal of his nation has waned,[7] even if his puzzlement about interracial tensions between fellow Mexicans still remains. A reproduction of different facets of the nation is still engrained in people's lives.

The tensions between the CCM and the MLA have been mainly because of the viewpoints of the Scalabrinians priests heading it. The Scalabrinian missionary order is playing a central role in translating emergent migrant demands for social and labor inclusion. Founded in 1887 and originally dedicated to supporting Italian migrants in the Americas, by the turn of the twentieth century, it had more than 600 priests across North America, Brazil, Italy, the Philippines, and Australia. The history of the evangelization of transnational Latino migrants in Rome is closely connected to the efforts of this order. Scalabrinians are playing a central role in the institution of Capillania (chaplaincy), which was designed as a mission of *cura animarum* (the obligation and task of the diocesan clergy to care for souls), promoted toward migrants initially by the *Exsul Familia* of Pius XII in 1952. The Capillania, as in the case of the MLA, serves the diocesan church by transforming its care from monoethnic to pluriethnic[8] and by ensuring that the center of evangelization becomes the person and the promotion of his or her dignity.[9]

The Scalabrinian Order

The order of the Scalabrinians was founded by the Italian bishop Giovanni Battista Scalabrini, under the name of the Missionaries of St. Charles Borromeo (with a female counterpart of Missionary Sisters established in 1895); it is the only order in the Catholic Church exclusively dedicated to the cause of migrants. Following on the debate generated by the publication of the Encyclical *Rerum Novarum* by Pope Leo XIII, Blessed Giovanni Battista Scalabrini contributed to the reflections on Catholicism, the rights of laborers, and the "love for immigrants."[10] He posited that the paramount problem of migration was a potential loss of faith because of deprivation and loss of religious instruction.

The appeal of Scalabrini pivots around a belief that migration is an opportunity for the improvement of human relationships and the relations between nations. Beyond a vision of the migrants as the "children of indigence," Scalabrini promoted a rethinking of migrants as the holders of cultural values. But in order to be good Catholics, migrants need a religious environment that fosters a transnational practice of faith. For Scalabrini, the pastoral charisma was not in opposition to national belonging, but the reason for a mutual strengthening:

> The national sentiment becomes a support for religious sentiment, and the poor immigrant receives not only the assistance of a Catholic priest but also the endearing care of an apostle, who will foster in him or her the old tradition of the nation (patria) and of the family; this tradition is the basis of his or her faith.[11]

For the Scalabrinians, migration is part of divine providence. As Father Battistella puts it:

> In the Scalabrinian tradition, migration is considered part of a holistic approach, which requires combating the causes of migration, which so often is not a choice, but a constraint, and promoting respect for migrants' rights and dignity. At the same time, migration is not just a problem but an opportunity for society and church, and migrants are not simply victims to be helped, but persons with much to offer and to con-

tribute to the community, subjects of transformation and mission. We need to understand the providential optic of migration in its positive and negative aspects. Of course, there are negative aspects such as the suffering in migration, but we should dwell not only on the suffering of migration; we should also understand it as God who is leading history.[12]

The Scalabrinians also emphasize the importance of learning the language, the culture, and the religious expressions of migrants both of their countries of origin and of their country of residence. The capacity of religious actors to understand the cultures of origin/departure and residence/arrival of the migrants is seen as strength not weakness. This is so because Scalabrinians conceive of a culturally relativist, migrant perspective as a fundamental part of an integrated church:

> In the complex, laborious, and often contradictory process of integration [*inserimento*], the migrant needs to be recognized as a citizen of the church who receives the incitement of Catholicity: While with autochthonous people, the migrant is called to enter the path of cultures' death and resurrection; he becomes capable, together with them, of a Pentecostal communion of reconciled diversities.[13]

In more recent debates internal to the order, migration is for the Scalabrinian pedagogy a challenge to resist a homogenization of migrants through "unity in diversity."[14] Recent and sophisticated Scalabrinian reflections are now also taking into account the transforming ethical horizons of migration. They also see that migration has been normalized as a state of exception. However, in these reflections the nation and the affective forces associated with it are still minimized.[15] Yet the strength of Scalabrinian pastoring lies in the strong relation it draws between migrant, national, and religious affective terrains, but this is also its Achilles' heel. I say Achilles' heel because in the recent practices of the MLA, the role of the nation has been an unspoken point of dispute. If Scalabrinian pedagogy has in the past fostered migrant cultures by using the original languages of the migrants in sacramental and evangelical celebrations, today the MLA shows an increasing tendency to perform sacraments and masses in Italian, despite the complaints of some of the migrants who attend. Nonetheless, there is more to an approach of a celebration of the nation than the use of a native language.

Until 2007, the second in charge of the MLA in Rome was a Mexican Scalabrinian priest, Father Manuel. Clearly influenced by Brazilian liberation theology, Father Manuel pointed out a disjunction between the

Catholic hierarchy that preaches rigor in matter of sexuality, contraception, and out-of-wedlock sexual relations and the realities of migration. Often in a passionate mood he defended migrants who lived in unstable economic and familial conditions and who had sexual and affective ties outside of wedlock; he saw these as the result of social isolation. For Father Manuel, such realities and the response they seemed to demand of the church contradicted sharply with the guidelines that, as a missionary priest, he was directed to follow by the Archdiocese of Rome.

In 2006 a rift emerged between the lay organizers of the CCM and the MLA while Father Manuel was taking care of the spiritual side of CCM. The CCM, which informally began its activities in 2000, but officially registered as a civil association in 2003, had grown by that time not so much in numbers as in its capacity for promoting events and gatherings that went beyond strictly religious and sacramental celebrations. After a verbal confrontation in a meeting, a split occurred, and a Jesuit took charge of the association while CCM meetings began to take place in the Church of Caravita, rather than in the church premises that were coordinated by Scalabrinians. In the wake of these events, Father Manuel complained that the CCM was no longer interested in evangelizing and had become too interested in celebrating secular national events. In contrast, the organizers continued emphasizing that in a profound Mexican way those national markers could not be separated from the Catholic identity of Mexico as a nation. The severity of this rift was such that the two sides did not speak to each other for some time. The CCM criticized some of the Scalabrinians of Santa Maria della Luce because they felt ordered around and treated as children. Even the Jesuit spiritual head of the community that followed recognized that:

> there is a need to respect the differences of the [migrant] groups. They are not parishioners, they do not want to be controlled and to follow orders (do this, celebrate that . . .). They have their own life; they are not children; let the people celebrate their cultural and national feasts, the day of the dead . . . let them lead their lives.[16]

However, the tensions were also organizational. Father Manuel helped draft the constitution of the CCM as a civil association, but in the end, and somewhat to his disappointment, he was not nominated as its president. He had hoped to be able to organize activities and gather funds for initiatives free from the gaze of his superiors and with more room to maneuver for a way of practicing a Catholicism that was more involved with the real lives of people. Instead, Father Alfonso, his direct superior, asked for "numbers": bodies to fill up the church, baptisms and confirmations to count in the church's archives to prove to the diocese that the Scalabrinians were looking after a consistent number of devotees. Since leading CCM members started to complain that he had lost interest in their work, this disagreement over the function and future of the organization became rather tense, and Father Manuel eventually left the staff of the CCM and focused on another migrant group part of the MLA—the Brazilian group. Father Manuel was eventually moved to Germany to take care of another Spanish-speaking congregation.

It is important to mention, though, that Father Alfonso was in some instances also critical of the Catholic hierarchy and diocesan forms of governing priests' lives. He did not openly voice his criticism, for instance, that the top floor of the living quarters of Santa Maria della Luce was still being used by a relatively young diocesan priest, whose life in Rome centered less on the church and more on selling secondhand furniture. Father Alfonso felt that the interests of the migrant church were always secondary to the diocesan Roman apparatus, and that too often the care for migrants "was more in words than action." But Father Alfonso as well as some of the other Scalabrinian fathers living at Santa Maria della Luce had difficulties with the composition of the CCM leadership. They could not accept Rogelio's gently but surely disclosed gay identity, nor could they fully understand the support and the influence that the Colegio Mexicano[17] had in the CCM. For Father Alfonso, though, the central problem was that the leaders of the CCM "do not feel they are immigrants; they feel different; they feel self-sufficient. So they have taken advantage to celebrate their [own] culture; they are not interested in evangelizing."

But if the CCM was accused of celebrating the popular side of Catholicism, it also meant it looked after the "*locuras de la vida*" (crazy things of life), in the words of Martha, one of the organizers. The association has also taken care of Mexican women who have been subject to domestic violence and has become involved in a few cases when violence was perpetrated against gay people. They have aided Mexicans in Italy who have been robbed, and they have attended to Mexican clergy who wanted to leave their orders but who had originally arrived in Italy on a religious visa. It is clear then that, beyond the ritual celebrations of Catholic and national events, the CCM has also engaged with those who do not fit into the picture of the normative family, the idealized narratives of the process of migration, or the "path of suffering" of migrants. If their dispute with the Scalabrinians was about not being evangelical and apostolic enough, they themselves have nonetheless attended to the socially less than accepted margins of migration.

Many in the CCM expressed resentment toward the infantilizing character of Scalabrinian pedagogical practice. But a top-down wish to turn migrants into (childlike) agents of new evangelization is not the only vision of migrant Catholics that the organization had to contend with. Take the position of Cardinal Biffi in an infamous and much-debated intervention in 2000, when he stressed that the Italian government should favor Catholic over non-Catholic immigration. He said, "The criteria for admitting immigrants cannot be only economic. It is necessary that one seriously concerns oneself with saving the identity of the nation itself."[18]

The debate over the Catholic roots of Italy and the Christian underpinnings of Europe is, of course, polymorphic, but it is critical to point out that Biffi's position is an expression of a wider spectrum that has on one (and more militant) side a strong call for Catholic apologetics (*apologia Cattolica*). This is a theology that strongly defends the truth of the Catholic faith. Social expressions of Catholic apologetics have been gaining renewed strength in Italy, and they all condemn what they perceive as an increasing laicization of society. I refer here to movements (and forums) such as Forza Nuova, a neofascist, grassroots organization, present in some neighborhoods of the municipality of Rome, which has a strong association with family-oriented Catholic policies.[19] Forms of Catholic apologetics have continuity with the ideology of the fascist regime. Members of parliament at the time too, such as Alfredo Mantovano, have often contributed to the discussion generated in Catholic forums, such as Alleanza Cattolica and Totus Tuus Network (connected to the magazine *Il Timone*).[20] Italian historians and sociologists such as Giovanni Cantoni, Massimo Introvigne, Franco Cardini, and Roberto de Mattei are also well-known intellectuals who have strongly supported an idea of militancy against laicism. These are all multiple Catholic voices, which, more or less adamantly, have strongly spoken against a perceived laicization of the Italian nation-state.

Hence, in the realm of Vatican's interventions, Biffi's voice is a "defense" of Catholicism and falls within the spectrum of what John Paul II called "the urgency of not squandering this precious patrimony and helping Europe to build itself by revitalizing its original Christian roots."[21] These words index a reality and an anxiety that Europe might lose its Christian and Catholic roots. This call, in John Paul II's words, is an allegedly positive reading of Eurocentrism. Instead, Benedict XVI has emphasized a negative impact of the loss of Catholic roots and the elevation of technology as a site of misplaced worship when not combined with a proper moral compass.[22] Hence, it is really important to see, and open up from different angles of inquiry, why and how different forms of transnational migration and immigration unsettle the church's focus on Europe as historically and religiously Christian.

In a similar vein, Luis Garza Medina, the Mexican vicar-general of the Legionaries of Christ until 2011, warns about the danger of ideologies that "divinize" concepts that belong to secular language, such as freedom or democracy, and dissociate them from realms considered worthy by the Catholic Church, such as family and faith.[23] Voices such as Garza Medina's are representative of a part of the church that has, since the mid 1990s, tried to reconquer a space in the public sphere by abandoning overt and unilateral political affiliation, instead placing its bets on emphasizing a communal Catholic culture based on a particular anthropological reading of the defense of "human values."[24] This is an important shift that cannot be overstated.

If orders such as the Scalabrinians have developed their pastoral care around ideas of cultures as diverse heritage backgrounds that migrants bring with them and transform in a host society, there is another part of the church that is using culture, in the singular, defined and circumscribed by a notion of human culture, or more specifically a condition of being human that is perceived as universal. This notion of human culture as the "Culture of Life" gets translated into a perspective of the church that animates a defense of life (see, for instance, anti-abortion stances) and a defense of the sacredness of the heteronormative family (see hostility toward the introduction of same-sex marriage laws). The voices of this part of the church are not new, but well rehearsed. More than ever, however, transnational migration and the Catholic pastoral toward migrants in the heart of Rome highlight a collision within the church between understandings of *culture* conceived of as the articulation of Christian heritage with a perceived-as-universal condition of being human and cultures as the diverse practices of identity articulated often, but not exclusively, in terms of affiliation with nations and languages.

Under the pressure of the conservative discourses of a Catholic culture of life the heterogeneity of migrants' lived experiences and fantasies is constantly threatened with reduction to a form of Catholic humanitas, where the human person is understood as part of a universal, single heritage, an offshoot of the roots of European, Roman civilization. Michel de

Certeau has explored an aspect of this tension in the production of knowledge. In his view, the "scriptural economy" is the violent act of disavowal performed by patriarchally orchestrated textuality against the multiplicity of embodied and often feminized experiences.[25] Being a Jesuit himself, de Certeau was aware of how the Catholic Church generated and also tried to break from different forms of scriptural economies in the long durée of its monastic, colonial, and modern history.

Numerous Italian intellectuals have voiced concerns about the move of the Roman Catholic Church, and particularly of Benedict XVI, of inserting a particular value of the human into a universal and totalizing notion of truth.[26] Gustavo Zagrebelsky, a prominent judge and briefly the president of the Constitutional Court, questions how an ethic of truth can really be a contribution to a national democracy, where ethics (rather than morality) should be informed instead by the possibility of doubt and questioning. Francesco Remotti, an Africanist anthropologist and leading academic figure of the University of Turin, raised related concerns in an extended letter to Benedict XVI, specifically addressing the sedimented cultural historicity of the family structure and the need to embrace a less reductive working notion in Catholicism of what can be considered a household unit. This is to be aware, in Remotti's view, of the forms that an "imperialism" of "the family" may take, and of the dangers of an abstract and unhistorical notion of human nature.[27]

Interventions such as Zagrebelsky's and Remotti's champion a notion of human nature that emerges out of multiple and historical forms of kinship, ethics, and, I would add, desires: Human nature is enfleshed, so to speak. Migrants' fears about being discriminated against if they speak their own language on a bus or while talking to their own children in public or the necessity of getting in step with one's Italian counterparts in a procession of El Señor de los Milagros on the streets of Rome or the openness or closure of civil institutions as the felt-in-your-veins openness or closure of Jesus's heart; the *indio* (the pejorative term used in Mexico to indicate a person of lower status) that sticks, with its multiple meanings, on the bodies of some Mexican Catholic migrants (often browner of skin and of perceived lower social status) rather than others in Rome; the understanding of the relation between faith and national, cultural celebrations, which impels a particular form of Catholic civic association (CCM) to break from a missionary form of the church's governmentality—all of these are examples of a surplus that cannot fit easily into Cardinal Biffi's evocation of the stronghold of a Catholic Europe.

Migrant itineraries and experiences may fit at times within the Sameness of the Catholic Church's clerical imagination about a common Catholic humanitas; at other times, they clearly do not. Their pluralization and enfleshment constantly challenge Catholic migration pedagogies.[28] Those are pedagogies that imagine, wish, represent, and create migrants as sacrificial carriers of family unity and sufferers in the process of migration.

On Sameness, Otherness, and Migration

What does the modern discourse of Christian humanism have to do with current Latin American migration in Rome? Some may see this line of questioning as a daring jump to take, but thinking about migration beyond a strict sociological paradigm of migrant faith-based communities can help expose the political subtlety of this connection. This is why Catholicism and transnational migration in contemporary Rome, with its multiple facets, demand to be examined within an Atlantic frame of analysis, as part of an Atlantic Return. As I discussed in the introduction, approaching Roman migrant communities in terms of a study of an Atlantic Return enables a detailed focus on exchanges, circulation, presence, and absences that shape the relations of people, ideas, texts, fantasies, and materialities that link the Americas, Europe, and the Mediterranean. It is through this perspective that the discourse of human nature (irrevocably linked to a sixteenth-century debate about slavery in the New World, as I discuss below) still resonates for a Catholic Church that situates the humanness of twenty-first-century immigration in an increasingly prominent area of action and reflection.

This take on human nature is intimately connected to histories and debates on conversion. However, rather than query a debate on conversion, agency, and the notions of self-transformation, I would like to interrogate the nature of Sameness and Otherness from debates on slavery, labor, and dominion. In a famous article revising Locke's theory of the modern subject, Talal Asad rightly argued that a medieval notion of the saeculum as a sense of the timing of history gave way in the Enlightenment to a "domain of 'purely natural' human action opposed to a domain of 'supernatural' belief."[29] In the wake of Asad's argument, Webb Keane argued that 1920s Dutch Indies Calvinists criticized practices of Catholic liturgy as a deceiving formula that claimed that the supernatural could be transformed into the material expression of the body and blood of Christ (the Eucharist). For them a practice of conversion was located instead in the "physical locus of the individuated subject" and in "sincere" acts of everyday speech.[30] Agency in Protestant conversion was seated not in human interiority or in God as such but in the effectiveness of extrahuman mediations in human life. Important debates in the anthropology of Christianity have emphasized action, agency, and material and linguistic mediation and their histories in the Reformation as critical vectors in the shaping of subjects, whether converted or converting. However, I argue here that it is also important to foreground pre-Reformation debates on Sameness and Otherness in order to explore present-day forms of Catholic subjectivity, labor, and mobility—and to a certain extent the study of distributions of subjectivity, beyond the subject, through a focus on the circulation of affective histories and (religious) materialities.

There have been competing takes on Catholicism and human nature. The Christian humanism formulated by friars such as Bartolomé de Las Casas[31] and Sahágun in the sixteenth century is marked by a resignification of paganism (embodied in the otherness of the "Indians") not as heresy, but in terms of an anticipation of fulfillment of Christian subjecthood (both in term of self-mastery and subjection). This meant that the otherness of the New World was resignified through the sameness of Christianity. The Americas, as described by Johannes Fabian, were recast as a pre-Christian Rome. The heterologies of the New World were translated into a social imaginary of a universal (and teleological) temporality, the basis of a 'humanistic' discourse.

The 1550–51 Valladolid debate presided over by Charles V staged two competing interpretations of Aristotelian thinking about the Spanish empire's enslavement of the Indians in the New World. The theology of Ginés de Sepúlveda inscribed the Indians within the "great chain of being," confining Indians to a subhuman category of irrational beings. On account of this irrationality they could be enslaved as productive subjects and subjected to a form of territorial control through the legislative frame of *encomienda*, a trusteeship granted to individuals, where the forced extraction of indigenous labor became central to the reproduction of Spanish elites. In opposition to Sepúlveda, Bartolomé de Las Casas relied on his witness of the mistreatment of the Indians in the New World to argue against Sepúlveda's claim of indigenous irrationality, barbarism, and transgression of natural laws (e.g., cannibalism), emphasizing instead the common humanity of the Indians and their basic sameness of spirit beyond their paganism and their unenlightened mores. Indians, in Las Casas's view, were not heretics (as radical others to the Catholic and Christian civilization) but potential converts; they might be pagan, but they were open to conversion.

Las Casas's views prevailed in principle in the Valladolid dispute, but in practice slavery survived in the New World long after Valladolid. Nonetheless, the language of conversion was used to justify the conquest of the New World. The Valladolid dispute had built on Pope Paul III's 1537 bull that subscribed to a vision that "those living in all the vast regions of 'the Indies' were human beings with liberty and dominion, capable of faith and salvation, and they were to be drawn to the Gospel by preaching and good example."[32] In this Augustinian view, no human being could have natural dominion over any other; only God has this power and right. It is on the basis of the concept of *natural dominion* (in the sense that it was divinely given by being children of God), and its *inalienability* (not to be taken away by other humans) that the subjectivity of the unconverted Indians was thought through and constructed.

The concept of dominion understood in its Augustinian formulation and elaborated by the Dominican Franciscus de Victoria (1480–1546) and Las Casas relates to the "capacity of human beings to own material goods and exercise legal jurisdiction."[33] *Dominion* is not part of natural law but rather what humans possess in relation to nature, and it became the basis for Las Casas's refutation of Sepúlveda's application (and justification) of Aristotle's conception of a natural slave to the indigenous population of the Americas. Dominion is also the basis for early elaborations of human/individual rights, for instance, in the work of Locke and his outlook on animal and property rights, insofar as an entitlement to possession is a condition that characterizes the individual as the subject of a right.[34] Interestingly enough, this characterization emerged in an even earlier dispute within the Catholic Church between Pope John XXII and the Franciscan order about the latter's right to embrace and exercise full poverty as part of a natural right (I return to this in the epilogue).[35]

Las Casas's position provided a way in which Indian "difference" could be read as "cultural" and thus within a sameness of humanity guaranteed by potential conversion to Christianity. He, together with others such as Franciscus de Victoria, helped develop a framework based on a Thomistic universal nature which preceded cultural difference, where "the notion of a common human nature embedded in the medieval discourse of natural law and natural rights points the way toward the toleration of cultural difference."[36] I emphasize here the word *toleration* and the manner in which the concept of a common human nature precedes that of cultural difference. In short, natives in this reading and through conversion could become part of the human family rather than be considered part of the category of the subhuman and the animal, in the Aristotelian great chain of being.

Much has been written about the power of mimesis in the early descriptions of the New World and the linguistic reproduction of imperial relations of production.[37] I am interested here in only one particular question: What do these "humanist" debates within the church in the sixteenth century and the concept of conversion as the basis for the possible fulfillment of Christian apostolic ambitions have to tell us about the contemporary return of Latin American missions to Rome? How do "returns" from the Americas resonate with this project of "humanist" appropriation? And how does this Atlantic understanding challenge the study of Catholicism and transnational migration? These are, of course, on one level open postcolonial questions. Postcolonial subjectivity has queried the Other/Self tension and analyzed the disjointed circulation of desires that co-constitute both Other and Self, colonized and colonizers. Postcolonial critiques have rightly pointed out the potential and the difficulties in formulating new terrains where the Other is recognized for its true complexity and plurality, without being fully known.[38] However, I am also asking about a particular aspect of the governmentality of the Catholic Church that centers on the tension between the authority (*potestà*) and divine power of the church, on one hand, and its capacity to regulate the praxis of the world, or its social manifestations, on the other.

I see the exploration of these questions as part of a genre of cautionary tales, paraphrasing Irene Silverblatt, who very cogently reads aspects of the Colonial Spanish Inquisition in Peru from the sixteenth century to the eighteenth century through Arendt's analysis of the deadly combinations of bureaucracy, modern rationality, and extreme violence, which link European colonialism in the nineteenth century to the birth of totalitarian states in the twentieth. Silverblatt calls for us to locate the inception of that modern state even further back to the birth of racialization in the New World, the bureaucratic work of the Spanish Inquisition, and anxieties about the purity of blood.[39] My own questions seek to draw constitutive linkages between modern church governmentality and the emergence of a primitive racial logic in the encounter of the New World. However, while these continuities remain rooted in the Americas for Silverblatt, my interest is rather to excavate their transatlantic articulations.

New Blood and Migrants' Catholic Pedagogies

Blood is important, indeed. Many Italian legislative framings of migrant terrains have their underpinnings in the principle of jus sanguinis, or the right to citizenship connected to blood descent, rather than jus soli, the right of citizenship related to the place of birth. The defense of a blood family is a central concern of the Roman Catholic Church and a key to its transnational migrants' pedagogies. The cautionary tale I am interested in exploring conjures a process of conversion and of apostolic mission that was not fully achieved; I reads migrant itineraries in continuity with the anxiety around the possibility of partial failure of the colonizing project.

Concern over the purity of blood, central to the interface of Christianity and empire in the colonial Americas, has bred an anxiety about another potency of the blood. In the eyes of the Holy See, the influx of Catholic "migrant blood" can be turned into a positive asset for a New Evangelization that is badly needed in Europe. But this new blood potentially escapes the church's projection as a blood of renewal, a new apostolic blood for existing and potentially new Catholic communities. As I explain in more detail later in this book, issues of national affects and belonging, on the one hand, and sexuality and eroticism, on the other, challenge this project or projection of the Catholic Church. From this point of view, migrant itineraries are not only reminiscent of the past; they also open aesthetic, sensorial, and spatial routes to becoming otherwise (as an open-ended process of transformation) in the present and the future.[40] This is why a study of migrant itineraries is central to see and foresee how the center of the Catholic Church can be transformed from some of its margins and how its Catholic humanitas can be challenged by the opening up of other forms of being Catholic.

Since the 1950s the Vatican has issued several official documents specifically dedicated to the migration phenomenon. The International Catholic Migration Commission was the very first major institution created by the church to pursue the cause of the migration phenomenon and the needs of migrants. Founded in 1951, the commission was designed to provide guidance and support to national governments and institutions in finding solutions for the world's migrants and refugees. The following year, Pope Pius XII issued *Exsul Familia*, the first encyclical on this issue, which is still considered the magna carta of the church's teachings and guidelines for the pastoral care of migrants.

In 1969 Pope Paul VI amplified and adapted the encyclical's doctrines to the new directions indicated by Vatican II. The pope issued the document *Motu Proprio Pastoralis Migratorum Cura*, which introduced the instruction *De Pastorali Migratorum Cura ("Nemo Est")* to the Congregation for Bishops. The adjustments were primarily a response to the Second Vatican Council's documents *Lumen Gentium* (1964), which focused on the church's commitment to evangelization and human promotion, and *Gaudium et Spes* (1965), a compendium of doctrines and guidelines that positioned the church as a promoter of charity and social justice in the world. The 1969 papal instructions recognized the migration phenomenon as a new "sign of the times." In the instruction, the church recognized both the necessity of helping a growing number of migrants in need and an opportunity to evangelize the migrating world through ecumenical dialogue, charity, and advocacy. This was a shift within the church after Vatican II that opened the church's teaching to a new alignment with changing events.

In 1970, Pope Paul VI created the Pontifical Commission for the Pastoral Care of Migration and Tourism, which in 1989 became the Pontifical Council for the Pastoral Care of Migrants and Itinerant People. The commission/council was entrusted with the coordination, management, and pastoral encouragement of the cause of migrants, refugees, and itinerant people, especially in relation to the local bishops' conferences.[41] The recognition of the migrant population as a core priority for mainstream Catholic evangelization in Italy, however, is relatively new. It was only in 2003 that the Permanent Episcopal Commission officially dedicated both diocesan and missionary resources to the evangelization of migrant communities in Italy. Though based in Italy, the foundation Migrantes and the CEMi (Commissione Episcopale per le Migrazioni) are playing important roles in the process of Catholic evangelization worldwide.

In 2005, the Pontifical Council for the Pastoral Care of Migrants and Itinerant People issued a key instruction titled *Erga Migrantes Caritas Christi* (The Love of Christ toward Migrants), in which the migration phenomenon is identified as a "structural component of society." Such acknowledgment is not a new notion for the Roman Catholic Church, but it is the result of a long process of adjustment to the growing phenomenon of migration on a world scale. In this instruction, migrants are portrayed as individuals who are particularly exposed to human rights discrimination and racism, who often suffer from the separation from their own families and culture, and who are exposed to labor exploitation, social neglect, and, at times, persecution. While condemning these conditions of migrant life,

Catholics are called on to be apostolic and charitable subjects by welcoming and assisting immigrants in their new countries, and at the same time by assuming an evangelical role that promotes Catholic values among foreign residents.[42] Broadly speaking, then, in Italy the church works as the "state's nurse," in charge of mending the social wounds caused by the lack of civic engagement and adequate sociopolitical measures toward immigration.[43]

A large part of the responsibility of welcoming and assisting newcomers is entrusted to the care of dioceses and parishes, which are tasked with providing a variety of charity and social services. The parish, in particular, has become the primary social subject of the church operating in the territory and *the* home open and available to anybody. Pope Benedict XVI underscored such issues by identifying the twofold role of the church. In his words, as a common house, the church provides support to all migrants from all faiths and cultures through organizations and institutions that offer missionary services and solidarity. At the same time, as a congregation of Catholics, the church is called to assume a role of advocacy to ensure the respect of human rights of migrants at the local and international level.[44] In *Erga Migrantes Caritas Christi,* a divine parallel is established between the figure of the migrant and the figures of Jesus, born in exile, and Mary, the "living icon of the female migrant." Migration becomes, through the mystery of Easter, the death and resurrection of humanity, a transformation from otherness into sameness via a harmonization of differences. In principle then, the particularities of migrants are an appeal for other Catholics to live again the solidarity of Pentecost, when the Holy Spirit harmonizes differences and charity becomes authentic in accepting one another. The experience of migration should be the announcement of the Paschal mystery, in which death and resurrection make for the creation of a new humanity in which there is no longer slave or foreigner.[45]

In principle, in the church everyone must find his or her own patria; hence, the Holy See's position on migration articulates a language of cultural pluralism, which upholds the right to dignity, promotes "fraternity, solidarity, service and justice," and sees the migrant family as the "domestic church." However, as is spelled out in the same *Erga Migrantes*, the Holy See discourages mixed-faith marriages and actively encourages marriages between people of the same faith. Again, the tensions between an imagined common human nature and the toleration of cultural differences reemerge. Or, as Benedict XVI puts it in the epigraph for this chapter, the migrant family becomes the cradle for "humanity's development."

An understanding of the heteronormative family as a cradle of life and the primary context for human development and adaptation is a terrain of ambiguity and contestation. The Catholic Church wishes to provide pastoral care to migrants, as well as humanitarian support—and in countries such as Italy, the church provides the bulk of the humanitarian assistance available to new immigrants—but the church's assistance is often paternalistic, and sometimes falsely inclusive.[46] The ambiguity is not only theological but also anthropological. The Holy See has focused its political intervention on the resacralization of specific forms of life vis-à-vis the life of individuals in specific political spheres and cultures—somehow basing this defense on a notion of traditional Christian civilization. Benedict XVI's rhetoric emphasizes a church as a direct *defensor hominis* (protector of man). The role that the Holy See has played in the UN debate over the abolition of the death penalty is a clear example of its efforts to appear to be a protector of people's lives under threat.[47] The resacralization of human life, however, is embattled terrain for the church. From a politico-theological perspective, this is so because life is always a form of "living state" that has to be constantly articulated and divided from within by a tension between organic (as natural) and relational (as social) living. Giorgio Agamben explains this tension and disjunction as one intrinsic to humanism:

> But if this is true, if the caesura between the human and the animal passes first of all within man, then it is the very question of man—and of "humanism"—that must be posed in a new way. In our culture, man has always been thought of as the articulation and conjunction of a body and a soul, of a living thing and a logos, of a natural (or animal) element and a supernatural or social or divine element. We must learn instead to think of man as what results from the incongruity of these two elements, and investigate not the metaphysical mystery of conjunction, but rather the practical and political mystery of separation. What is man, if he is always the place—and, at the same time, the result—of ceaseless divisions and caesurae?[48]

For our purposes, then, this articulation is a constant point of tension within the church, between human rights (as belonging to a polis and to the social) and the culture of life (as a right to life as "natural"). As Asad suggested, we encounter an interesting paradox between physis and polis: the notion that the inalienable rights that define the human and relate to a state of nature do not depend on the nation-state, whereas the concept of the citizen, including the rights a citizen holds, presupposes a state that Enlightenment theorists called political society.[49] As I have explained, a tension between animality and humanity, as a debate about the human person (where to place the natives, so to speak) became central in Catholicism with the first colonial missionary encounters in the New World. The articulation of the human as a conjunction of a supernatural spirit, an organic animality, and a socialized materiality has always existed as a set of potential disjunctions with high political relevance—what Agamben calls the *Mysterium disiunctionis*.[50]

Hence Benedict XVI's perspective on migration as seated in a cradle of life and in a "culture of life" has been in continuity with a Thomist understanding of a universal natural and rational dominion. However, it has to wrestle with this disjunctive mystery. Those aspects of migrant itineraries that cannot fit into this culture of life call into question the limits to Catholic understanding of migration under the rubric of Catholic Sameness (the other is always recognizable as "us," as a "human person," a child of God). More questions beg to be asked here: If disjunction is at the heart of life, as Agamben shows, how can we read politically the Roman Catholic Church's impulse for a *specific conjuncture* of life, as the Culture of Life? And, further, how can a historically seated disjunction between animality and humanity, and related anxieties about sameness and otherness, still linger in the current Catholic Church's dealing with Latin American transnational migration in Italy?

On Mary and Jesus: Dancing in the Basement

In December 2009 Jessica and Juanito got married in the Church of Santa Maria della Luce, not a very common event in this parish where people's stories are riddled with marriage betrayals rather than tying the knot. Jessica already has a child back in Peru; Juanito too has a child, and neither of them has been married before. They now have a young daughter together, and they are both household workers in a villa on the Casilina. There are guests whom I don't often see attending this church. They are the *compadres* of the couple—*gente de dinero* (well-off people)—as they have businesses in the area of Rome close to Piazza Vittorio Emanuele. The crowd of the parish is excited about this marriage. At the mass, Father Alfonso repeats that Juanito and Jessica are poor, they do not have anything, but the most important thing is that they have the love of each other. They also have friendship and faith here: The two go together, Alfonso insists.

Alfonso continues that they are the "blood" of the mission and the Latin American community of migrants—and when friendship goes together with faith, he insists, then no rumors can divide the community. But *el chisme* (gossip) is unavoidable here. Some women complain that the women close to Father Alfonso run the church. Others say that you should be very careful to whom you pass on your job to replace you while you are away, because they could take advantage of you and spread gossip about you with your employers while you are not there. Others observe that some are able to get emergency small loans from the priests, whereas others do not have access to them at all. And the words go round.

Jessica is moved when she describes that her mother sent the shawl that is wrapping her child (not his biological one), as the girl gets baptized in the same ceremony as the wedding. Jessica speaks to the crowd with a microphone at the end of the ceremony, thanking the church, the priest, and their friends there, and vowing that from now on she will live the life of a "true" Catholic: *"Me comprometo a vivir desde ahora como la Iglesia manda"* (I vow from now on to live as the church orders). Father Alfonso smiles, and we all clap and follow the newlyweds to the doorstep of the church. With the group we get into some cars and follow the winding roads of central Rome close to the Metro station of Porta Furba. Then we arrive at the Hijos del Sol, a Peruvian basement restaurant in a residential area—basements are often the living alterity of daylight cities.[51] A blast of music receives us. I am hanging out with Dalia, who looks rather sad on such a festive day. She is a history teacher in Peru and has three children whom she is now supporting and paying for their education. It is tough as her husband in Peru has not been keeping in touch, and things between them are not good. She is working as a caregiver for a *nonita* (an elderly woman), and money is very tight. She keeps her coat on; she will keep her coat on for the few hours we stay at the restaurant. We eat and talk, and then a Peruvian woman in a tight dress starts to dance onstage—a rather explicit dance—women from our group glance at her and do not seem disturbed. I ask Francisca what she thinks about the music and the ambiance:

> You know, Valentina, you need some romance, and here in Rome it is so difficult, because you live in [at the employer's] most of the week, but also because men are not to be trusted here. Italians do not really want to be with us, and Peruvian men often have double lives . . . what double, triple at times! But you need to take your mind off, especially if all is crumbling around you [*si es un desfase*]. Father Alfonso does not fully

understand our life either. I am a very devout woman, but in the mission they do not understand we need some fun, some healthy fun, sometime an *apapacho* [a hug], and we are here on our own, so that is why the mission is important, but the fathers do not understand enough. In some of the celebrations we make in the church, or take the Day of the Migrant,[52] there is no music or dancing, or if there is, it is so late that we have to leave to be back home, where a *nonito* is waiting for us. Sometimes we can dance for a while in the church, but not all priests like that.

I then get up to dance on my own—I like the salsa music—but I make a mistake. After a short while Juanito comes up to me and dances with me. I realize the code is not to just get up and dance. In this group you dance in a couple, as it is inappropriate to be seen dancing on your own. I sit down again and Dalia is still sitting there; she has been asked to dance too for a short while. But she still wears her coat. I gently ask why she does not take it off. She smiles at me with a glance, holds my arm, and I understand we will speak about later. The music is really loud now; the woman on the stage is half naked and surrounded by some men who in turns are coming up from the audience and dancing with her mimicking a sexual act. Our group rather openly invites Juanito to go up. He is tentative, shy to start with, but then he goes up for his turn too. This is definitely a big day for him. Francisca laughs and says that probably some Italians do not even know that there are places like this in Rome, where "we" Peruvians have fun. The problem for many attending the church is that there is no public place to gather, and you may have to end up in these basement clubs, that at times she likes, but that at times are "places of troubles," where violence can erupt unexpectedly.[53]

After a few hours Dalia and I walk back to the metro together. She takes my arm and complains that where she has been working she eats pasta, pasta, and pasta; she loves it, but she has put on weight. I smile back, a common problem for women: not fitting in your clothes. We are in the subway now; before departing, I give her a hug and promise to see her the following Sunday in church. While she gets out, her coat gets partially snagged and opens on her back. I can see a tattered dress that looked much better in the front. She is definitely going through a hard time. I wonder if she is still sending all the money she earns back home.

If "suffering" is part of life for many of these Catholic migrant women, it is not the only register. Father Alfonso is not the only priest in the Scalabrinian community of the MLA who does not mince words about the municipality of Rome's interventions and government policies toward migrants. However, his religious order's interventions implicitly still support a very Christian-confessional mode of granting legal residence for undocumented migrant that is implicitly consonant with the official discourse of Italian immigrant regularizing practices. As Cristiana Giordano has argued, within the frame of current Italian legal discourse, an account of oneself (as an illegal migrant)—*la denuncia*—cannot be given (or legalized) but through a procedure resembling a confession. Moreover, where cultural citizenship constructed by ethnopsychiatric experts tends to focus on the "retrieval" of a migrant "tradition," what is often lost is the powerful drive for rupture intrinsic in some of the migrants' processes of individuation.[54]

Hence Scalabrinians emphasize a vision of the MLA as a *pan-American community,* where the expression of devotion to the church and active participation in evangelization and sacramental life should unify the body of the migrants under the umbrella of Latin Americanness. But on the ground, interruptions of national affect, forms of subtle racialization even within the migrant's body, betrayals at the start of migration, and the proliferation of out-of-wedlock erotic relations (see following chapters) do not allow a neat closure of identity to the process of migration. Neither the culture of life nor an attempt to mold a pan-American community identity onto the bodies and stories of migrants is fully successful as a Catholic pedagogy.

Migration and Vatican II

To understand the relationship of migration, the culture of life, and an MLA fantasy of pan-Americanism, we need to return to the particular historical context in which a revision of Vatican II is taking place. This context contains both a reinforcement of a medieval conception of Christendom—a romanization of world Catholicism and an internationalization of Rome—and advocacy for universal human rights. The implications of this revisionism are not limited to the internal politics of the church around the promotion of a canonical liturgy and the reassertion of a centralist and hierarchical decision-making structure. The revisions have a wider implication for debates on secularism and for the concrete politics of immigration in Italy.

A large debate is taking place across many disciplines, including anthropology, in response to a critique of secularism as having been (although not totally) oblivious to its own religious Christian underpinnings—for instance, the binarism of transcendence and immanence. Scholars have addressed how understandings of gendered affective subjectivity, moral injury, and the nature of transforming multiculturalism in plural societies has required engaging existing exclusionary forms of universalizing secularism.[55] With this scholarship in mind I argue that the numerous debates about secularism need also to be understood through specific national histories of church-state relations.[56]

If some Italian intellectual debates have emphasized the ethical nature of secularism and the historical formation of human nature, interventions from historically Protestant countries have also shown an interest in secularisms in the plural. Janet Jakobsen and Ann Pellegrini, for instance, have compellingly argued the view that not all secularisms are a result of European colonial history, nor are they all based on a universalist transhistorical reason. They instead see a plural conception of the secular as decentering the tacit association of secularism with a specifically Christian context: the division of public and private and Protestant-infused market-centered political economy. "Telling time and histories" of secularisms as "ways of living out, of embodying, secular possibilities" calls for a new openness of the continuum of the secular and religious and of the possibilities for envisaging different futures.[57]

The notion of a Catholic humanitas pivots on an universalist understanding of human nature and Catholic civilization that has been mobilized in debates on secularism. It is also playing a role in apparently secular spaces of (Italian) national policy, producing, from the point of view of the Catholic Church, paradoxically exclusionary legislation on migration. If thought in continuity with secularist debates, rather than in isolation from them, untangling some of the working of Catholic humanitas in the field of migration contributes to what Simon Coleman and Joel Robbins think of as the potential of anthropology of religion to "[make] reports of otherness effective at home,"[58] and I hope a contribution to a queered, radical pluralism, which "need not banish religious possibility from its midst."[59]

For Benedict XVI, the revision of Vatican II emphasizes canonical liturgy and rites as the ultimate way into Catholic faith. In this view, by understanding the canonical ritual essence of Christ's presence (as a truth and incarnation in the liturgy), Catholicism as a faith and teaching is already inculturated. For Benedict XVI, Catholic truth is inculturated as *precultural*, seated in the body as the culture of life. Hence, it is a particular regimentation of the body that becomes the cradle of true Catholic subjectivity and the precondition for what the same Vatican II explored as the inculturation of faith and the spiritualization of culture. Moreover, in his work on the spirit of the liturgy, Benedict XVI argues that liturgical rites are certain; creativity is not seated in spontaneity. Instead, the whole essence of the body in ritual motion is its lack of spontaneity, and participation in the mass is not about what is visible, but about what is spiritual in essence. A particular boundary between the social and the spiritual emerges from specific orientations of the body:

> Unspontaneity is the essence. In these rites I discovered that something was approaching me here that I did not produce myself, that I am entering into something greater than myself, which ultimately derives from divine revelation. This is why the Christian East calls the liturgy the "Divine Liturgy" expressing thereby the liturgy's independence from human control.[60]

But privileging this reading of inculturation as a *precondition* (the presence of Catholic Truth in the liturgy) rather than as an *effect*—an index of diversity of cultures (the incarnation of Jesus and his teaching have different human, cultural manifestations in the world)—is not confined to the teaching of the former pope. The same ideas are taken up by conservative wings of the Roman Catholic Church, rooted in some diocesan enclaves, which emphasize the Aristotelian/Augustinian roots of European civilization and see migration, at least within the Italian political context (articulated first by the 2002 Bossi-Fini law and in 2009 by the Security Decree) through a prism of criminalization and illegality. It is to these long theological and pedagogical lines of Catholic interventions that a pluralization of secularism(s) should respond.

The case of the Mexican order of the Legionaries of Christ, which I discuss at length in the following chapter, constitutes a transnational perspective on this articulation, and another conservative dimension of the return from the New World in the twentieth and twenty-first centuries to the heart of the church. Legionaries of Christ mimic some of the positions of the preconciliar Jesuits. Parts of the Jesuit order have been actively involved with Vatican II in trying to understand this inculturation as a precondition of culture. This is what some Jesuits have pursued while also clarifying the differences between a concept of relativism and a concept of pluralism in contemporary society, in conversation with what they see as a too-radical revision of Vatican II by Benedict XVI. In the words of F.L., a long-time director of the Jesuit College in Rome and a much-loved spiritual adviser of the CCM for a few years:

> The second extreme would be an excessive identification of the church with itself, to the point of drawing a radical division between the church and the secular world. In other words, to put the church at the center, and stress what divides her from the rest of humanity. This would be to stress excessively the *difference of the Christian,* stated strongly by Romano Guardini in the postwar years, rightly with a defensive attitude. If we were to go down that road, all the debate about the inculturation of the Gospel, the inculturated evangelization, the necessity to permeate all the aspects of human life with the value of Jesus Christ will be meaningless and useless.[61]

F.L. is claiming that for the Roman Catholic Church a danger of self-aggrandizement remains. But this language of difference is also a language of the recognition of plural sociality. F.L. is thus also skirting around an important aspect that is awakened by the presence of migrants within the Catholic Church related to the circulations of narratives and experiences of (lay and religious) migrant betrayal. Simply and maybe very boldly put, the lingering danger for the Roman Catholic Church is that it can become captured in its own narcissistic fantasy. The other side of betrayal is to get too attached to the object that it is perceived to be betrayed by. Without a narcissistic attachment there cannot be betrayal.[62]

Twists on Catholic Humanitas

Multiple Catholic migrant pedagogies are nested in long-term tensions between the diocesan priests and the priests of the religious orders operating over the same spatial and symbolic terrains. Diocesan priests (such as Father R., the priest in charge of Santa Maria degli Angeli) are not always on the same page on issues of migration. There is a real impasse visible in Italy within the Catholic Church toward migration. This was illustrated to me by Archbishop Marchetto, the secretary of the Pontifical Council for the Pastoral of Migrants and Itinerants until 2010. A day after the ratification of the 2009 Security Decree, when undocumented immigration became a felony, newspapers reported that he denounced the chain of suffering that this law would engender.[63] Predictably the following day saw Father Lombardi, Pope Benedict's Jesuit spokesman, announcing that

Marchetto's remarks were *a titolo personale*, or his own opinion, and that they did not reflect the official posture of the pope and the Holy See.

Archbishop Marchetto, in a personal interview, pointed a (diplomatic) finger at the lack of integration of different areas of the church and their different receptions of the *Erga Migrantes Caritas Christi*. He argued that in some quarters of the church it has not been received at all. He saw one side of the church fully immersed and committed to *l'accoglienza* (reception/organized welcoming), but this lacks, he insists, "a more complex work of evangelization." He argues that the Roman Catholic Church needs to develop a *pastorale d'insieme* (an integrated ministry) that would entail both a process of advocacy, which would serve as a hub for a dignified national vision, but also a diocesan communion, a religious diocesan dimension. For Archbishop Marchetto, there was and still is a lack of integration between different structures of the church and a lack of "ecclesial integration of the immigrants into the local church." In other words, Marchetto subtly pointed out how closed part of the diocesan world in Italy is to the presence of migrant life in their own constituencies: The case of Father R., which I describe at the beginning of this chapter, is a clear example.

Moreover, for Marchetto different migrant waves bring a "vital dynamism," which is part of *his* understanding of the culture of life. We need a new "humanism," he kept arguing, "that can be religious, lay, doesn't matter," that is based on a "dignity of the person that is universal." Nonetheless, a slip between "human dignity" and social normativity is still present in his words. Hence a dominant part of the Roman Catholic Church and the Roman Curia ideologically promote a normative family and family unity as an anchor to migration and the culture of life. Another part of the church, which at times gets silenced (as in the case of Marchetto), still take seriously the generative force of cultural difference. Religious orders such as the Scalabrinians and the Jesuits are not always on the same page either. At the grassroots level—such as the interventions of the Scalabrinians—cultural differences cannot be ignored. Priests such as Father Manuel are torn by dissonances and by the incongruity that requires him to follow a pastoral teaching that, in important ways, runs counter to the everyday reality of migration in Italy. This is so because the territorial responsibility within the Catholic Church is well divided and the Scalabrinians have to negotiate with diocesan priests for any help they wish to receive from the Diocese of Rome, help which they absolutely need.

Within the widespread disenchantment with secular governing institutions during the papacy of Benedict XVI, we can see one Catholic social imaginary that expresses itself through the notion of a "right" liturgical body and an ideally sexualized body of Catholic migrants. Benedict XVI's theology spoke and continues to speak of a Catholic humanitas in relation to migration that is based on a reading of the human person derived from an interpretation of the Augustinian dominion that turns thought away from an understanding of the human as the product of a dialogical practice, wherein sexuality, race, gender, and also disability play important roles.[64] Benedict XVI's positions may appear to be different from those of Pope Francis interventions into the church's discourse on migration. Although the latter are beyond the scope of this book, it is important to understand Pope Francis in the light of the history and the tensions that I am highlighting here, not as separate from them.

To sum up, a paradox runs through the Catholic Church, which treats migration through a communitarian and contextual approach (human dignity for all, a clear rebuff of violent forms of governmentality, and an interest in migrant cultures, an approach actively practiced by Jesuit and Scalabrinian priests), and yet theologically grounds human rights for migrants in a precultural, universal understanding of human beings. The theological impulse of Benedict XVI to think of Catholic migrants as a community of humans based on a "true" and universal Catholic humanitas requires an imagined universal tradition, a specific notion of the heteronormative family, a belonging of the Nation (to the People), not nations, to History, rather than histories. But as I explain in the following chapters, Catholic migrants' itineraries are also constelled by divisive affects toward different nation-states, eroticism, and uneven racialized histories. And this proliferation at its margins can be a challenge to the core of the Catholic Church.

3. *The Legionaries of Christ and the Passionate Machine*

This chapter explores the Atlantic return from a return of the mission and the specific perspective of a religious order founded in Mexico, the Legionaries of Christ.[1] Specifically, I focus on the attachments and the mimetic drives that mediate the relationship between the Legionaries of Christ and the pre– and post–Vatican II Jesuits.

Although the two orders—the Legionaries and the Jesuits—are in many respects different, I argue that they are connected via a shared death/life wish: The self-fashioning of the Legionaries of Christ has developed out of the partial death of some aspects of the Jesuit order. Those aspects relate to the key role the Jesuits had before Vatican II in the education of the elites. When analyzed in light of the revisions of Vatican II during the papacies of John Paul II and Benedict XVI, the symbolic and historical relations between the two orders show that a Catholic integralist church[2]—born in reaction to modernism and the social doctrine of the church, and to which the Legionaries are associated—has acquired strength in Europe, in part because of an Atlantic return.

The affective dimension of the relation between these two religious orders emerges out of, and extends through, a complex set of historical and political contexts. Here I pay particular attention to the manner in which a renarrativization of the Cristero War in Rome takes root in and revivifies a love for an apostolate of the Roman Catholic Church. At the same time, the constitutive relationship between these two religious orders is firmly located in affective histories of confrontation between Church and state—in this case, between the Mexican state and the Catholic Church. The strength of the histories of confrontation between Church and state (in particular, in the 1920s and the 1930s in Mexico) is transnationally reanimated in Rome through a rehearsal of a narrative of a Catholic Church under attack by the hands of secularist forces. The Legionaries of

Christ, a Mexican order, have played a role as an integralist force within the Catholic Church in Rome. They have concrete linkages with Italian politicians and administrators, who have themselves been involved in "secular" governments over migration in the Italian territory playing a role in the design and implementation of particularly restrictive legislation, promoted under Berlusconi's governments, which have criminalized undocumented immigration, but which are still in place after the end of those governments.

As in the preceding chapters, the relation between different souls of the church and multiple Italian local and national governments is complex and not as homogenous as an official position of Roman Catholic Church in Rome wishes to portray. It is important then to pay attention to the institutional and ideological alignment of conservative and integralist factions in the church within the Italian political scene. What appears out of this institutional and governmental analysis is a larger story, that echoes in different ways throughout this book, in which the preservation of an *Italian civitas* is too soon identified with a *Catholic humanitas*.

None of this should suggest that the migration of Catholic clerics, missionaries, seminarians, and nuns from the Americas to Rome has not existed for hundreds of years. My intention is not to claim that this phenomenon is new but rather to read specific forms of this migration in light of the intersections they may have with shifts in laws about migration in Italy and Rome. In this sense I want to place both religious and lay organizations under the same analytical gaze of transnational gendered labor, to explore how they may have more in common than readings that divide "secular" from "religious" migration have highlighted.[3]

The "Old" Jesuits and the "New" Legionaries

The nearly five-hundred-year history of the Jesuits is very complex and has been debated and characterized by an ambiguous relationship to papal authority. Popularly, the Jesuit General has been addressed as the Black Pope, to emphasize the mimetic and antithetic nature that links the Jesuit order to the Roman Curia. The order of the Jesuits, the Society of Jesus, was founded by St. Ignatius of Loyola in 1540 and was originally dedicated to missionary and pedagogical endeavors. It has been transformed through different crises. The crisis of the order's vocation that coincided with Vatican II was thus not the first. In the early seventeenth century, the crises of the Company, as the Jesuits were then known, appeared at the same time as the first internationalizing of the order. Tensions grew between new, emerging political patriotisms, the role of the Roman Catholic Church, and the order's religious unity and activism. Pierre Coton, a seventeenth-century French Jesuit, wrote about saving the order from its Jesuit activism, while Antoine Artaud, a contemporary Jesuit, wrote about defending the "motion of the heart" and expressed a call for a clearer Jesuit posture on the work "from the inner to the outer."[4]

Anxiety over the right balance between the apostolic life and the inner/spiritual formation has driven different reformations of the Jesuit order. Within the first, the sixteenth-century Jesuit reformation, the inner formation not only of individual Jesuit spirits but of the spirit of the Company became one of the building blocks of a renewed doctrinal corpus. Under General Acquaviva, stricter and longer process for the training of novices, a strengthening of the *ratio studiorum*, and the production of a canonical Jesuit spiritual literature were put in place. However, this internal reformation was subtly but consistently weakened by the proliferation of "extraordinary devotions" both within and outside the Jesuit order in the first part of the seventeenth century.[5] These mystical devotions incarnated a religiosity that had become marginalized by an institutionalized and rational apostolic Jesuit endeavor. Mystical devotions within Catholicism have a complex and profoundly gendered history.[6]

The continuing anxiety within the Jesuit order concerned the fear that the love/desire for the absolute Other and one's own dissolution in it may have been alienated in its members by a Jesuit-driven vision of a post-Tridentine church (the 1545–63 Council of Trent, at the time of the Lutheran schism, was intended to reaffirm the unity, dogmas, and sacraments of the church). In other words, the notion of a mystical speaking *to* God was irremediably separated from the mastery of speaking *of* him. Therefore, the practice of minor sixteenth-century mystical devotions represented a thorn in the side of the Jesuit order, indexing a more general anxiety about the connection between visibility and invisibility, a potential schism of the "God of the heart and the God of a society at work."[7] I argue that this anxiety did not go away, but runs through Jesuit history to the present.

The sixteenth-century tradition of the Ignatian spiritual exercises to some extent embraced a self-inquiry rather than a mystical root of Christianity and medieval Catholicism and opened a decisive path into the modern shaping of self-inquiry and self-identity.[8] In Ignatius's spiritual exercises (which Roland Barthes defines as a "psychotherapy" that awakens the dullness of a body through the production of a phantasmic language), Loyola stressed imaginative views and terrains as language vectors of direct divine communication and a subsequent will to action. It was the constitution of a field of images as a linguistic system that kept at bay the potentially unruly aspects of mystic experience.[9] Speaking with the divine had been entrenched in the use of language as a gradual path to illumination, not as a bewilderment of the emptiness of experience, typical of mystics such John of the Cross or Teresa of Ávila. In this way, the Jesuits designed a new form of mysticism of service entrenched in the energy of language, not in the absence of it.[10]

Even if Jesuits reacted against the mystical line of Quietism[11] in seventeenth- and eighteenth-century France, they were the clerics associated with those dimensions of Catholic religiosity linked to the secrecy of the confessional, the emphasis on interiority, and the enigmatic language of mysticism.[12] However, it is a reading of mysticism as secrecy and obscurantism vis-à-vis the transparency of legitimate secular authority that actually signals the history of transformation (and the internal death[s]) of the order. It also runs through other momentous conjunctures in the history of the Jesuits, such as when the order was suppressed and then restored (between 1767 and 1814). Hence, the ambiguous relationship between mysticism (as *ravissement,* witnessing the divine in the absence of language) and the apostolate (as the language of a mysticism of service) runs throughout the history of the Jesuits. I argue this is a tension that runs through the Catholic Church at large.

Finally I bring attention to a later potential schism within the Jesuit order that took place in 1960s Spain, the implications of which shaped the order's transformations during and after Vatican II. This is the crisis of the *true* Society of Jesus, which had its historical roots in the revisionist, antimodern doctrinal posture present in the order since the 1814 restoration and which can be read as parallel to the history of the Legionaries.

It is no secret that Vatican II represented a particularly important historical conjuncture for the Jesuit order, and that it marked both a transformation of and a crisis in the order's public role and image. The order lost more than ten thousand members (both seminarians and priests) between 1961 and 1970. What is even more striking is that while there were more than ten thousand Jesuits dedicated to education worldwide in 1970, their number fell to nearly half (6,528) by the end of the 1970s. Even in the view from the higher spheres of Vatican, this crisis had repercussions not only in the formation of new priests and seminarians worldwide but also in the Catholic education of the laity.[13]

An anxiety about Jesuits moving away from education is captured in a letter sent by a group of parents of students in the Sicilian Jesuit College Pennisi in June 1977 to Cardinal Gabriele Garroni, the prefect of the Congregation for Catholic Education:

> Exhorted by a profound attachment to the Mother Church, we parents of students at the College Pennisi of Acireale, which has been the pride and glory of Sicily and Southern Italy, take the license to direct our prayers to you, so that your knowledgeable intervention would lead the General of the Jesuits to stop the worrying resolution to suppress the Catholic cultural center which has been so important to the College Pennisi. This would indicate a major defeat of the Christians, though, to the advantage of the enemies of the church. . . . The lack of vocations and therefore the lack of personnel are the false excuses, without credibility, that the Jesuit Fathers can claim. But the reason is that they do not want to dedicate themselves to education and to the work with the youth; hence we take the license to object: Why not give this difficult and delicate task to other religious orders?

This letter points to a crisis, not confined to the Italian case, in the field of Catholic education promoted by the Jesuits. This crisis about the demise of this historical role of the Jesuits was not confined to Italy. It was also behind the tensions around a potential schism that happened in the 1960s in Spain.

The Spanish "revolt" of the *true* Society of Jesus began in January 1969, when a group of eighteen senior Jesuits, led by Luis González, openly challenged the work of General of the Jesuits, Father Pedro Arrupe.[14] A document signed by the so-called Group of 18 pointed out emerging obstacles within the order to practicing ascetic traditions, and criticized the company's turn toward secularization.[15] The Group of 18 led a movement that sought recognition and autonomy from the Spanish state to carry out a life through precepts and postures considered by them traditional to the Jesuit order. The petition was received by the Spanish archbishop Casimiro Morcillo González, who asked the Spanish episcopate to respond to the request. Pedro Arrupe acted quickly and appointed a commission to analyze the situation of the Jesuits in Spain. The episcopate responded in favor of this Jesuit minority group. However, a year later, it emerged that this decision might have come on the strength of a personal crusade by Archbishop Morcillo, who it seems forwarded the petition to the Spanish episcopate without of any explicit request from the petitioners.

Soon after, in February 1969 Arrupe wrote a letter to express his view on the recent incident, invoking the principle of Jesuits *en fidelidad* to call on the internal cohesion of the order under the umbrella of the fourth papal vow (more on this below). With the effect of that letter, Arrupe reconsolidated the order as an apparently unitary force out of the XXXII General Congregation.[16] Today the "real" source behind this alleged petition is unclear: Some even point to Father Dezza, a very powerful Jesuit close to the pope in Rome (a Jesuit who was much later appointed by John Paul II as the pontifical delegate to lead the company in September 1981, when Father Arrupe was suddenly incapacitated by a stroke). What is at stake in this question of authorship is the possible interference by the Holy See into the state of the Company in Spain.

However, I read the presence of this counterreformist dissent group as an expression of a trauma and a profound religious shock generated by the aggiornamento of Vatican II[17]—an interpretation that partially echoes the broader interpretation of Vatican II itself as a not-free-of-conflict transformation of the church from within.[18] This internal battle within the Jesuit order and an impulse toward restoration was a traumatic confrontation that implied a "death" of the traditionalist and conservative wing of the order—a silencing within. I read this as a psychic death, a phantom that haunts not only the Jesuit order but also the Roman Catholic Church at large. Moreover, I argue that these crises of the Jesuit order—in the 1960s as a loss of its tradition and in the sixteenth century as a loss of the "motion of the heart"—were also about different directions of apostolic renewal within and outside the Catholic Church and the passions that motivate these directions still today.

As in Mexico, the Italian Jesuits' post–Vatican II turn away from educating elites toward an interest in the church of the poor has had a profound effect on the Catholic education of the ruling classes. In turn, along with other orders like the Salesians, the Legionaries of Christ have tried and are trying to fill a void in the Catholic pedagogy of the laity that has been left by the Jesuits' post–Vatican II transformation. In a letter from Pope John Paul I to General Arrupe, never sent during his papacy because of his premature death but endorsed and released by John Paul II the following November, the pope reflected on the perceived changing direction of the Company of Jesus:

> But in the solution of these problems [we must] be able to distinguish the tasks of the religious priests from those which are of the laity. The priests

have to animate the laity to comply with their duties, but do not have to substitute for them, forgetting their specific task in the evangelical action. . . . Together with the doctrine we have to *keep to our heart the religious discipline*, which has also constituted a characteristic of the Company and which has been indicated as its secret and strength. Achieved through demanding Ignatian asceticism, fed by an intense spiritual life, and backed by a *mature and virile obedience*, this is naturally manifested in the authority of life and the exemplarity of religious behavior.[19]

Compare Pope John Paul I's letter with one written a few years earlier by the head of the Jesuit Seminary in Puente Grande Jalisco, Mexico, to Father Janssens, Jesuit General in Rome, anxiously describing the shifting behavior of some of the Seminarians:

In dealing with people outside the seminary, a tendency which is less austere and somehow dangerous is notable among some of the junior seminarians of the south. In order to strengthen the link with the families of their fellow seminarians they are allowed noticeable familiarity. For instance: they talk to young ladies in the gardens of the house, sometime unaccompanied, *sometimes hugging them with one arm*, sometimes hugging them under their arm, while they talk to them.[20]

A perceived lack of "virile" support for the Mother Church and too much interest on lay pursuits, combined with perceived "dangerous" emerging forms of eroticization, produced anxieties in senior Jesuits, the Roman Curia, and the pope. An othering of the Jesuit order, which was in the sixteenth century the mystical, erotic, and feminized love that spoke *to* God, is indexed here in a fear of a male eroticization of bodies that are lacking their (necessary) virile austerity. And it is also feared as too much interest in worldly matters, which should belong to the laity.

On the Legionaries

There have been uncanny parallels, as well as tense encounters, between the Legionaries and Jesuits since the early 1940s. The Legionaries of Christ, originally called the Missionaries of the Sacred Heart of Jesus and the Virgin of Sorrows, were founded by a Mexican, Marcial Maciel Degollado,[21] in 1941 and encouraged by Pope Pius XII. It was only in 1965 that the *Misioneros* changed their name into the Legionaries of Christ and obtained the Decree of Praise, or full legitimization as a religious order. However, the official blessing of this newly formed congregation did not go smoothly.[22] Marcial Maciel was a contested figure, who died in 2008 in Florida, after having been asked by Benedict XVI, a few years earlier, to retire from public engagements, because of sexual and drug abuse allegations.

The Legionaries were very highly regarded by Pope John Paul II, and Maciel was the leading organizer of the first successful papal official visit of John Paul II's pontificate—in Mexico in 1979. Before that in 1970, Paul VI entrusted the prelature of Chetumal-Cancún to the Legionaries of Christ, whose missionary work focused on the Mayans of the Yucatán and Quintana Roo. At a stroke, one of the most racially selective religious orders[23] in the modern history of Mexico had been chosen as a missionary order in an area of Mexico populated mostly by indigenous people. Years later, in an interesting twist of Vatican politics, it was the Jesuits, rather than this local, "Mexican" religious order tasked with evangelizing the indigenous poor, that assumed such an important role in the EZLN movement (Zapatista Army of National Liberation) in the nearby region of Chiapas.[24]

In Rome, the Legionaries have been informally called the "new Jesuits." This expression is sometimes uttered with disbelief or amazement, but its implications are intriguing for current and possible future directions of the Catholic Church. Prior to the demise of their founder in 2008, the Legionaries had become a very powerful order in Rome, with important transnational connections not only in Mexico but also in other parts of the Americas. Part of a counter-Enlightenment tradition of Catholic integralism, which embraces the nuclear family, anti-individualism, and a denunciation of the dehumanization of a perceived "culture of relativism" in Benedict XVI's words, the Legionaries are at the same time "modern" and among the first orders in the Catholic Church to grasp the importance of mastering new communication technologies.[25]

In the words of a former rector of the Scalabrinian order in Rome in 2008, "They are the modern Jesuits, and they feel they are like the Jesuits at the time of the Church crisis in the fifteenth century; they see now the Church in crisis and they think to save it." The Legionaries, then, speak to both medievalist and hypermodern readings of Catholic humanitas, through the embrace of a neoliberal ideal of prosperity, but also through attention to relationality against capitalism's atomism and relativism— shortcomings that Benedict XVI highlighted as the evil of capitalism to be fought with renewed social and divine love for human integrity.[26]

Aspirations and fears of emerging integral Catholicism do not align with clear-cut extremist political formations. Instead, they have tended to percolate, at least during the last two governments of Berlusconi, through political discourses and pedagogical interventions that "can render them as a far more significant peril that any overt 'fascist' or 'neofascist' movement."[27] In other words, it is reductive to talk about a binarism within the Catholic Church in terms of opposing liberal and integralist takes on transnational migration. Yet it is important to focus on the kinds of alliances that have been forged by different religious orders with political groups that have been involved in the field of migration. Scalabrinians, Jesuits, and the Legionaries of Christ are the three orders that I focus on in this book and that have a particular relation to the Latin American mission and the Comunidad Católica Mexicana. Of course, there are other religious orders that interface with Latin Americans in Rome, but I focus ethnographically and historically on only these three as they stand for parallel yet different approaches within the church. The Legionaries in particular produce and embody imaginaries and actions that aim to reanimate the force of Militia Christi—a conquering and missionizing religious spirit that has circulated within the Catholic Church for centuries, and most clearly since the foundation of the Jesuits.

This spirit is one aspect of the historical conditions of possibility that allowed for the emergence and consolidation of the Mexican order of the Legionaries of Christ in Rome (not only there but also in other countries such as Spain and Chile). One of these conditions is nested in imagery of national martyrdom that is then transnationally resignified into an embodiment of the fear of a church and faith under attack, which has found a particularly powerful referent in the history of Mexico's Cristiada War during the early twentieth century. This history of Mexico, I argue, is not confined to Mexico, so to speak, but it is currently "resignified" in Rome, and this resignification is part of an Atlantic return. If so then also a surge of contemporary Catholic integralism at the heart of the Holy See in Rome can be, and should be, understood through such a transnational prism representing a return to the center of evangelization.

A focus on the reemergence of integralist Catholicism at the heart of Europe (as something connected to ideas of European civilization, as I argued in chapter 2, that are challenged but also fueled by increasing transnational migration) finds an illuminating parallel in ongoing debates concerning Islam and secularism. Indeed, in the case of Italy, the debate about the government's political views on Muslim immigration cannot be separated from a close analysis of different anxieties and perspectives that animate the Catholic Church from within. Moreover, the politics of moral injury, which produces projects such as the Observatory of Religious Freedom in Rome, is intimately connected to anxieties about the integrity of the civitas and its reproduction within an increasingly racialized and plurifaith society. This is also, as Saba Mahmood argues, connected to the broader problem surrounding how conceptions of the law may be biased by a normative disposition toward a majority culture.[28]

To understand the formation of the "new" Legionaries requires situating the birth of this order at the conjuncture of a particular moment in Mexican history and in the relationship between the church and the Mexican state known as the Cristero War. Historians and journalists have claimed there is a connection between the suppression and killings of Catholic priests and lay people at the hands of Mexican government forces during the Cristiada (or Cristero War) during the 1920s and the emergence of the Legionaries of Christ. The Cristero War (1926–29) was sparked by the conflict between local Catholics and central state governmental forces over the application of the Calles Laws. These laws, named after their chief architect and champion President Plutarco Elías Calles, and particularly article 130, were changes to the 1917 Mexican revolutionary Constitution concerning the control that the Constitution exerted over the Catholic Church in Mexico. The Calles Laws, which took effect in 1926, established a stronger control over and even an impediment to the formation of Catholic congregations, mandated the closure of existing ones, increased control over priestly participation in public life, and increased taxation on the Catholic ministry.[29] These legislative changes were seen by many as an anticlerical move by the new postrevolutionary state against the church. Others, though, saw it not just as a forced laicization of the state, but as a challenge to the Catholic monopoly of religious faith and practice. The Calles Laws spurred a series of heated reactions, including the formation of the Liga Nacional Defensora de la Libertad Religiosa (LNDLR) in 1925 to try to unify different Catholic forces to call for freedom for religious cults. Responses to the laws, coming from a mixed class base, were often violent in nature.[30]

The Legionaries of Christ seem to rearticulate ideas sown during the Cristiada to save an endangered Catholic Church and to follow the pope's teachings closely. This renarrativization is a small part of a larger confrontation between lay and religious forces over the matter of freedom of Catholic religious cults in the public sphere, and the ramifications of this conflict were felt well before and after the war. At the core of this rearticulation is an implicit but fundamental tension between a secular state and the church that holds a universal (Catholic) truth. The modus vivendi expressed by the Legionaries of Christ is clearly positioned across this divide, in a way very different way from the Scalabrinian connection between migration and the relativism of culture(s). The Legionaries are "defenders" of the teachings of the popes, such as John Paul II and Benedict XVI, especially in matters of culture of life and bioethics.

The history of the Legionaries of Christ has associated itself genealogically to the martyrs of the Cristiada as can be seen in their active role in the recent beatification of José Sánchez del Río, a fourteen-year-old boy killed on 6 February 1928, while in a company led by the Catholic general Guízar Morfín.[31] The Legionaries of Christ have played a key role in the canonization (performed by John Paul II in 2000) of the martyrs of the Cristiada or Cristero War and the sanctification in 2006 of the first Latin American bishop, Rafael Guízar y Valencia, who was also the uncle of the founder of the Legionaries. Other canonizations are potentially on the way, though they are less clearly bound to the heart of the Cristero War, which historians locate in the regions of Jalisco and Michoacán, but which spread to more racially mixed regions, such as Veracruz. Broadly then, the role of the Legionaries in those canonizations indexes the order's position toward the history of the Cristiada—to be a strong supporter of an integralist church that promotes the centrality of the clergy to Catholicism and allegiance to the pope.

The tensions of this history are possibly engrained differently in female bodies. A paradigmatic case of this emerges in the story of Leonor Sánchez López. Hector, a very smart diocesan priest training in Rome at the Gregorian University, recounts her story in his words as follows:

> In Orizaba, Veracruz, in 1937, when the law passed by Alejandro Tejada prevented the public from celebrating mass, the mass was then celebrated in private homes. One day the police broke into a home after a fight and they shot a fifteen-year-old woman, Leonor Sánchez, and then her parents and other people, who were mainly factory workers in the textile industry, marched to the palace of the governor and asked that he "*diera la cara*," but "*el no la dió*" [that he come forward, but he did not]. So the people went to open the temples [churches] and carried the fathers on their shoulders and brought them back into the temples. They are trying now in Orizaba to promote the cause of beatification of Leonor Sánchez, but [this] has not happened yet. The people maintain the memory of those events that happened around the temple, and this is still very strong

there; people talk about it; it is in their memory; for some, it is engrained in their bones. The Cristiada was not only in Michoacán and Jalisco.[32]

In this interpretation innocent women and their martyred bodies were the bastion and the carnal symbol for the defense of Catholicism in times of encroachment.

If the Legionaries of Christ repurposed ideas sown during the Cristiada in their own call to arms to save an endangered Catholic Church, these efforts appear decidedly reactionary in the eyes of some Mexican fathers in Rome, one of whom I quote anonymously here:

> The Legionaries of Christ say "I am faithful" [*soy fiel*]; however, they are repetitive, they do not make steps forward. . . . They wish to go back to the Christian church where there are churches and public buildings, where the Catholic space is total, where there is a crucifix everywhere, where there are Catholic schools, to the point of even having Catholic cars! This is the Cristero spirit: have a powerful church facing a strong state.

But there is also a side of the Legionaries that has led to much critique both outside and inside the Catholic church. The fourth vow of the Legionaries of Christ, which was temporarily revoked by Pope Benedict at the time of the death of its founder in March 2008, professes a hermetic secrecy about, and a total dedication to, the acts and words of the founder. Repeated reading of lengthy scripts and letters by the founder are key parts of a Legionary member's formation and daily discipline. This has led to critiques about a "cult" of the founder within the order, which actually seemed to have led the group of leaders of the order around him to cover his illicit behaviors for many years. A special commission of the Roman Curia headed by Archbishop Velasio de Paolis carried out in 2009–10 an Apolostic Visitation to evaluate whether the order could survive in the same form after the demise of its founder or if it had to be taken under the firmer and closer apostolic and disciplinary wing of the Holy See. In 2012 the constitutions of the order were revisited and the figure of the founder recalibrated, while key figures in its leadership in Rome and Mexico were changed. The order was not dismembered then but allowed to grow again under renewed directions.

Regardless of these powerful real and potential restructurings of the order, the Legionaries of Christ have had and still have an important role in Catholic higher education and the development of diocesan priests in

Rome and in Mexico. The motto of the Legionaries is "teach, educate, and form." Their skills are focused on attending to the individual and the whole human being as *integer homo*. Although they have become the confidants of some members of the higher Mexican and Italian social classes, they nonetheless dedicate themselves to ordinary people. Or, better, they attend to people as individuals:

> I do not know much about their ideas about migration, but I know that [the Legionaries of Christ] are very sensitive to those who are in need. I was walking with Padre Rodolfo and when a beggar asked him for money, . . . he stopped to talk to him; he asked his name, where he was from, how long he had been there; they had a long chat. He showed a real interest in the guy, who was definitely a foreigner, sitting there begging. . . . I do not know but they have a particularly good manner with people; they make you feel important. (Soledad, a Mexican student at the Gregorian, a Jesuit university in Rome, personal communication)

It is this emphasis on the care of the individual that has made the Legionaries so successful in recruiting wealthy elites and in creating a feeling that, by being a member or sympathizer of their lay movement, they belong to a "club."

The Legionaries operate two major universities in Rome. The University Reginae Apostolorum, founded in 1993, is a pontifical university dedicated to training diocesan priests and clerics of different orders with a Legionaries of Christ mandate. The inauguration in 2004 of the Università Europea, which is situated on the same campus and is dedicated to lay peoples' study, was attended by key Italian politicians including Marcello Pera, the head of the Senate Chamber at the time. All ordained Legionaries have to spend at least a few years of their thirteen-year training in Rome.

Important Italian politicians have been connected to the lay movement of the Legionaries of Christ, including Alfredo Mantovano and Antonio Fazio, the governor of the Bank of Italy between 1993 and 2005. Mantovano, an MP of the right-wing party Alleanza Nazionale, wrote the main text of the 2001 Bossi-Fini law, which, as I explained in chapter 2, regulated immigration until the Security Decree of 2009. Mantovano, who until 2011 was an undersecretary for Home Affairs, asked for an even tighter version of immigration law against what he terms "liberal attacks"[33] and resigned his post because of an ongoing conflict with then Interior minister Roberto Maroni regarding the proposed relocation of newly arrived illegal migrants from Northern Africa across the whole Italian peninsula, a move that Maroni, a key player in the separatist Northern League, did not want to embrace politically.

The influence of the Legionaries of Christ on the Berlusconi government since the early 2000s can also be traced through their role in shaping policy through educational and research institutions. Through their connection with the Università Europea the Legionaries have hosted congresses of Catholic intellectuals and politicians dedicated to forging pedagogical and political avenues for an integralist Catholicism. Alfredo Mantovano, for instance, had a central role in crafting a master's degree program in migration studies hosted at this university in 2005/6. The master's courses were focused on understanding the current and possible future legal and social pitfalls of illegal and legal migration to Italy, with conspicuously little reflection on any contemporary cultural perspectives or on migrant flows might contribute to the destination country's growth. The master's program imagined migration not as a part of divine providence, but as a state nightmare. More than fifty people initially enrolled in the master's program, mainly individuals working then in the Italian ministry of internal affairs in Rome (which paid the tuition fees), so it had an impact on social servants working directly, at this time, on immigration issues.[34]

Guest speakers to the course included intellectuals such as Giovanni Cantoni and Massimo Introvigne, who are both at the forefront of a small but powerful movement of the Italian Catholic right called Alleanza Cattolica.[35] In the inaugural speech of the master's program in the university of the Legionaries, Giovanni Pisanu, then minister of the Interior, confirmed his connection with Alleanza Cattolica and Alfredo Mantovano, reflecting on the centrality of Catholicism to the politics of immigration, and the spirit of conversion:

> So no to whatever form of syncretism, no to any form of confusion between religious cultural identities, but yes to a dialogue for the defense, since I am a Christian, and proud of my identity. Moreover, if I can speak for a second as a believer, the truth is only there, in the cross of Christ. I have kept a vivid memory of a childhood reading that has marked me deeply. It was a sort of letter of instructions that was given to the missionaries . . . : When you meet a pagan, a nonbeliever, one who has other religious beliefs, do not tell him his God is false, or mendacious, but help him to reflect because you will see that at the end of his reflection he will find Christ. Hence I think that our identity has to be nourished by this

certainty, and, in being sealed to this certainty, we can gently and peacefully engage in a dialogue with other religions.[36]

So there has been a clear group of political interests that have benefited from an affiliation to the Legionaries of Christ. There are thus multiple lines of political alliance that connect players in Berlusconi's governments, integralist Catholic intellectuals, employees in the Roman municipal government of Gianni Alemanno, and the Legionaries of Christ, especially via their educational efforts. I am not suggesting that these are secret alliances, as a journalistic mode of writing might imply. Through an anthropological lens instead, I want to open up a reading of these threads as potentially at the core of one of the many souls of the Catholic Church in its transnational returns.

Parallels between the Jesuits and the Legionaries

In this chapter I am drawing a parallel between the "old" Spanish-founded Jesuit order and the "new" twentieth-century Mexican order of the Legionaries of Christ. I want to explore here how these two religious bodies may be phantomatically connected via the presence and the mimesis of the haunting spirit of the other.[37] Phantomatic refers to a spectral presence of something that was there before but is not there anymore—a haunting sense of belonging (here as attachment to the spirit of another order), that some scholars have productively investigated as reposed in materialities.[38]

A phantomatic presence here takes the form of the embodiment of someone's secret, or can be the haunting and living repository of somebody's else unspeakable drama.[39] This unspoken drama is partly situated in a historiography, contested today, that locates the death of an "old" church as intrinsic to the birth of a "new," post–Vatican II church. A phantomatic relationship between these two orders is based on mimetic analogies affectively active in the histories, formations, and pedagogies of the transnational reproduction of the orders of the Legionaries and Jesuits. This relationship exists within a Roman Catholic Church that is able to contain within it what Carl Schmitt called a *complexio oppositorum* (complex of opposites). Current revisions of Vatican II with its focus on charismatic renewal, Marian devotions, and antirelativist perspectives have direct implication for forms of governmentality and "passions" that are cultivated by the Roman Catholic Church. This passionate machine—the articulation between governmentality and the production of passions—is moved both by transnational Marian mobilization of affects (see next chapter) but also by militant ones—Mary and the militia have often gone together.[40]

The Legion's close ties with the elite are even more conspicuous in Mexico. Monterrey, the financial hub of Mexico (also called the "Houston of the North"), is dominated by a group of business families that are the most powerful in Mexico and throughout Latin America—the so-called Group of Ten. The Jesuits played a major role in educating the children of the wealthy in Monterrey, but in 1968 the local bishop, Alfonso Espino y Silva, drove them out of the archdiocese with the accusation they were backing a group called Movimiento Estudiantil Profesional and its leftist call for strike at the Instituto Tecnológico de Monterrey. Since then, the Legion assumed a similar role to that formerly played by the Jesuits, setting the social and intellectual tone for Monterrey's wealthy through a web of schools, clubs, and charitable organizations.

The Legionaries' educational work in Mexico parallels the work of the Jesuits on two fronts. They are particularly strong in the *pastoral de la Juventud* (youth pastoral work) and have had a strong and growing influence on Catholic higher education since they created the Catholic Anahuac Universities Network. Work on both fronts can be read as a conservative strategy aimed at counteracting the effects of liberation theology in Mexico and in Latin America by gaining direct access to the future Catholic elites of the country. Whereas the Jesuits moved toward an *opción preferencial de los Pobres* (preferential option for the poor), the Legionaries have been described as holding a *teología de la prosperidad* (theology of prosperity).[41] John Paul II's difficult and somehow alienating relationship with the "new" postconciliar Jesuits, and in particular with General Pedro Arrupe, should be interpreted alongside his privileged relationship with the Legionaries of Christ in Mexico and Rome. During the papacy of John Paul II and the mandate of Angelo Sodano as Vatican secretary of state (1990–2006), the Legionaries of Christ gained a strong degree of influence within the Curia Romana. Although many forces are involved in the relative successes of the two orders in Mexico and in Rome, their sharply contrasting relationship with the Holy See during John Paul II's papacy has undoubtedly contributed to their parallel stories.

Central to the argument of this chapter is that an analogical mimesis has taken place between the two orders, and that the spirit of the militia, a legion for Christ, is a key aspect of this mimesis. This analogical mimesis takes different forms: the centrality of the apostolic work, the pedagogical formation, the importance of the Ignatian exercises, the devotion to the

Sacred Heart, and the charisma of the founder. Apostolic work has been central to the formation of the Society of Jesus since its sixteenth-century inception. St. Ignatius felt the need to create an order that was devoted neither to monastic life nor to the parish. Hence, the vow of the Jesuit dedicates him to a special obedience to the missionary vision and directions of the pope. The Legionary practice and vocation are also firmly rooted in apostolic work, especially with the educated classes. This orientation translates ethnographically when lay members of the movement are repeatedly encouraged (in quasi-soldierly tones) to take up this apostolic task in their everyday life, to turn from being a lukewarm Catholic into an active agent of the apostolate.

The training, or formation, of a Legionary of Christ is remarkable among the religious orders in its similarity to the formation of a Jesuit. In both orders, one initially joins the novitiate, after which the first "simple" vows are taken. As a member of the juniorate, one engages in a period of theological study, which is followed by a period of philosophy. A period of regency, or work, follows, and then a return to theological studies. Finally, one enters a period of tertianship, which St. Ignatius called the period of the "school of the heart," before the one is presented with the option of professing perpetual vows. The Ignatian spiritual exercises are also central to both orders and consist of a unique and lengthy thirty-day silent retreat carried out by members of both orders before ordination, although this occurs at different stages in the priests' formation in the two orders. Both orders also practice a yearly eight-day silent retreat. The militaristic tone of the specific images evoked by this Ignatian exercise could forge different interpretations of an "unconditional defense" of the Roman Catholic Church against "evil" forces.

The charisma of the founder of the Legionaries of Christ, Marcial Maciel, has characterized, for better and for worse, the history of the order, and it is around a clash of charisma that the first tensions between the Legionaries and Jesuits appeared. This clash first became apparent during the early 1940s, when Maciel attended the Jesuit seminary at the University of Comillas in Spain, as well as a few years later, when he was expelled from the Jesuit seminary of Montezuma in Texas. As a letter from the head of the Jesuits in Comillas read:

> But it is regrettable that Father Maciel has shown so much distrust for our Society and to some extent has given signs which render him suspect to us about the insufficiently virtuous means he is using to achieve his own

ends. Moreover, since he also has novices there (even if the house was not canonically erected) and since he possesses a great power of attracting them, there is a danger of the bishop's displeasure if more vocations to this new recently and approved religious congregation emerge. In fact, in 1947 three pupils and in 1948 another three entered this institution. (My translation from the Latin)[42]

In the words of another Jesuit supervising the Comillas province of León:

> Since his arrival, Marcial Maciel, a young Mexican priest and the founder of a certain religious congregation, has greatly fostered this separation among the Americans and the Spanish. Lest I say too little, I am soliciting information from the assisting priest received from Father Rodrigo (who knows the man very well), about this singular and dangerous man, and about the necessity that he depart entirely from the Seminary of Comillas with his pupils. (My translation from the Latin)[43]

I am interested here in the fact that Maciel is described as having "dangerous" power and "greatness" in these and other Jesuit letters. There is a real fear of a powerful and charismatic force that championed a group of "young" Latin Americans and could take Jesuits "away from their order." To an extent, there was a perceived betrayal here as well. Senior Jesuits in Comillas felt that this young Mexican priest was given hospitality, was embraced with open arms, and then began to bleed forces away—his actions were perceived by senior Jesuits as dangerously duplicitous. If the Legionaries of Christ have been key for John Paul II in reaching out toward Latin America and its rejuvenation of the Catholic Church, fear and betrayal, between the Legionary and the Jesuit orders, are also affects of an Atlantic Return.

Since the inception of their order, the relationship of the Legionaries to the Jesuit order has been characterized by an anxiety about the former order's mimetic powers over the latter one. Parallels exist between both orders, in their militaristic interpretations of the apostolate, in their emphasis on education and intellectual formation (which can become an attractive force for the formation and control of diocesan priests and the laity), and in their understanding of the Sacred Heart as the foundation of the spirituality of both orders. These are some of the building blocks of both orders, emphasized or de-emphasized at different historical moments. At one level, the mimetic relation between the Jesuit and Legionary orders is an anxiety about "too much proximity" because of similar elements between the two, in the present as well as in their pasts. Before I further explain these connections, I want to elucidate some key elements of the bioreligiosity of the Legionaries of Christ in relation to the history of the Jesuits I have presented.

Legionaries' Modus Operandi

Michel Foucault has given us tools to understand how bodies act and are acted upon. Through a study of how bodies are normalized in social practices, we can discern situated and profound relations between politics and ontologies. In this way, for Foucault, biopolitics is a form of government over those conditions of life produced by normalizing technologies of population, as well as a power over human conduct through particular political technologies. Those technologies of the well-being of the subject are seated not only in material conditions, the distribution of the rhythms of labor, but also in the demarcation of transcendental boundaries—boundaries of mediation with an otherwise.

However, I think we need to consider the affective presence (not the embodied practice of a belief), the modus operandi of theological horizons in religious life and the way in which these too are entangled in the presence of lived and "un-lived" histories. In chapter 2, I analyzed how the Holy See has recently focused its political energies on the resacralization of individual life, with a hypostatization of a "culture of life" vis-à-vis the lives of individuals in specific political spheres and cultures. In the light of this historical conjuncture, the modus operandi of the Legionaries shows at least three key elements.[44] First, the heart has to be cultivated with a mix of humility, virility, and apostolic heroism. As it says in one of the order's internal manuals:

> What is my love of Jesus Christ like? Is it genuine, profound, based on faith and reason? Is it virile? Or is it shallow and prompted by feeling? Rather is it passionate, leading me to accept the sacrifice of the religious life joyfully? . . . [Does my love for Jesus] keep the meaning of the cry "Adveniat Regnum Tuum!" always foremost on my mind, on the tip of my tongue and embedded in my heart? . . . Do I think I can be a follower of the Sacred Heart without a deep, practical, and sincere self-denial? Does the thought of Christ incline me to happy, prompt, and heroic obedience? To minute and perfect fulfillment of the Legion's call

to love others? Does it foster imitation of his meekness and humility, and bring me to union with Him through strict control of my affections and purity of mind?[45]

The true "man of the kingdom" has to love the mystical body, in the form of the Legion itself, through his imitation of the ideals of Christ's heart as a redeemer and a conqueror. The mystical dimension of the Legionaries' bioreligiosity dwells in this mystical body that governs the inner practice, and other practices, of surrendering with unlimited self-denial to the cause of the apostolate of the Legion. The affective force of and the love for the apostolate acquires, as for the Jesuit, a mystical power. As we know, affects are transmitted through the social, but they also prefigure social relations themselves. They are constitutive of the latter without being fully acknowledged by individuals.[46] So the force of this apostolate becomes an affective field that moves the Legionaries practice as a whole, not just the individual priests of the Legionaries. In turn, this is a force that shapes the Roman Catholic Church as a passionate machine.

Marcial Maciel required that all the Legionaries of Christ in training, from any part of the world, should spend some part of their formation in Rome. They may not be able to do so in the future, but in the words of Father Jesús L.C., with whom I once visited in the inner chapel of the Regina Apostolorum:

> Father Maciel wanted this chapel to be a space for *recogimiento*, but also a space of inspiration. . . . You see that light coming through [pointing to the skylight over the altar]? Father Maciel wanted the light to be like the one created by Bernini, as the descent of the Holy Spirit, but this Church is open, like a fan, as the inclusion after Council Vatican II, we are opening new missions in the Philippines and in Africa . . . and we all pass through here. I love this chapel, it reminds me of the Tepeyac. Every time I go to Mexico I try to visit the Virgin, even if it is for a short visit.[47]

The church is decorated with onyx and alabaster brought from Mexico, the benches are of solid handcrafted wood, the colors are brownish, and somehow the strong light of the outside contrasts with a protected, dimmed-down ambience. When I shared with Father Jesús my feeling that this church seems to me to be like a "womb," he said:

> Yes, it is like coming back to the mother; that is why I like so much this chapel and the Virgin of Guadalupe; it is this light and shadow that make one feeling he is coming home. There are more than 450 Legionaries liv-

ing now here in the Regnum Christi,[48] and more than 1,250 here in Rome. All of us are different, but I think that for each one of us this chapel is really special.

Hence the Legion (La Legión), as a "she," may have its spatial "womb" too. The Legion is also a "she" in a liturgical sense and as an affective agency, and the legionary is the cultivator of a love that streams forth from an ideal total identification with the order. In the order's daily book of prayers (used by every Legionary as a guideline for prayers before the death of the founder in 2008): "Can I say that I think like the Legion, love as she does, feel as she does? Do I feel responsible for the plan God has for her?"[49] There is a strong gendering of the order here, and a totalizing identification with a female, passionate quality. But my conversations with Father Jesús, a Mexican Legionary of Christ, make me understand that there is a "soft" side to the Legionaries, one that is as intimate as its journalistic image of an order led by a fierce apostolate and its power-seeking within the Vatican is hard. Vernacular realities are always more complicated.

The second element of the modus vivendi of the Legionaries requires a technique of the body that pays particular attention to a careful posture of the body and to an appropriate presentation. A Legionary should always eat with style, not too much, so as not to "show passions" in eating, as another Mexican diocesan priest who lived in a Legionary-led Mater Ecclesia in Rome explained to me. Or when involved in the football championships of the priests' league, a Legionary team is always recognized for its "tidy" look and "shining" outfits—and seen as such by other priests who play in the league. Again, in the words of the same priest, the Legionaries need to have "discreet glances," especially with women, and they need to be careful about their looks during outings so that "self-control helps them keep feeling the presence of God in their soul."

Legionaries are also recognized in the Comunidad Católica Mexicana for their outfits. Whereas Mexican Jesuits, diocesan priests, and other seminarians may dress rather casually, the Legionaries are always dressed in clerical collars and immaculate grey or black priestly suits. Legionaries move around in pairs, and when coming up to strangers or people known to them, they "act as a team." Critics of the Legionaries have said that this is a subtle but very strong form of peer control, so strong, in fact, that it minimizes the potential for Legionaries to interact with the "outside" world on their own. They are also very diligent. Legionaries often carry a notebook, and while conversing they are always very ready to get a person's contact details and invite them to events. The use of the media by the Legionaries is very effective.

Third, the modus operandi of the Legionaries stresses the believer's individuality, his or her own uniqueness in the path of finding and uniting with God, while maintaining a very strong sense and aesthetic of the mission of the whole body of the Legion. In the words of Gaston, a young Legionary from Puebla whom I met at a Comunidad Católica Mexicana event in 2010:

> I grew up in Puebla with many brothers and sisters, and I have been used to helping at home. Now here in the seminary we have to study very much and it is very long, and we all help, we do all by ourselves. We do not have sisters [religious nuns] doing it for us. Father Maciel thought it's important we keep it that way; we need to be very organized, and pay attention to details. We have to study to be very prepared, to speak well and to strengthen the church.[50]

But to "speak well" is a function of education or erudition and also an imitation of the aesthetic of Christ's love in the being of the Legion. The love its members feel for the Legion is also *a love for the "spirit of combat"*:

> Do I practice the Legion's spirit in my conversations? Do they radiate the "sweet fragrance" of Christ? Do I argue? Do I know how to give in, even thought it hurts me? Am I humble in this respect? Are my conversations frivolous? Do I make an effort to speak of Legionary themes? . . . Can I say I am at one with the spirit of the Legion? Is my love for the Legion strong enough not to omit even the most trivial details? Do I uphold the primary demand of the spirit of combat, blind faith in my Cause and in its eventual triumph, as well as burning love for my spirit and my fellow combatants?[51]

It is clear in passages like these that the Legionary modus operandi has a less public, even "intimate," aspect and endorses a regimented individual and communal apostolic body. Moreover, as I've suggested above, it is also anchored in specific geopolitical terrains and often based on the affective return of transnational stories of Catholic martyrdom. Through its unique claim to these stories of martyrdom, through its occupation of renewed spaces of Catholic education in Italy,[52] and its closeness to some conservative political elites in Rome, this order, and the orientation within the Catholic Church it stands for, actually, more or less implicitly, supports a perspective that sees a connection between immigration, illegality, and integration to a strong, Catholic notion of national identity. The Legionaries have invested themselves in educating the Catholic political elite in Italy and Mexico. While mixing with and acting as the spiritual advisers of some in those elites, they have been a group of references for politicians who have played a role in the drawing of Italian immigration policy, which has unfortunately become increasingly exploitative and exclusionary during this time.

The Church as a Passionate Machine

It is in this light that contemporary voices of the members of the Regnum Christi in Rome are still strongly supporting the order of the Legionaries, even after the revelations of their founder's second life (fathering children in two separate relationships).[53] However, in the eyes of the Italian and Mexican women who belong and participate in the activities of the Regnum Christi at the Università Europea in Rome, the story of the "weakness" of human nature (and, specifically, of the founder of the order) should not spoil the higher ideals, practice, and apostolic work of the order of the Legionaries of Christ and its lay movement. However, in the group that I followed, this attitude was not easily accepted, but came out of renewed discussions between priests/animators and the women lay members.

To sum up, then, the Legionaries of Christ are *not* the new Jesuits. The two orders are not homologous, but they are connected by revelatory details and the affective forces that animate them. Sigmund Freud talked about how a methodology inspired by the work of an artist such as Michelangelo draws attention to unnoticeable details that actually reveal other, less evident possibilities and intentionalities.[54] Finding in Freud's speculation the basis for a rethinking of method, Giorgio Agamben suggests that the form of scrutiny Freud intimates is an *archaeology of signature*, which emerges in the interstices between the semiotic field (what we recognize as a sign) and the hermeneutic (the interpretation of signs). We can understand the signature as dwelling at this interstice, in the moment of schism, by embracing the presence of what could have been, as a constitutive force:

> In other words, archaeological regression is elusive: It does not seek, as in Freud, to restore a previous stage, but to decompose, displace, and ultimately bypass it in order to go back not to its content but to the modalities, circumstances, and moments in which the split, by means of repression, constituted it as origin.[55]

This understanding of schism, of what it could have been as a genealogy of the present reveals a methodological way forward for understanding the relation between the Jesuit order and the Legionaries of Christ. The co-presence of "lived" and potentially repressed elements of each one of the religious orders is illuminated by focusing on details, such as the potential internal schism of the Jesuits in late 1960s together with the anxieties around the presence of Maciel in a Jesuit-led seminar in 1940s Spain. The detail as a signature reminds us, or better yet, takes us to the moment of the inception, of an oblivion—the forgetting of what it could have been, but that is nevertheless constitutive of what it is now. The oblivion of the Jesuit order is itself a complex historical formation, but I have highlighted here at least two components: the oddity of the Jesuit's sixteenth-century mystic devotion and the "disappearance" of the *true* Society of Jesus in twentieth-century Spain. These two apparently minor moments in the order's history are considered by many historiographers as receding elements in a Jesuit history.[56] However, that conflict within the order was in a sense a "true" killing, as the "mystic" space in the Jesuit apostolate is still one of contention.

The history of the *true* Company of Spain (which was dismembered and quieted by the voice of the company that emerged after the XXXII General Congregation lead by Father Arrupe) was the suffering of a death within. I argue that the details of those "inner deaths" should illuminate the Legionaries of Christ's analogies with the Jesuit order and the filling in of the latter evacuated spaces. Those spaces have also been historically masculinized (and eroticized). By filling in/taking over affective spaces (promoting a virile posture of priesthood in the church, where Jesuits were perceived as lacking), the Legionaries may have implicitly benefited from the strength of the "death" within another order and captured some of their historical affective power, some of their virility. To describe it differently, they captured some remainders of a (symbolic) capital that the Jesuits had accumulated in more than 450 years.

A "simple" rivalry between two different Catholic religious orders in their transatlantic reproduction helps explain how affective forces can be harnessed from realms of both official and leftover translocal histories, which, for anthropologists, both shadow and enlighten contemporary and coexisting ethnographic encounters. A study of a translocality of the Roman Catholic Church at this particular historical conjuncture of a new Romanization of the Catholic Church and a universalization of the Holy See as a political/moral subject needs to engage with the particular articulation of these affective forces. The Atlantic return is illuminated here by an attention to mimesis between orders in the Americas and Europe. This is an attention to both the lived experience of Catholicism and the role of phantomatic presences—of a past call of the Jesuits in a present call of the Legionaries—shaping each respective order.

Just as affects circulate, intensify, and "stick" to the skin[57] of particular religious orders, they are also hijacked for the agenda of a particular Catholic project. Celebrating this harnessing/hijacking mainly as an understanding of affects that signal eruptive, creative potential and liberating forces—as some theorist of affects have done[58]—may well obscure more than it reveals. In fact, affects mobilized in the relation between the histories and practices of both Legionaries and Jesuits are also the haunting imprint of very conservative and, to a certain extent, hypermodern projects of a ("universal") Catholic humanitas. So Catholic humanitas is not only a theological project of the church, it is also a pedagogical apostolic one that is affectively transmitted through religious orders. This affective articulation of apostolic (and virile) forces and the anxiety of their loss throughout history are parts of what constitute the Catholic Church as a passionate machine, marked by forces and weaknesses within an Atlantic return. The powerful ways in which theologies are affectively transmitted (and incarnated) are central to an anthropological understanding of Catholicism, and so to an understanding of the forces of histories in the present.

Coda

I am not interested in debating the scandals that have been attributed to the founder of the Legionaries of Christ or in examining journalistic interest in the internal discipline of the order and its particular inclinations in recruiting members among the very wealthy and powerful for its lay movement, the Regnum Christi.[59] However, it is important to note that the Legionaries have undergone a major crisis, and an apostolic visitation (an internal review by a higher commission of the church). Less in favor with the papacies of Benedict XVI and Francis than it was with John Paul II,[60] the order was audited internally to the church between 2009 and 2010. The visitation also evaluated the order's reliance on the charisma of its (now dead) founder Maciel, in the light of recent revelations concerning his fathering a child and earlier accusations of drug abuse and pedophilia.

The Legionaries of Christ, whose project is entrenched in that of a Catholic humanitas, have received much attention from the media. The accusations of pedophilia laid against Marcial Maciel have marked both the early and later parts of his priestly career. Maciel was suspended from his ministerial functions between 1955 and 1957[61] and after another investigation of allegations of pedophilia and drug abuse by the head of the Council of the Doctrine of the Faith (Cardinal Joseph Ratzinger then, now Pope Emeritus Benedict XVI) he was advised that he should retire to private life in 2006. When he died two years later, one alleged daughter in Spain and one son in Mexico appeared, the second suing the order for compensation. Cracks in the ideal of the purity of the Legion had begun to emerge just before Vatican II.[62] The case of Maciel became one of the key examples of Benedict XVI's annus horribilis for the priesthood in 2010.

However, in order to address this constellation of events properly, we would need to analyze the phenomenon of the Legionaries of Christ in a broader register of the eroticism of the church—the subject of another work to be written. I want to signal here that in the Catholic Church boundaries between eroticism and abuse may be thin, and a focus on the return of the missions can be helpful. To understand abuse within the Catholic Church we cannot confine the (painful) debate to lay-clerical relations (see abuse taking place in parishes by the hands of priests). I think we need to focus also on a history of the Catholic Church from within its clergy. We need to understand sexual abuse of the clergy in the light of a suppression of a force of eroticism.

A rubric of historically informed relationships between the "suppression" of Jesuit mystical impulses (in the sixteenth century), the increased eroticized expressions of the order (with and after Council Vatican II, when many Jesuits left the order and some married), and particular forms of "virile" postures and "love" for the Legion may help us address eroticism as an ambiguous force. Its lack of containment within the clergy when transformed into abuse is, of course, a very worrisome aspect. But eroticism, in its symbolic and fleshy forms, is also an embodied and passionate force that is present in a renewal of a communal "apostolic" body within the Church—eroticism as ever, has an ambiguous position. The chapter that follows will focus on further emergences of eroticism at the intersection between migrant itineraries and the Catholic Church.

4.   *Migrant Hearts*

It is a warm afternoon in April 2011. I am getting out of the San Giovanni metro station in Rome. I am going to visit Eloisa and Roberto for a meal in their one-bedroom apartment, a place that took them forever to find to rent but is still not really affordable. Eloisa[1] likes this flat, although it is a bit damp and right at the entrance of this lower-middle-class condominium building, so the curtains have to be kept shut for privacy. Eloisa attends Santa Maria degli Angeli and Santa Maria della Luce, two churches in the Latin American Mission (MLA) network of national churches in Rome, and she shares with the many other women who attend these churches a great devotion to the Virgin of Chapi and to the Sacred Heart, or Corazón de Jesus. She keeps a beautiful representation of the Virgin on her vanity table, together with the many other devotional representations she has received from friends and priests both in Rome and in Peru. Space in the apartment is limited. The Italian owner of the flat did not want to move out the old furniture, so Eloisa and her partner have created storage space along the upper parts of the walls. The place feels cramped but also full of memories. After her partner has gone to a meeting, we start to share stories of migration, love, broken hearts, and Catholic faith while curled up on the sofa, with a nice blanket over both of us.

We talk about women breaking the hearts of men—of good men here—with endless strings of betrayal. We talk about women involved in the church, who sometimes gather in migrants' houses where beer drinking is taking its toll and where new sexual liaisons are formed and others broken. We share stories of other women who have left overnight, one in particular who took all of the furniture from the flat she was sharing with a "good" man. Eloisa recalls the love of her life, a Peruvian priest in a religious order, who stole her heart. Or better, they stole each other's hearts. He met her in Peru a long time ago, and she saw him again in

Rome. She remembers his laugh, his articulate speech, but also their shared sense of isolation here in Rome, and then a touch she felt from him one day here, the hand she felt on her lower back, and then a kiss. That left her in the air for days—affects that circulate between (forbidden) bodies and that make the hunger for contact and warmth very real here: "I felt I was melting, Valentina, but at the same time I was finally alive again, my heart was alive again, my skin was alive again." I am reminded again that affects are transmitted through skin; they can open new horizons just as they close others; and they arise between people rather than within them.[2]

Anthropological studies of Catholicism and migration that focus on tension and division between popular religiosity and Catholic hierarchy have taught us to pay attention to life-cycle rituals and the hegemonic and counterhegemonic forces that are at play in ritual performances, symbols, and the discursive practices that constitute the everyday life of Catholic faith.[3] These studies have shone light on the gendering of popular devotion, the relationship to saints' lives and local clergy, the embodied and ethical directions that identification with the life of Mary means for migrants in new social and geopolitical terrains, and the way new local shrines reinforce a sense of community identity in the diaspora.[4]

This chapter—through the analyses of ritual celebrations, including devotions to the Sacred Heart (a fifteenth-century devotion to the suffering of Jesus)—captures (re)emerging struggles for the colonization of "new" territories within the Catholic Church. It argues that Latin American migrant itineraries and Roman urban landscapes reveal the circulation of deep-seated anxieties, first about pollution by a migrant Other but also about the possibility for renewed forms of Catholic centralization and counternarratives of the periphery.

A key difficulty in studying forms of Roman Catholic pedagogy vis-à-vis migration centers on the celebration of the strength of the Latin American Church within the global Roman Catholic scenario, a strength that is so often identified with its passions. Desires, passions, and fantasies are important focuses for understanding migrants' religious experiences. Migrant hearts are what drive the church, but they are also a thorn in the side of the church; for example, the embodiment of sexual desires outside of marriage is a problem for the church, which constantly advocates for a stable Catholic family. As I have already suggested in the second chapter of this book, the culture of life is founded on a specific idea of the family, which stresses heteronormativity and condemns out-of-wedlock sexual relations. Migrant erotic longings for inappropriate intimacies, whether transgressing marriage or clerical chastity, haunt the normative idea of the family and the culture of life anchored in it. This comes into striking view in Rome.

Although a pastoral evangelization at the MLA in Rome stresses a drive for a pan-Latin American church, my analysis here does not wish to address "migrant communities," a concept of community that, in its fulfillment of a holistic longing, has too long fascinated anthropological inquiries on migration. Migrants instead, taking a de Certeaunian angle of analysis, are those who "teach us to circulate in our language and our customs, and adapt to our material and symbolic universe"; they point to itineraries that are difficult to contain, but also potential engines of revitalization: "All we have to do is invent with them [the migrants] a 'culture in the plural' in offering them the condition of a plurality of *mixed itineraries* that are diverse, changing and constantly being re-shaped."[5]

Migrants' subjectivities are forged in a process of mobility and a cultural swarm, as the ensemble of that which can proliferate at the margins and that, at the same time, in de Certeau's view, actively undermines centrality. Migrant itineraries constitute a making and unmaking of margins and centralities.

Questions of centralities and peripheries, and of the recomposition and decentering of the Roman Catholic Church pass obligatorily through migrant terrains today. Such terrains are often elided from view, their constituents seen as unskilled and unnecessary by Italian publics. Yet just as migrant labor has become indispensable for the reproduction of advanced industrial economies, migrant passions are in fact central to the rejuvenation, as well as, paradoxically, to the decentering of the Roman Catholic Church today.

In this chapter, I explore these questions in the return of affective histories of the Church of Santa Maria della Luce and the articulation of these histories across the MLA network in Rome. These stories are history and spaces of new orientations of hope, but also of betrayals. As one of the key sites of Catholic worship for Latin American migrants in Rome, the Church of Santa Maria della Luce thus functions within my study as a prism, allowing me to address some of the strengths and difficulties of Catholic migrants in Rome.

A second and, as I will show, related thread in my analysis centers on how migrant itineraries become embedded, more or less problematically, in erotic desires that "stick to the skin" and how the devotion of the Sacred Heart, with its long history, captures some of the tensions of divine love, the incarnation of passions, and the aesthetics of tactility and presence. Finally, I turn to what I describe as hearts in motion to discuss, through the examples of a pilgrimage to Il Divino Amore and a procession of the El Señor de los Milagros, how the affect of national devotions intersects in contradictory ways with a notion of common Catholic Latin American identity, a "common identity" (adopting the language used by Scalabrinians) that is seen by the Catholic Church as central to its own apostolic renewal in twenty-first-century Rome. My aim in drawing together this apparently diverse range of phenomena and experiences is to point to a deeper continuity of being Catholic and migrant that is not tied to a common and universal Catholic identity, but rather to multiple conditions and aspirations to the homey in migration and faith, and their intersections with conditions and experiences of betrayal.

Hearts Emplaced

The Church of Santa Maria della Luce is tucked away in an old barrio of Rome, Trastevere, just south of St. Peter's and the Holy See. It is the only church dedicated full-time to the whole Latin American population. There are other churches in the city that are part of the MLA, but each one of these is dedicated on a part-time basis to the evangelization of particular national groups, normally carried out through a Sunday mass in Spanish and regular Sunday *convivencias* (gatherings).

Catalina, the Peruvian churchwarden at Church of Santa Maria della Luce is a widely trusted, yet very private Peruvian woman who has been working in the church since the Latin American Mission was established in this parish in 2003. Through my conversation with Catalina, I have come to realize that it was not Santa Maria della Luce but Santa Cecilia in Trastevere that Pope John Paul II had originally intended as the center of the Catholic Latin American community in Rome. That beautiful edifice, referred to by Catalina as a museum church, stands only a short hop away. It was the perceived preciousness of Santa Cecilia, however, that led a group of archbishops to redirect Pope John Paul II's original plans in 2002. Catalina added that this is because "they think the migrants will ruin the place; they will spoil and dirty it." As I explained earlier, in chapters 1 and 2, the clear evidence that the Catholic hierarchy in Rome do, in fact, see migrants in this way is part of a wider tension between culture as a "historical heritage" and culture as lived, embodied experience that plays out in multicultural Rome. This tension is not confined to the politics of sacred domains, but emerges in the discourse of municipal authorities as well.[6]

Santa Maria della Luce may not be an important church in the Roman landscape or a particular asset for the urban religious cultural heritage, but it definitely has a rich affective labor history, which has emerged through practices of migrants' reappropriation. Santa Maria della Luce is a very old church. It was originally founded by Santa Bonosa, a Roman heiress, on the remains of what was possibly an even older Augustan court or a Jewish tribunal. The zenith of its social significance in Rome occurred from the eleventh century to the thirteenth, when the area was populated by migrant women and men coming from the provinces, who provided services for the Vatican. During this period, it was a church of secular laborers for the papal court. In the latter half of the sixteenth century, the church entered into a period of decadence (like hundreds of other churches in Rome), during which time "della Luce" was added to the name of the church, after the miracle of the apparition of the Virgin to a blind man. Father Manuel, insists that this has always been a church of laborers, whose work, often unrecognized, was actually the engine of a local as well as a larger economy. The historical continuities in the current role and constituency of this church—Latin American laborers employed in Rome's informal and service economies—is striking and appears so to me and to Padre Manuel as we discuss the church's history.

Yet the church has also experienced a history of deaths and reincarnations. It was closed to the public during the 1990s and the early 2000s, and only revitalized by the settling in of Latin Americans in the summer 2003. In the words of Leticia, one of the more active Peruvian helpers at the church, the story of the church's recent rebirth often emphasizes the prior decadence and the dirtiness of the church before the Latino community and the Scalabrinians moved in. It is also the story of the work a group of women: "*para hacer un hogar a El y a nosotros*" (to make a home for Him and us). Leticia recalls huge shopping trips that Padre Manuel makes regularly to one of the big shopping centers in Rome, bringing back cars "full of soap and everything to clean," as well as the back pain and the strained wrists of migrant women who had just helped clean the church, the ritual silverware, and the Crucifix in preparation for the celebrations of Good Friday. Dirtiness and the labor of cleaning seem to be continually evoked in secular and religious migrant itineraries. And this evocation is gendered.

Cleanliness has a long history in colonial racialized labor, articulated through the subtle imposition of internalized spatial segregations.[7] This internalization of cleanliness (often as a marker of value) is transmitted and inscribed in the everyday care of the church. But it is also through the materiality of this labor that a reproduction of otherness sticks to the migrants' skin and is at times challenged. The stress on cleanliness and the acts of cleaning a church that once was left shut and uncared for and now is the migrants' "home" is thus neither a private domain of self-care nor a public act of compliance. It is an affective material transmission and the making of homely and unhomely via "official" and competing histories. Santa Maria della Luce is a place with competing histories and values— one is a certain idea of (Italian) culture as heritage, the other has to do with history in the making. This history in the making is an active revaluing and reinscription of the church through a new apostolic blood and labor that is affectively transmitted more than ever through the handling and rubbing of soap and the breathing and sweat of the workers.

Erotic Hearts

Rosalba is an educated Ecuadorian woman who has been working as a *badante* (caretaker) since 2001. She was unmarried and in her early forties in the spring of 2005. The trajectory of her story is not unique, but it is revealing. Rosalba came to Rome after her best friend was murdered in the streets of Guayaquil. She followed her married sister and brother who were already living in Rome. She benefited from one of the early regularization processes, and she obtained a *permesso di soggiorno* (residence permit) in November 2002. She remains a legal resident in Italy. Yet despite the relative bureaucratic ease of her arrival, her life in Italy has not been easy. Before she arrived in Italy, her siblings warned her it would be hard: "But nobody can conceive how hard it can be, before you arrive here."

In four years, Rosalba changed live-in households four times. She finally started sharing a flat with her brother and sister in one of the peripheral neighborhoods of Rome. Although this afforded housing security, she had to spend more than an hour and a half on the buses to arrive at work by 8 A.M. For her, the major problem in Rome is the "humiliation of the heart." She talked at the time about the complexities, the abuse, the anxieties, and the pettiness of the bourgeois Roman families with whom she happened to live and work for more than three years. For example, an older man whom she looked after bothered her at night for sexual favors; the elderly wife of an ex-general arrogantly assumed that Rosalba could not read and write; another older woman, afraid of solitude, demanded company in front of the TV until the early hours of the morning; and the daughter of one of her employers envied Rosalba's education and English-language skills. Rosalba was also puzzled about Italian family relations: The son of an elderly person in her care lives around the corner but seems to visit his parent only infrequently.

Along with many other migrants, Rosalba is obsessed with time: "There is no time," she repeats. When you manage not to live *puerta adentro* (literality "inside the door," meaning live-in), you have to hold multiple jobs, often on different sides of town, which requires much juggling on public transport. There is often not even time to eat between jobs. Time, or its scarcity, is what kills women here, she claims. This was quite literally the case of an Ecuadorian acquaintance of Rosalba's, who was killed while running to the bus stop, because she was rushing to work.

If Rosalba's acute sense of the scarcity of time reflects a general experience among other women in the parish that the time between jobs seems to rush by, never slowing or stopping, it is a relation to time that is accompanied by the equally common feeling that time scarcely moves at all. When I was chatting with some migrant women on a Sunday at the parish of Santa Maria degli Angeli, they recalled looking at the clock as if "time never passes." When one is puerta adentro, the uninterrupted and single-minded attention required to care for their often elderly clients can begin to absorb every minute of these women's days. In contrast, as soon as they begin living away from their place of work (what is called *puertas afueras*, living outside the house), their wages are inadequate, and they have to take up more work; so time that goes too fast becomes the bad master of daily life. Rosalba, like other badanti, is an intimate witness to the breaking down of older structures of Italian family care that has accompanied the aging of Italian society. Her accounts are full of amusement, sadness, disbelief, and a sense of moral superiority, since in Guayaquil "we do take care of our *papis* [fathers]."

Although Rosalba's tone is often upbeat, there is much insecurity and precariousness in her life, starting from her work contract: "They can throw you out of the house overnight, and you may not even have time to come back for your things; so it's better to not possess anything of value here." Her sense of powerlessness emerges from being the weak and disposable link in endless Italian family sagas. Migrant workers, in their role of badanti, can often turn into the sacrificial carriers of intimate Italian familial odysseys. The term *sacrificial* here evokes Mayblin and Course's ideas about sacrifice beyond ritual in the wider spectrum of social life and labor.[8]

Hence within specific social and labor relations, and in contingent Italian immigration policies that have made migrant family reunions increasingly harder than in the past, a perceived migrant moral superiority emerges. When the story is about other migrants, a different moral economy seems to apply though. Rosalba and her friends often mention the multiple relations that Latin American women and men have here. Starting with Rosalba's sister whose child is in Ecuador and whose husband is in the United States, but who has now got a younger and "lazy" Peruvian boyfriend living in the house: "Is it because people are lonely here? . . . There are no roots here?" Rosalba asks herself. Or in the words of a friend of hers who is a Peruvian domestic worker, "People's hearts here are getting colder." The cooling of the heart is about a lack of caring too. A lack of caring toward others is perceived by some migrants as being at the heart of some Italian families. Thus the Catholic Church and the clergy see much potential in transnational Catholic immigrants to Europe to reinvigorate family life.

Father Roberto is a Mexican diocesan priest who has helped at times with the evangelization of the migrant women in Santa Maria degli Angeli. In preparation for Easter Sunday in 2010, he stresses in the Sunday meeting group that women "should be like the Virgin mother, you should have the courage [*valor*] that she had as mother of Jesus, and do not feel alone. You are all a living sacrifice." In that same week, for the exposition of El Santísimo in Santa Maria della Luce, Father Josefino, a Scalabrinian priest from Guadalajara, reminds twenty or so women at the Thursday mass that, during Pentecost, it is the love of the community that is important, as well as the "presence of Mary with us, the migrants." Receiving the sacraments and praying to Mary are important; "Sacraments are a chain of love" that link the father and the mother with the child, the golden link that "makes us a community." That love for the church, El Santísimo, and Mary is what makes us endure this path, Father Josefino continues. It makes women "*firme en la dificultad*" (steady in the difficulty) and able to cope with the "path of suffering" that is turned into love for the community. For Father Roberto, Father Josefino, and other Scalabrinian priests, migrant women become "sacrificial carriers" (since they "carry" the sacrifice of migrating, enduring difficult jobs, and leaving their family behind) in a world where the heart is getting colder. But the *comunidad de verdad,* the real community, is often a fantasy and a longing. Father Josefino remarks, during the washing of the feet on Holy Thursday, that "we do not only have to wash our feet; many here have also to wash their ears and mouth; we need more community here." Migrants' sacrifice is built on a rock, but the rock turns to sand, he adds, if women do not pray, and it will soon turn to quicksand—if mouths and ears are left unwashed. Language excesses and the proliferations of gossip and rumors become the signals of divided communities.

In that same church's oratory, on Pentecost Sunday, we cut a cake in celebration for one of the women's birthday. Noemi, a Scalabrinian nun who helps with the evangelization of migrants, stops us all before we eat and asks the women around the table to pray:

> Put your distresses [*penas*] in the Sacred Heart, and let your sacrifice be like that of the worthy Virgin, as the mother who gave life to us, so you will not be selfish. Take advantage [*disfruta*] of the love within your circle and share with all. This love allows us the sacrifice of our life of work, which turns into love, the love of the Sacred Heart.

Then Dalia and I step out in the courtyard with pieces of cake in our hands. She recounts her recent trip to Peru to meet her children and her husband after nearly two years of absence. It was a disaster: "He did not even buy me a coke," she says sadly. As soon as she arrived, he started to sleep on the couch, pretending it was because of the heat; then he expected her to buy all the food. The house was badly maintained—junk everywhere, old appliances rusting in the courtyard. It took her days to clear the junk away. And he was constantly on the phone texting. One day she checked his phone and realized that he was texting a lover. She was so upset that he did not tell her to her face.

In the past Dalia and I had sat together or walked around Trastevere eating Italian ice cream, recalling often that she was "ready to go" while working as a live-in maid. Like other women, she has a suitcase ready under the bed. Dalia was a secondary-school teacher back in a suburb of Lima, but the money did not last to the end of the month there, so she made this sacrifice (her word) to migrate for her children and her husband. But now all has been crumbling down, and she does not understand where it went wrong, where the heart went wrong. For years, she bought nearly nothing for herself, to the point of near obsession; she sent so much of her earnings home that her friends in Rome began to worry. They thought she was doing too much for her family abroad, nearly killing herself from work. Her friends could read in her a deception that is part of other women's lives here.

While we eat cake, Dalia insists that when she is with the Corazón de Jesus she feels a warmth and renewed call; she insists that she has to do this work for her children but also for her husband. But now her husband, who is much older then she is, is with somebody else, and she does not understand what happened. She feels betrayed. She has accumulated nothing here, and when she was back home in Lima she just cleared away unwanted junk and without any help. "I just needed an *apapacho* [a hug]," she adds. In the MLA the clergy and nuns see the migrant working experience as moral and emotional suffering, which produces a moral force that migrant women are bound to acquire—a journey of the soul and a trial of the spirit, like the biblical experience of Jesus and Mary in the desert land. However, a language of sacrifice for family and children back home obscures the presence of a lack. This is a lack of affective proximity and erotic warmth animated by the "fleshed" entanglements of hopes and attachments in the present.

Noemi's prayer to the Sacred Heart does not always work; it can also leave migrants at an impasse, a melancholy impasse of betrayal and affective disorientation. Evocations of labor, love, community, and sacrifice ride high in the affective terrains of these migrant spaces; but these spaces are also littered with betrayal and broken hearts.

I have kept in touch with Dalia, and three years later, she is no longer the bouncy, bright-eyed woman I met when she had recently arrived in Rome. The color of her skin is duller; her hair is shorter; she has put on some weight; and the tone of her voice has grown weaker. Her hands show some allergic reaction to the house-cleaning substances she uses in her work. She now wears clothes an employer has left her. Those clothes can be recognized by other migrants as "simply out of fashion." In the words of Catalina: "Italian women look generous, but they always give you clothes that they do not use anymore that are out of fashion, and you know when a migrant woman has either just arrived here or when she is struggling with money because she wears out-of-fashion clothes." If Dalia looks less attractive and eroticized, her devotion to the Sacred Heart is still there.

This is an expression of an affect that Father Manuel has rightly noted among many women here, that for them "*hay un desfase*" (there is a mismatch or gap) so that "*la señora suspendió que vivió aquí*" (the woman suspended the fact that she was living here). There is a temporality of suspension: a suspension of disbeliefs (a withholding of a realization that one's hopes for a better life as a migrant have not materialized), which can take place in migrants' experience of actual de-skilling. This suspension can be a space out of one's own control, a desfase, where an experience of migration fails to be linear, accumulative, and positive. Migratory experience becomes a gap, a condition of misrecognition, as Dalia's body and story at certain conjunctures of her itinerary suggest. Scalabrinians often insist on the power of making community and admonish women for never fully creating a pan-American Catholic community. However, this pedagogy contributes to a misrecognition of the forms that migrant life takes; it cannot acknowledge fully this gap and how it works out in (especially female) migrants' subjective experience, rather than community.

It is difficult to place within those pedagogies the unexpected erotic vitalism that is injected by a casual male stroke on the lower back of these women, or the convivencia, such as with Rosalba's sister's out-of-wedlock-relation, or the affect of betrayal and desfase woven into Dalia's life. These disturb the matrix of a community of "good" Catholic subjects, which then in turn imagined and referred to by the Catholic Church as a new apostolic blood for the reconversion of shrinking congregations of the faithful in Europe. Maybe it is the narcissistic projection that the Catholic Church is a stronghold of unity and a cradle of family life that makes betrayal such a powerful affect in these Catholic migrant itineraries. I am referring here again to Freud's idea of narcissism as the other side of betrayal, where he reads an experience of betrayal as the impossibility of standing up to an image of narcissistic love—explained as the child's introjection of his or her parent's sexuality expressed as a form of separation and betrayal.[9] The anxiety that has plagued the Catholic Church about its own unity cannot be confined just to a narcissistic reading, of course; but the connection between a fantasy/love of a normative family and the impossibility of its fulfillment makes the experience of betrayal an important analytic aspect of the relation between Catholicism and migration.

Moreover, Dalia's desfase and betrayal emerge at a particular conjuncture of transnational labor and exploitation of the labor of love, in an Italian context where migrant legislation on immigration and migrant labor conditions can be very constrictive, as I have addressed in earlier chapters.[10] For many migrant itineraries, these forms of transnational labor require the refinement of an affect of constancy, respectability, and familial love in their workplace. At the same time, women often have to deal with transforming transnational intimacies: they have been and are affected by betrayal.

Against the official position of the Catholic Church that stresses the existing, psychologically detrimental effects of transnational migration on the family and its reproduction, it is crucial to recall that betrayal in kinship and family relations is present well before transnational migration. To understand an affect of betrayal in different migrant itineraries is an important shift of focus away from a psychological reductionism of migrants' lives, toward an analysis of the situated (and therefore historical) affective field of migration. This analytical shift builds on existing historical and political economic analyses of the relation between female migration and the Catholic Church, as an embattled terrain of sexual deviancy from normative, family-bounded sexuality.[11] In short, nuanced forms of betrayal are the products of an intersection between migration, labor, and Catholic faith. If that intersection produces and contains different forms of love, so it also produces betrayal. Studying this intersection, I argue here, is central to seeing how the heart is animated and invoked in different forms and migrant itineraries.

Heroic Love

Hearts live because blood circulates. If the Sacred Heart is originally a fifteenth-century devotion associated with penitence, suffering, and its expiation, divine blood is both a sign of community and of cruor, blood spilled in violence and for revenge. A spilling of blood is not confined to the Sagrado Corazón de Jesus; in the Church of Santa Maria della Luce it is also present in the Virgen Dolorosa (Lady of Sorrows) who looks on majestically from the first left apse of the church (see the frontispiece of this book). The two-meter tall statue is moved to the central altar on particular occasions, such as Holy Friday. The Dolorosa is a baroque image of the Virgin at the foot of the cross. The Virgin is shown with a dagger-pierced heart, an iconography that originated in Spain, but which spread in New Spain in the sixteenth century. In some representations she also cries blood from her eyes.

A heroic dimension of suffering is sacralized but also destabilized in the iconography of the Sacred Heart of Jesus and Mary as La Dolorosa. During sermons, priests and missionaries repetitively stress the importance of the family, the solidity of (monogamous) marriage, and the central role that migrant women play in reproducing these institutions.[12] During one of the Via Crucis organized by the MLA in 2008, Carola, a Colombian woman, stands out from the group as the only one carrying a small baby on her back. She showed little fatigue in our nearly two-hour walk, interspersed with many stops, reflections, and prayers. During one of these stops, Father Josefino stresses a parallel between the Via Cruces of Jesus and the Via

Cruces of all migrant women here away from their children. I ask Carola whether she agrees. She was in a different position from that of many of the women in the MLA. Coming from Colombia with her husband, they both helped out in the parish in exchange for some temporary accommodation. Nevertheless, she reflected,

> Yes, family is important, but it is also what chains you. It is your source of joy but also of sadness, because many here cannot follow their children, and you see what happens to Latin American children who grow up here—often they are lost [*se piérden*]. So it is a blessing but also a limit; we women cannot do it all, and everyone calls on you, the children and in the job, especially here in Italy where it is so expensive to live. But it was also difficult back home, so it is never easy for women.

The following Saturday, I am sitting with Father Manuel having a coffee in the upstairs quarters of the Santa Maria della Luce, where a group of Scalabrinian priests lives. Catalina was preparing the coffee, and Father Manuel was "cross" with Pope Benedict XVI. He had written three letters to him recently, but he had received no reply. He wrote the letters because "continuing like this is not possible" (*hací no se puede*):

> In the recent encyclical, the pope says that the Fathers cannot give communion to those who are separated or divorced. But there is not a pastoral for the woman migrant who has come from Latin America. They have left because there is domestic violence, family prostitution, and the father there does not have time for them. They [the priests there] tell them: Why did you get married? Now *aguantate* [cope!] and you will go to heaven. But this is not useful anymore. And we have more and more women arriving here, and we do not know enough; we are not enough [of us] to attend to them, and we do not know enough of what they are going through. The ritual we follow in the church is often too masculine; there is a need for a *pastoral feminina*.

We finish drinking our coffee. It tastes bittersweet. In the meantime, the preparation for a later mass continues; flowers are arranged by some of the women who have their day off or who are unemployed and thus are helping at the church. Some men are cooking simple food in a little room on the side of the church that normally hosts migrants' gathering. They are called *los pollitos*, a small group of men who, because of the way the migrant labor market favors women, or due to their age and physical health, cannot find jobs. The church provides a place for them to be and occasional unpaid work to keep them busy. Feminization of male transnational migrant labor is not new here either; many men who would wish to work in the construction industry end up caring for elderly or sick, bedridden Italian men.

Later that same year in November, the mass of Todos los Santos (All Saints' Day) was celebrated by Father Joselito, who, like Father Manuel, is originally from Guadalajara. He is an energetic priest with a witty sense of humor. This is the "feast of all of us," he mentions, a day to celebrate each and every saint's name, and the saint within each of us. This is also a celebration of remembrance, different than the Dias de los Muerto for the Mexicans that I have attended in Rome[13]—less public and somehow more intimate.

Father Joselito is leaving soon. He has been posted to Switzerland after a year of service here. Young missionary priests are moved around so that they do not get too attached to a given situation or to a particular group of people. You cannot get too comfortable in missionary life. Father Joselito reflects that some of the women at the Church of Santa Maria della Luce love him, he thinks, because he gives his time and has been good at "listening to them." They often live *encerradas* (lit., locked in, meaning as live-in maids), he adds, and he has made a point of taking them around, to discover a bit of Rome and have fun together. In that year, Father Joselito has taken a group of women to open air concerts at the Capannelle, organized trips to museums and gardens in Rome, or just taken them for an ice cream in the Piazza Risorgimento. Some of the Peruvian and Ecuadorian women feel that he has helped them experience a little freedom, a moment of laughter *"para olvidar las penas"* (to forget their worries). Hence missions such as MLA can become important places for socialization, springboards to "explore the city," "get out of depression," and *"rencontrar el ambiente"* (lift one's spirits).

But by the end of that mass something different happened. The women in the church gathered close to the altar and surrounded Joselito, a group of around ten, tighter and tighter. He makes a joke that they are going to kidnap him. A woman took an Andean shawl and wrapped it around him. The women become quieter and raised their hands over Joselito's head, but they are also touching his body, one woman begins speaking a benediction for him, or literally over him. It is a benediction for his family, his health in his new place, as well as for all the women who follow him here. Some women begin to cry silently. The irony of the women blessing the priest is not lost on anyone. The women disperse around him and come down from the altar; two worry that maybe they did too much in taking the lead to bless the priest. The normal arrangement of roles is quickly put back in place.

Maybe Father Manuel was wrong: There is already a feminine pastoral in action in the migrant churches in Rome; it does not await Benedict XVI's recommendation, nor is it contained in the migrant pastoral teaching designed by the Archdiocese of Rome, or the Pontifical Council for Migration. It just happens. It arrives unexpectedly, a matter of female presence and of affective forces that circulate in this and other migrant churches: forces of love, benedictions, erotic desires, and attachments.

So if "the heart grows cold" in migrant itineraries, it is reignited in multiple spaces of Catholicism. This reignition is part of a history of gazes and touching, exposure and veiling of the flesh that permeates Catholic aesthetic culture and devotions, especially mystical ones. Mystical devotions are not only visual; they are also manifested in bodily and language excesses.[14] In a complex hagiographic tradition, reread by feminist scholars, mystical devotions are sites of creative freedom away from a patriarchally imposed identification with Jesus's flesh and its suffering, toward a lived heart and blood of interior and loving passions.[15] Yet histories of female mysticism and suffering can be as concealing as they are revealing.[16]

Eloisa, who is an organizer of the Peruvian and Ecuadorian group that meets at the Basilica of Santa Maria degli Angeli, reinforces the idea that for some women it is a matter of the heart in a particular way:

> The affectivity of the woman here is crushed [*la afectividad de la mujer aqui se destroza*]. It is so difficult for women here, so when people live in close proximity in a rented flat very many things happen. Many times it happens that a man sleeps with the cousin of his wife, who may be living there too. So there is much *mezcla de la familia* [mingling/mixing up of the family], and it is such a mess for the children. . . . When I pray to the Sacred Heart, it is like finding a peace, a great love, but also to not forget that the heart unfortunately shuts here, because migration in Italy is so difficult. The Fathers do not get sometimes that when they put their arms around the shoulders of women, it can be difficult. They do not realize what they do, but then women in the parish get stuck in a net of affects [*se quedan enredadas en los afectos*].

So the heart is shut at one level to cope with the reality of living in migration; but a touch, an embrace from a priest can open the gate to the heart, allowing one to feel how dead one has become within. The body of the priest is a presence that can open remembrance of vital but also haunting attachments. Lay and religious migrant bodies are a complex "fleshy" presence, woven together through particular historical conjunctures.[17]

Kevin O'Neill has noted the way that in Guatemalan evangelical Christianity, eroticism permeates a language of call for Christ and his coming.[18] The eroticism of language deepens the evangelical call. In the MLA context eroticism, in the affective presence such as that of the Sacred Heart (and La Dolorosa), is more an absence of words; it embraces both the suffering and affective physicality of life, through an identification with Christ or the Virgin's life. But it is also a reminder of living with betrayal as an inception of the process of migration.

Sacred Heart(s)

Erotic passions are a dimension of the cult of the Sacred Heart. The symbolism of the Sacred Heart has a long history: from early apparitions revealed to the French saint Marguerite-Marie Alacoque in 1680s, to the use of the Sacred Heart as a protective symbol during an outbreak of plague in 1720s southern France, to its wide circulation as a counterrevolutionary and countersecularist symbol after the French Revolution and well into the early Republic. The secularist histories, against which this symbol is counterposed, were part of the modern project of the nation-state and the supremacy of secular powers over Catholic religious and mystical practice.[19] In Paris, the cult of the Sacred Heart was galvanized during the contestation of the building of the Basilica of the Sacré-Coeur and its symbolism as a site of martyrdom that embraced both conservative allegiances to the ancient regime and communard revolutionary commitments.[20] Paradoxically, in a strange quirk of fate, the basilica openly commemorated martyrs of the right and, unwittingly, "in its subterranean depths a martyr of the left"—Eugène Varlin—who was a respected and committed socialist, brutally murdered in May 1871 during the Commune repression on the exact spot where the basilica was finally built.[21] From its inception, the Sacred Heart was an embodied image, a verbal and visual living image,[22] that contained and called upon both official and unofficial histories.

The histories of the early female saints that championed the need for the church's (male) establishment to embrace such devotion reveal interesting tensions. The cult of the Sacred Heart has historically worked as a call for the chosen people in moments of historical and devotional upheaval. It has also been a call for a bodily and intimate experience of the divine and in particular the love for Christ: Through the symbolic door of Christ's wound, believers could reach the dwelling of the divine heart incarnated in a human form. This symbolic evocation of the divine in a human dwelling (the heart) indicates a movement from the periphery to the center, from the unhosted (away from the heart), through the wound, to the hosted (into the heart).[23]

Michelle Molina has pointed out that in medieval times Catholicism cultivated an openness of the heart and its readiness to be inscribed by God's presence. With St. Ignatius's spiritual exercises there is a shift, however: The heart becomes the "seat of religious being." Containing a tension of penetrability and impenetrability, Catholic heart-centeredness encompasses by then both the carnality of the heart, the cultivation of its capacity to be inscribed, and the site for a possibility of the passionate subject's self-renewal.[24]

In late nineteenth-century Italy, devotion to the Sacred Heart had at least two natures. It was an individualization of devotion, a personal search for sanctification that has championed the stability of the family and marital union above the corruption of the senses and contemporary habits.[25] But it was also a devotional symbol in time of cholera, epidemics, and wars, especially during World War I. For Italian soldiers on the front, the Sacred Heart was a powerful point of collective, devotional, and nationalist identification. Similarly, it functions as a unifying and protective shield for particular labor guilds and factory workers. The Sacred Heart has been a devotional *"point de ralliement"* (lit., the point of winning over), a moment to abandon oneself into the hands and protection of Jesus.

Robert Orsi noted that, among American Catholics, the Sacred Heart icon has been more than a "meaning-making" representation. For American Catholics, he argues, it has much more to do with the making of kinship and the phenomenological and transformative nature of retelling stories.[26] The Sacred Heart is a form of mediation, between the social and the divine worlds, and its affective potential is not set in stone, but rather arises in unpredictable ways. It is present, but not always as part of received and official church histories. The multiple and contradictory natures of this devotion emerge in different encounters in the MLA, but also among the Legionaries and the Jesuits. In fact, the central role held by the cult of the Sacred Heart in both orders is also rather telling.

It is illuminating to briefly explore the way that devotion to the Sacred Heart marks the complicated relationship of the Jesuits and Legionaries of Christ. The key yearly celebration of both orders is that of the Sacred

Heart in June. However, there are similarities and differences around this cult. A reemergence of the cult of the Sacred Heart took place in the Jesuit order around the time of Vatican II. For the Jesuit theologian Karl Rahner, the Sacred Heart is a "primordial word," a primordial symbol that indexes, through the corporeality of Christ, the center of life. For Rahner, the heart is not divine love itself but a "container," filled with evocative powers that we, as humans, have to direct toward divine love. For General Pedro Arrupe, too, the Sacred Heart becomes central once it is stripped of its excessive piety, and revitalized by finding its meaning and relevance in the contemporary context. I encountered references to the Sacred Heart in the Legionaries and their lay movements specifically in relation to the "Great Promise," which is a series of devotional practices to the Sacred Heart performed over a period of nine months that help the seeker to the path of "grace of the final penitence toward heaven," in the words of a Mexican member of the Regnum Christi. In both orders, the Sacred Heart encapsulates the strengths and limitations of a personal and individual experience of divine love and forgiveness. But the Legionaries stress in their prayers the promises that Jesus made to Saint Marguerite-Marie Alacoque and her obedience to him, while the Jesuits stress the Sacred Heart as a primordial symbol that needs to be revitalized in contemporary contexts.

In the MLA the Sacred Heart, or Corazón de Jesus, appears in both Father Manuel's and other Catholic priests' evangelization as well as in the migrants' stories. Itineraries such as that of Marialuisa are exemplary.[27] An intelligent Ecuadorian immigrant who started out in Italy as many others, as a badante for a nearly blind *nonito* (a term of endearment for a grandfather), Marialuisa is equipped with strong motivation and a commitment to self-improvement. She trained in communication at the Gregorian University in Rome and has been working in Spanish-speaking broadcasting for a while. Married to an Italian man who is younger and less educated than she is, she refers to the Sacred Heart as that which helps her to navigate the difficulties of everyday life, but also as that which is there when everything else fails. The turning to El Corazón de Jesus is for matters of the heart, to "*encomadarse a El*" (entrust yourself to Him); it is the presentation of oneself to the warm gaze of Christ ("He is looking at you; He is with you").

Marialuisa is active in an organization of migrant women and the leader of the first radio program for Spanish-speaking migrants broadcast from Radio Vaticana, which I introduced in chapter 2. Her approach to this devotion is not merely a form of prayer to ask for a blessing. She describes the Sacred Heart as a sense of the homely (in the sense of being at home). When she is before his image, which hangs in the entrance hall of her flat, it is like "being back in Ecuador." The Sacred Heart is thus not only a representation that can evoke a believer's pledge, but it is also a sense of homeliness in transnational migration. In Ecuador, this image is in "so many houses," but it is also in Italy. The Sacred Heart becomes uncanny because it brings one home, as it is also reminds one of the estrangement from one's own home:

> When you see Him [in the portrait] in your house, you think you are in Ecuador, but then you turn around and look out of the window, and you know you are not home. [The Sacred Heart] is so beautiful, He takes you [*te lleva*], and then still, you know you are not home.

As with the Freudian uncanny, it is this paradox that makes the Sacred Heart such a powerful site in these migrant itineraries: It is both location *and* dislocation.

The Sacred Heart in some migrant itineraries becomes a vessel, which contains the believer, where a sense of the presence of home and peace is felt, but at the same time, it is talked about by the clergy as playing a role in the reproduction of a particular Catholic *hogar* (household). For the priests and nuns, the evocation and reminder of the strength of the cult of the Sacred Heart (both of Jesus and Mary) is, on one hand, professed as that love which keeps together and blesses a Catholic household as the "primary cell of society." On the other hand, it is a promise of absolution. In the words of John Paul II:

> The day after tomorrow we will be celebrating the Solemnity of the Sacred Heart of Jesus. This feast recalls the mystery of God's love for the men and women of all times. Dear young people, I invite you to train yourselves at the school of the Heart of Christ to deal confidently with the commitments that await you in life. I thank you, dear sick people, for the spiritual help that you give to the Christian People in accepting to do the will of the Crucified Jesus in a fruitful union with his saving sacrifice. Lastly, dear newlyweds, I hope that you will feel the true joy that stems from daily fidelity to the charity of God, of which your conjugal love must be an eloquent testimony. (John Paul II, General Audience, 16 June 2004)

A commitment constitutes then a devotion to the Sacred Heart. It is so in the case of Jorge, a Costa Rican man who plays an active role in the MLA and at Santa Maria della Luce. Jorge comes from a poor family of twenty-two children, and he has five children and an ex-wife, ten years younger than he is, back in Costa Rica. Prior to leaving Costa Rica ten years ago, he owned a small hotel, a "good business," but his ex-wife "betrayed him," left him and then wanted to come back. However, "Her love was too passionate, and that was no good [she started to see another man]. Women let down [their] men, and men let down God, and man is the head of the woman, so in this way it is not possible." Then he adds he went to live with another woman with whom he fathered a daughter in Costa Rica, before coming to Rome.

Living conditions were hard, and ten years ago he made it to Italy on a tourist visa and started to work as a badante for a string of different elderly men, and then stayed for more than five years as a badante of a relatively young widow. Unexpectedly, her children asked him to leave the job one night, but he did not want to elaborate why, so I can only infer that he and the widow may have become "too close." For Jorge, rallying to the Corazón of Jesus is tinted by a commitment to God's plan:

> In a dream that I had recurrently for three years, I dreamt about a prop-
> erty I had. I was walking toward the house, and when I entered there was
> the Corazón of Jesus, and then a man, a friend appeared at the threshold
> and he was very tired and sweaty and was saying "Jorgito, this is not
> mine," and he took me under his arm because he was worried. When I
> asked my brother about this dream, he said that this was a sign of Him,
> that I had to dedicate things to El Corazón de Jesus; it is the sign that you
> dedicate yourself to Him.

The Sacred Heart is an orientation of commitment, a mediation, as well as an uncanny presence. In the words of Benedict XVI the presence of the Sacred Heart is in the mediation of the liturgy and is an emulation of the love of God, but it is also the celebration of all priestly mediations. The Sacred Heart is an outward and inward bridge of the sanctification of priests and a reminder of their apostolate, and Jesus's spilled blood is a gift of grace:[28]

> We are celebrating the feast of the Sacred Heart of Jesus, and in the lit-
> urgy we peer, as it were, into the heart of Jesus opened in death by the

spear of the Roman soldier. Jesus's heart was indeed opened for us and before us, and thus God's own heart was opened. The liturgy interprets for us the language of Jesus's heart, which tells us above all that God is the shepherd of mankind, and so it reveals to us Jesus's priesthood, which is rooted deep within his heart; so too it shows us the perennial foundation and the effective criterion of all priestly ministry, which must always be anchored in the heart of Jesus and lived out from that starting point.[29]

But commitment is not all. The Sacred Heart is also an affective domain that includes the humanized, erotic, and aesthetic dimensions of faith. And its devotion is seated in histories of betrayal too. That is so in the case of Ricky, a Peruvian man in his early forties from the Selva, who when I spoke with him in 2011 had been in Italy for about six months. His wife, who arrived in Italy more than eight years before him, put in the papers for him to come after his having raised their two daughters in Peru with her financial help. However, when Ricky got to Rome he realized that she was betraying him and living with another man. She had asked for the *ricongiungimento familiare* (family reunification) really because she was tired of caring for all the family, and wanted him to come to Italy and work to provide for the kids too.

Ricky now works on and off in the construction industry, but work is really scarce for a migrant man. He keeps on repeating that it is really harsh to leave the adolescent daughters on their own in Peru. His estranged wife, now living with a singer in a Peruvian band, seems to not realize that "girls need at least one parent with them there." He still hopes she will come back to him, but expresses his own crisis in terms of women's *libertinaje* (debauchery) in Italy. He recognizes that women in Peru often leave to come to Italy because, he thinks, they want something different that they cannot find at home, even if they do not know what it is. "There" it was a "simple" life, but "here" things get complicated for some women, because they follow a life of "pleasures" and their hearts change:

> [His estranged wife's] heart has become wrapped up, as if covered in bandages, and now it does not feel the same, migration is like bandages that cover up your heart, and then it is not the same. I pray to the Sacred Heart at times, to lift those bandages from her, so that the purity and simplicity of her heart can shine again.

The Sacred Heart is a material icon animated by the homeliness of official Catholic narrative and the unhomeliness of migrants' uncanny, embodied, and erotic journeys. In other words the Sacred Heart is an intimate and complex vessel for harboring affective betrayals and the embattled unpredictability of gender relations.

Eroticism is a lived affective force and a drive. Georges Bataille has argued that eroticism has a sacramental and sacrificial character. For him both eroticism and sacrifice pivot around the violence of opening up beyond a presumed separateness and discontinuity of individuals to a connection between individuals through a continuity of disrupted boundaries: "The whole business of eroticism is to destroy the self-contained character of the participators as they are in their normal lives."[30] Hence eroticism is a form of divestiture, a nakedness that calls for continuity between participants. With but also beyond Bataille though, eroticism of religious materialities (such as the Sacred Heart) can be read in continuity with a mystical, divine erotic experience. But mystical experience does not always require the absence of objects;[31] instead, it can be mediated by situated religious objects or images. Objects such as the Sacred Heart condense a force of circulation and sedimentation of affective histories; they *are* it, rather than merely representing it.

Caroline Walker Bynum, analyzing the material devotion of the late Middle Ages, has suggested that we need to rethink religious icons and relics through an expanded light that incorporates an ontological paradox. The paradox is that some Christian religious materialities are the "changing stuff of no-God and the locus of a God revealed."[32] Through a particular historically situated reading of medieval devotions and their struggling with complex ontologies, the reading of Bynum helps us understand some of the paradoxes and religious materialities in twenty-first-century migrant Roman terrains. If we need to go beyond the power of representation of religious imaginaries into the study of how they matter, we need to take into consideration the historical traces of a Catholic *corpus*. This implies going beyond the confinement of Catholic migrant personhood and seeing how affective circulations of histories engrave religious materialities and are woven into transnational migrant itineraries. Forces of Catholic histories ignite the affective paradoxical powers of Catholic religious materialities because "the expression of and reaction to Christ's humanity, even his bodiliness, were part of a larger religious discourse about the material itself and how it might manifest or embody God."[33] If visionary religious culture has been central to aesthetic and anthropological readings of religious Christian modernity, so the materiality of tactility, first, and sensorial dimensions of (divine)

matter, second, have been central to the Catholic visionary culture's healing powers.[34]

If the Catholic corpus, as Bynum has suggested, is manifested in pain,
perception, and survival,[35] then MLA's experience highlights a current
paradox in this corpus. Migrants are sacrificial carriers in a "heroic" and
community-oriented journey in priestly discursive practices. Together
with an invisibility of presence in Italian society, the Catholic migrant
experience is a sacrificial standing out, but it can also be at times a desfase,
a suspension of living here, an experience of betrayal, of betrayed intimacies. The paradox of the Catholic corpus is then about love and betrayal,
the homely (in the sense of homey) and the unhomely.

The Sacred Heart is a mediator, an index of materialities of love, of its
continuities and discontinuities, and marks a paradox of longing for, and a
stillness of, arrival.[36] Its devotion and presence in migrant itineraries is
both about a sacrifice of (in the sense of giving up) as well as a longing for
heartfelt bodily passions. If Carl Schmitt discussed the complexio oppositorum as the Catholic Church's capacity to combine (politically) opposite
tendencies in its governance and still prevent schism, here the oppositorum
works as a material and devotional tension entangled in affects of belonging, the (un)homely, and betrayals.

Hearts in Motion

In this last section I follow up on the reflections and refractions of the heart
and turn briefly to a 2006 MLA pilgrimage to the Sanctuary of the Divino
Amore on the outskirts of Rome and to the Brotherhood of the Señor de
los Milagros. This pilgrimage, organized annually by the MLA, was not
as well attended as in previous years; nevertheless, more than sixty Latino
migrants and a group of Mexican sisters of the order of Santa Maria Imma-
colata joined forces and walked overnight from the Coliseum in the center
of the city to reach the sanctuary by dawn, eighteen kilometers away. I
went together with Jorge and Eloisa, who reassured me that while it was
hard to walk all night, once I had made it, it would be "*bien bonito llegar allí
en la mañanita*" (so good to get there in the morning). We left around 11
P.M., and the Latin American Mission had planned a series of prayers and
chanting, but at the last minute the pilgrims' group was attached to a bigger Italian pilgrimage devoted to the Virgin of Fatima, which was walking
to the sanctuary that same night.

Once we joined the Italian group of more than four hundred people, there was some talk between the Scalabrinian priest, heading our group, and the priests who were in charge of the other pilgrimage. The result was that we had to forgo the Spanish prayers and follow the Italian pilgrimage, which disappointed some of the migrants. During the first part of the night we recited the rosary seven times in Italian, which was led by Italian pilgrims ahead carrying loudspeakers. The rosary, of course, is all about the suffering of the Virgin and the role of woman as the mother of Christ, and prayers were interwoven with songs for the well-being of the clergy, the strength of the Catholic family, and women as its pillars. Marian cults and devotion are definitely resurgent in Italy, but they are also a source of contention.[37]

Once we stopped midway for a rest around 2 A.M., and some took out something to eat; the night was demanding on the body. When we started again on the pilgrimage route, all of a sudden some MLA participants began to chant Marian and Catholic Latin American songs in Spanish, accompanied by guitars and drums. The lyrics were about the joy of life in the Catholic faith and the joy of receiving Mary's and Christ's spirit within, inside the body. The rest of the group, but especially two Italian priests who were are the back, were taken by surprise. The priest-organizer of the Italian section in the front, came back to the end of the procession and told our Scalabrinian priest—half whispering—to "be quiet" and stop the singing with the guitars. In a short while though, some of the Italian pilgrims began to join in. From then on, the spirit and the mood of the pilgrimage changed in our group: There were comments from the migrants about the joys of being there, shaking away the earlier suffering mood, and singing aloud their songs in Spanish—the soundscape had changed.

Lamentations of the rosary could still be faintly heard at the beginning of the pilgrims' group, but the sound of the guitar with the Spanish prayer songs seemed to be the energy many of us needed to fight tiredness and arrive at dawn at the Divino Amore. Once we had arrived, the Latin American group was directed toward the Old Sanctuary (built in the 1750s) at the top of the hill to celebrate mass in a small modern church added to the compound in the 1970s. The Italian group instead celebrated their mass in the larger and impressive new Sanctuary of the Divino Amore, which had been opened in 1999 by John Paul II, in the lower part of the compound. We were all exhausted in the early morning, but elated to have made it. Eloisa laughed, saying that "we" are always put in windowless basements, or in small rooms at the top. She was jokingly referring to the living topography of her past employments and the present ones of many of her mates, who were live-in carers, or badanti, in Rome.

These experiences of religiosity point to a transnational sense of the sacred, where Catholic religious identification is still crafted through common symbolism (the Virgin) and an experience of sacred inclusion (the invocation of a Catholic spirit moving into the body), but nonetheless negotiated in a transnational, at times exclusionary, space (the Italian pilgrimage). Devotional forms need to change with the migrant revitalization of the Catholic heart. That change is sometime perceived as a challenge. If devotions such as the pilgrimage to the Divino Amore are spearheaded by the Latin American Mission to create a sense of a unified Latin American Church in Rome, the goal of a pan–Latin American Church is not always successful. Attempts to create a pan-American ethos over a national one may be a pedagogy of the church designed to defuse rifts in some North American contexts about different homelands, but this is not particularly the case in Rome.[38] So if conflicts of racialization and national and class distinctions take place within and around the MLA and the CCM (Comunidad Católica Mexicana), there are also tensions around ways in which migrant Católic passions fit (or not), or threaten certain forms of Italian Catholicism.

Nonetheless, certain forms of migrant devotions are becoming attractive even to dedicated Italian Catholics. This is the case of El Señor de los Milagros and the Virgin of Guadalupe, which I discuss in the next chapter. The Peruvian confraternity of El Señor de los Milagros, with his presence, organization, and rituals, is gaining notable strength in the parish of Santa Maria della Luce, not always to the liking of other non-Peruvian migrant devotees. This lay religious brotherhood performs its rituals with militaristic and legionary passions that remind one more of the Legionaries of Christ than they do of lay religious associations such as the CCM. With their growing transnational presence, they signal other important aspects of a return of the missions within the cardiovascular paralysis of the Roman Catholic Church in Rome.

El Señor de los Milagros is one of the most important devotional Catholic images and was brought to Peru in the sixteenth century, possibly by the first Africans working in the plantations. The Cristo Morado, or Lord of Miracles (other names for the Señor de Los Milagros), and its undamaged survival through both the late seventeenth-century and the late eighteenth-century earthquakes in Lima, made him a very popular devotion with both mestizo and indigenous constituencies.[39] Its transnational devotion is strengthening in different parts of the world, from North America to Spain to Japan, showing a productive tension between the globalization of its devotion and the migrants' conquering of public spaces and moral status in often unwelcoming hosting societies.[40] The devotion is organized as a brotherhood composed of male groups called *quadrillas*—which take turns carrying the heavy representation when he is taken in procession—and by a women's group, which traditionally carries the incense and sings the litanies.

Interestingly enough, the Hermandad de los Señor de los Milagros (HSM) in Rome passes through the prison of Regina Coeli in Rome. The story that is told in the mission is that in 1986 a transsexual sex worker from Peru, who was detained in the Roman prison of Regina Coeli (close to the MLA), brought the image to Rome and began to spread its devotion among fellow Peruvians. A person whose sexual orientation would not clearly fall into the normative cradle of a migrant's family was the one who marked the inception of this devotion in Rome.

The brotherhood of the Señor de los Milagros is one of five Catholic Peruvian brotherhoods officially recognized and organized in Rome.[41] There are more than three hundred families active now in the HSM, and the organization attempts, for the most part successfully, to attend to the needs and the emergencies of fellow migrants. Many of the organizers think that that there is a crisis of the clergy in Rome, that there are not enough priests attending to even the basic needs of the people. So migrants who arrive here, Roberto explains in perfect Italian, have a "spiritual shock;" as the church does not give space: "It does not and cannot help."

Roberto is an articulate, perfectly bilingual lawyer in his late twenties who grew up in Rome from the age of thirteen, in a family whose grandmother was totally devoted to El Señor de los Milagros. He was the first general secretary of this organization in Rome, nominated directly by the Roman Curia; now he is a legal adviser for the institution and an outspoken advocate for immigrants' right in the Roman political scene. Others agree with him in believing that the Hermandad develops a parallel form of governance and evangelizes in very direct ways. In Roberto's words,

> One of [Hermandad del Señor de los Milagros'] aims is to transform
> from illegality to legality through the sacraments. One has to have proof
> of having received them, or to take them if one has not done so yet, so it
> is a form of evangelization or catechesis. It is a form of life. So it is not a
> legality of the state; there are people who belong to the Hermandad who

are in prison; we know they have stolen because they needed to send money to Peru, and they did not know how to do it otherwise, but we talk of the *legality of the soul*. (My emphasis)

The brotherhood has strict rules: People apply formally and are vetted in relation to their family values. Following admittance to the organization, they must maintain a strong Catholic discipline and put in frequent appearances at the brotherhood for rehearsals. Impeccably dressed in a violet tunic and a white cordon knotted around their waist, each man in the brotherhood is trained to carry the icon of the Señor de los Milagros on a sedan that weighs more than two tons. The carriers are divided into distinct groups according to their skills and physical strength. Each woman wears a characteristic white embroidered shawl. The women form the *sumidhoras* (incense holders) and *cantoras* (singers) who walk before and behind the icon in the procession. Normally there is a clear gendered division of labor, but since Peruvian female migration has been prominent in Rome, women here do carry smaller icons, as was the case of the "enthroned" Señor de La Justicia, in the Church of Santa Maria della Luce in spring 2011.

In the process of caring for and carrying these icons, these men and women give of themselves as true Catholics. They become the passionate engine of a renewed Catholic Church. Roberto again:

> Italy has to learned to give, to give even its dreams, as one gives himself when carrying El Señor. . . . We are not carrying a piece of wood; we are carrying *him*. In the procession we [men] are all bundled up, but often after the major procession in October, my shoulders are blue, and once I had a slipped disk. If you really cannot do it anymore, you ask for a change, but this is a shame [*vergüenza*], just as it is when you are not permitted to carry him because of discipline within the brotherhood. When you are carrying the Señor de los Milagros, you are not thinking that "this is just another thing." What we carry on our shoulders is not a symbol of the Señor de los Milagros, it *is* the Señor de los Milagros. For this reason we cannot touch him with our own hands; we just have to hold him on our shoulders. Because the hands are dirty, and would you touch a *señor puro* with dirty hands?

So the Señor de los Milagros, especially in the yearly celebration on the last Sunday of October, blesses the city. Some other carriers in the group describe the violet uniform as a form of protection. If you are wearing it

during the carrying of the Señor in the streets of Rome, you can get closer
to an Italian policeman and you do not feel threatened by the police. Even
if you do not have a legal permit of residence, you become a *regolare dello
spirito* (one regularized in the spirit). The power, presence, and proximity
to the Señor de los Milagros can grant a "legality of the soul."

A problem exists, however, since the Scalabrinian priests themselves do
not always agree with the governance of the HSM. Some of the members
of the brotherhood are not married in the church but live with their partners, and often have children (sometimes from previous unions or marriages in Peru). So there are different family configurations even among
strong devotees. In the words of an elder member of the brotherhood:

> The Scalabrinian priests had to turn their ideas around. It is better to be
> in than out, we told them; the church is stronger with us and with our
> presence, even if we do not reflect the ideas of the Scalabrinian priests
> and the officials of the Roman Curia. But the Roman Curia nevertheless
> loves what we are and what we do, not only for the evangelization but
> also for good behavior and caring of our fellow migrants. There are ten-
> sions between the different national churches here in Rome, and the
> spaces to meet are only a few, but this is our struggle, also the struggle of
> Christ and the Señor de los Milagros. We are also the new blood of the
> church here in Rome: We are the pulsating heart. Look at some churches
> here: No passions, no devotions—they would be dead spaces, if it were
> not for us immigrants.

In April 2011, during the Via Cruces on Holy Friday, these types of
conflicts within the church seemed to reach a high. Father Simon, a well-
informed Brazilian Scalabrinian priest who is now in charge with Father
Alfonso of Santa Maria della Luce, has his job on the line. A letter has been
sent to his superiors and the Roman diocese to complain about his work
and behavior. Gossip is circulating even during the procession that Father
Simon wants to stop the growing power of the Hermandad del Señor de
los Milagros; there are complaints that he does not allow Peruvians the
space they should have. In his turn, Father Simon complains swiftly that
these misunderstandings happen "when lay people are put in charge of the
church." This is, of course, one of the conditions generated by the changes
introduced with Vatican II, which emphasized the need to strengthen the
participation of lay people in the church's apostolic work.

During the sermon at the mass earlier that night, Father Simon emphasized that there is "no understanding, no meaning to the process of

migration, but one has to give himself or herself [*entregarse*] to the process," like Christ in his life, death, and resurrection. But this process is riven by tensions between nation and church. This Peruvian brotherhood wants its space in the MLA, and its leadership is not ready to negotiate with its Brazilian counterpart. Father Simon, though, is afraid that they are taking too much space and that other, non-Peruvian migrants feel marginalized. This brotherhood has a strong affective attachment to the Peruvian nation that does not work well within the project of pan-Americanism fostered by the Roman diocese and the Scalabrinian priests. For instance, an affective attachment to the Peruvian nation comes out strongly in the repetitive songs that are chanted through the streets of Trastevere on Holy Friday.

While carrying a smaller sedan with El Señor de Los Milagros to the Square of Santa Maria in Trastevere and back to Santa Maria della Luce, we are all chanting the well-known hymn of El Señor de los Milagros:

Señor, de los Milagros a ti venimos en procesión
tus fieles devotos a implorar tu bendición
con paso firme de buen cristiano hagamos grande nuestro Perú
unido todos con una fuerza te suplicamos no des tu honor.

[Lord, of the Miracles, we come to you in procession
Your faithful devotees to implore for your blessing,
With a steady walk of a good Christian we are making stronger our Peru
Altogether with strength we implore you to give us your honor.]

Non-Peruvian devotees of the MLA are part of the procession, but the voice of a woman next to me in the procession repeatedly dwindles on the "make stronger our Peru." I ask where she is from; from Salvador, she replies. Later, when the procession is nearly over, she points out that Salvadorans are few in number here, and that she is devoted to the Señor de los Milagros; she is moved by him, although she feels there should be a more equitable sharing of resources in the MLA and that "el honor" to be Peruvian is not really close to her heart: "The mission is not only for Peruvians, but it is difficult, as the love for your nation [*patria*] is like your first love, you never forget it." Once again affects of the nation interrupt Catholic migrant pedagogies.

On Migrant Itineraries

In this transnational landscape the Sacred Heart and national devotions such as the Señor de los Milagros become affective fields that move as well as interrupt the "good functioning" of the Catholic Church as a passionate machine. In contemporary Rome, threads of histories animate the Catholic evangelization of Latin American migrants' itineraries. They weave in reminders of the church's spatiality, migrant labor, Sacred Heart(s), hearts in love and motion, and erotic hearts, pointing to an ongoing but also unfinished project of Catholic evangelization. It is unfinished because part of the official pedagogy of the Catholic Church has pushed eroticism and carnal passions to its margins—something to be strongly discouraged if out of wedlock. But carnal passions, the passions of the flesh and the betrayal of the flesh, are what animate Catholic vessels such as the Sacred Heart of Jesus and the long history it carries—a long history that embraces the paradox of the incarnation of the divine: of Christ in a human body, of the divine presence in a fleshy vessel.

In twenty-first-century Rome, the Sacred Heart is paradoxically both a dwelling and an exiled abode. For the clerics it becomes a mediator that turns migrants into renewed apostolic actors for evangelization, to convert their passions into the passion to convert. It is also a subtle reminder of unhomeliness and the betrayal of nations and families. (Sacred) Hearts point to migrant subjectivities that struggle with but are also animated by different erotic, familial, and spatial vessels for a sense of homeliness. Thus, one of the Catholic Church's theological fears around the Sacred Heart occurs when the Sacred Heart's connection to Christ's humanity (the basis of the "culture of life," in Pope Benedict's words) is played down to favor a reification of earthly sentiments.[42] Transnational migrant itineraries and religious practices can tell us a story of renewal of the Catholic Church from within, but they are also stories of a struggle for inclusion and autonomy. As is the case of embodied devotional pilgrimage performances, such as the rituals of the Hermandad de Señor de Los Milagros, Catholic practices are often played out on multiple exclusionary national fabrics. Devotional hearts, Sacred Heart, and Catholic hearts in motion are all affective domains that are deeply connected to the movements of histories, to their condensations, returns, and hauntings—key tools of a renewed analysis to understand the intersection of religion and transnational migration.

To conclude the articulation of mobility, passions, betrayal, and desfase of the heart that I've elaborated in this chapter demands a few further remarks. First, the migrant itineraries presented here are about migrant subjects who are sacrificial carriers in the eyes of the church but also at times perpetrators of (erotic) betrayal and the victims of betrayals by others, and the betrayals of their nations. These migrant itineraries aid but also destabilize official Catholic pedagogies of migrant evangelization that emphasize the normative family and family reunification as the focal points of an imagined redemption of migrants' bodies and souls. This contradiction is better understood if we situate these cases within the larger system of desires and anxieties of the church toward the New Evangelization and the return of Catholic blood from the Americas, which (as I have suggested in previous chapters) is always also a spectral return of missionary histories.

Second, a study of the Sacred Heart and the Señor de los Milagros pushes at the analytical enclosure of a study of migrant communities, through a study of affective and religious materialities. Belonging to a brotherhood such as to the Hermandad del Señor de los Milagros can challenge the boundaries of migrant "illegality" and makes devotional hearts the center of a renewed affective politics of spiritual legality and purity. And the Sacred Heart points to a tension between the homely and the unhomely, fidelity and betrayal. If desfase is a misrecognition, a suspension of being here and ultimately an unhomely condition for some migrants who are actually employed in caring for elders and children, in making other homes homely, then desfase emerges as a transnational matter of the (sacred) heart.

Third, we must understand how transnational migration is both marginal and central to the Catholic Church in its multiple hearts and their articulation. Sacred material devotions and the tactility of their presence are the incarnation of passions, and, as such, they carry both histories of inclusion and exclusion of imagined relationships and communities. In the next chapter I discuss in more detail the church's pedagogies of a "common identity" of being Catholic and Latin American and how they are further challenged by affects of the nation.

5.   *The Virgin of Guadalupe*

A Nexus of Affects

A connection between Marian devotions and the (un)making of nations is one of the threads of an Atlantic return of the mission. This chapter focuses on Mexican transnational returns of histories and the affective politics of celebrating the Virgin of Guadalupe in Rome. I argue that these transnational Catholic devotions contain or exceed the affect of the nation. The analytical interplay between a fantasy of the nation and its political reenactment gives us important insights into how racialized transnational religious histories are intimately connected to national political affect. Broadly speaking, it allows us to think about how transnational religiosity becomes a symptom (in a Freudian sense) of what has been repressed within the birth of a "modern" nation. This chapter, then, continues to explore the changing heart of Catholic migration while engaging with presences of the Virgin of Guadalupe in Rome.

My exploration of these questions proceeds through an ethnographic attention to the forms that this transnational religious celebration has taken within a four-year period and foregrounds some of the gendered complexities and anxieties that these celebrations unleash as strengthening a conservative Roman Catholic Church. Extending this analysis, I turn to a TV production on the Guadalupe devotion in Rome that portrayed the Virgin of Guadalupe as folkloric, rather than a sensuous, affective presence. Finally a study at the heart of the transnational Roman Catholic Church needs to engage different haunting presences in the political imagination of transnational displacement and reemplacements. This is also illuminated by a focus on repressed and returned histories, histories that I argue come back sometimes in symptomatic forms around issues of the nation(s) and its relation to Catholicism.

I argue here that the celebration of the Virgin of Guadalupe becomes a nexus of affect that gives force to an ultramontane (in defense of papal teaching) and conservative part of the Roman Catholic Church, which is transnationally reproduced in Mexico and in Rome. This renewed force promotes Mexican notions of patria, faith, and family and a reappropriation of the cultural memory of a violent confrontation—for a long time "repressed" topic in Mexican historiography—of twentieth-century Mexican history, namely the Cristero War.

As I have already noted, the Mexican church plays an important role in the current rearticulation of conservative forces in Rome through the work of Mexican orders such as the Legionaries of Christ, and their articulation and mimesis with the Jesuit order. The celebration of the Marian and Mexican cult of the Guadalupe Virgin must be understood within a critical approach to Marian studies—an approach that does not separate a study of popular religiosity from the one of the institutional church but analyzes them as co-emerging. Such a critical examination of these cults of the Guadalupe helps us explore how affective forces and the return of histories are valuable focuses within the burgeoning field of the anthropological study of Marian cults, which complements, but also exceeds an emphasis on the study of lived religion. The study of the emplacement and phenomenology of religion as rich and complex sets of spatial, material, and kinship relations is an approach that benefits from a parallel one that focuses on the histories and fantasies that were never fully lived, or were forgotten.

To explore these histories and devotions I use the concept of symptom to indicate the expression of an *imaginative intrusion* that undermines a given form of political and social control. A symptom is a defensive mechanism generated by anxiety that is rooted in a traumatic event and reenactment of being-in-danger. The traumatic event connects to an impossibility to fulfill a desire, which is therefore displaced or repressed and comes back in a symptom-form, such as a prohibition, or in a "substitutive satisfaction which appears in symbolic disguise."[1] Symptoms have the character of interruption and the eruption of an unexpected and uncanny affect. Hence they also connect to a paradoxical potentiality of histories that never were, but still are.[2] In adopting an affective histories approach, I follow the proposal of Eric Santner (rereading Franz Rosenzweig) that a focus on the symptoms of history need not pay attention exclusively to the rise or fall of nations and empires, but "rather to moments of uncoupling—of *exodus*—from the fantasmatic 'holism' of epochal or cultural totalities"[3]—in other words when symptoms open up and liberate history from a totalizing interpretation and closure.

La Guadalupana

La Guadalupana has a complex historicity that fascinated early anthropologists.[4] There is a long, well-documented history of the Virgin of Guadalupe as a multifaceted Mexican symbol of inculturation and subversion of colonial powers, the struggle for the independence of the new nation, and anxieties around its secular and religious roots. The transformed use of the image of the Virgin of Guadalupe, who allegedly appeared to the indigenous (now Saint) Juan Diego in 1531, is indicative of changes in the collective imaginaries of colonial and postcolonial Mexico. The barometer of this imaginary and the mobilization of the Virgin as a contested sign span centuries.[5]

The Virgin of Guadalupe has been interpreted, on one hand, as a sign and a reflexive prism of the historical transculturation of a Mexican imaginary[6] and, on the other, as a survival of devotion throughout different periods of Mexican history.[7] With the publication in 1648 of the first book on Guadalupe by Miguel Sánchez,[8] she became a theological symbol imbued with an Augustinian tradition rooted in medieval Christian practices. However, the resonance of an immanent, indigenous presence of the divine through the Virgin's appearance also challenged and transformed the transcendental, Augustinian Catholic pedagogical impulse that characterized the first Franciscan missions in New Spain. An analysis of the emergence of the cult of the Guadalupe shows how a density of historical specifications helps us understand how any interpretation of believers' "consumption" of this image or its mobilization in national (and later transnational) localities should be read within and as a product of particular historical conjunctures: specifically that of Mexico in the latter half of the nineteenth century and the emergence of the social doctrine of the church, with Leo XIII's encyclical *Rerum Novarum* (1891).

The historical conjunctures of the second part of the nineteenth century, in fact, pointed to a new paradox developing within public perceptions of devotion to the Guadalupe. On one hand, the devotion to the Virgin of Guadalupe was seen as a negative expression of popular religiosity that had been strategically orchestrated by the clergy against liberal and anticlerical forces; on the other, her celebration was lauded as an embrace of an authentic indigenous and Mexican religiosity that dovetailed with emerging indigenistic and nationalistic discourses—for instance, in the work of the nineteenth-century intellectual Ignacio Manuel Altamirano—that promoted liberal modernity and progress for a newly born Mexican nation.[9] It was in this context, and specifically during the coronation of the Guadalupe in 1895, that she became the official patron saint of all Latin America. Yet behind the regional significance of this event, this coronation represented an important turn in the relationship of the Catholic Church and the Mexican state. It effectively symbolized an end to the self-exile of Vatican clergy from Mexico that had taken place in response to the liberal, and perceived anticlerical reforms introduced in the 1857 Mexican constitution.

In October 1895, when the new shrine in the Tepeyac was officially dedicated to the Guadalupe, prelates delivered a series of sermons about the wonders and the powers of the Virgin of Guadalupe in her capacity as "protector of the nation," the "Lady of Mexican history" and hence the bearer of both Mexican tradition and its future.[10] This articulation of the Guadalupe with the future progress of Mexico ideologically bore both social redemption for the popular masses and the advancement of Mexico as a religious nation. This articulation entailed an intense condensation of historical, political, and racial referents, making the Guadalupe the lady of national history, the mother of the Mexican mestizo, and the Queen (*La Reina*) of Mexico, while also the symbolic mother of all the Americas. Looking ahead thirty years later, during the Cristiada or Cristero War in the late 1920s revealed this exalted celebration of the Virgin of Guadalupe as an idealized and deeply problematic marriage between the public sphere of the nation-state and an institutionalized Catholic practice. Further, the (failed) pre-, and postrevolutionary Mexican anticlerical efforts to defanaticize and desacralize Catholicism, which at the same time sought to sacralize, in a rather Jacobin spirit, the "perfectibility of man and society through the rational applications of science and technology" represent what is perhaps an even more problematic legacy of this moment.[11]

In more recent twentieth-century history, the Guadalupana (another way to address the cult of the Guadalupe) has been interpreted as a mediator between liberation and submission, as a liberating symbol with significance for salvation. Within this view, and affirming the lasting influence of nineteenth-century nationalist discourses, some Latino theologians have played a key role in arguing that she is a central player in the process of the inculturation and *mestizaje* of Christianity in the Americas. She is then described as a popular religious symbol for evangelical transformation and life-enhancing processes rather than disruptive racial mixing,[12] providing a sense of origin of the "new Mestizo" of the Americas that signals a passage from "brokenness to integration through a conversion process."[13]

The Guadalupe has figured in recent discussions as a call for dignity and hope in social transformation, as seen in Timothy Matovina's ethnographic work on the U.S. Catholic South,[14] and as a potential to reinscribe human and immigrant rights in Mexican transnational communities' political struggles within a post–9/11 U.S. society.[15] However, new arguments for the liberatory power of this sacred feminine icon have been accompanied by criticisms of the way these perspectives effectively reinstate a patriarchal cosmology that ascribes to femininity a submissive aspect of the sacred. This critique has emerged from a Chicana feminist perspective, which has advocated a reimaging of Guadalupe that highlights her contested and warrior-like nature and her contribution to radical struggles for social justice that resonate with Latino women's experience in the United States.[16] In this sense, the Guadalupe becomes a liberatory symbol because she allows a space for founding a renewed Chicana (and more broadly) female speaking-subject position. By deconstructing the Guadalupe's patriarchal formation and exploring her as a healing enunciatory position, the Guadalupe acquires a capacity to embrace ambiguity as the "new mestiza."[17]

Yet the Virgin of Guadalupe is not only a liberatory icon or, like other Virgins across the Americas, a symbol of a nation in exile.[18] I would argue that she is also a nexus of ambivalent affect that are embodied and mobilized transnationally at particular historical conjunctures. I use the word nexus to indicate a *field of force* in the social imaginary,[19] which has current and possibly proleptic effects. In my previous work, I engaged with the production of prisms of belonging in urban Mexico in order to address the interface of cognition, history and memory as they are expressed by people's narratives of time and space.[20] Here, I am interested in a nexus of affect mobilized by a transnational social imaginary.

The *OED* defines nexus as a "bond, link; a means of connection between things or parts," but also as a "predicative relation." Affects have a material presence within a system of transmission between people and hence do not belong only to people's imagination and desires.[21] By awakening sedimented histories in the present, affects shape the social imaginary. To study nexus of affect is to study predicative connections in the circulation of histories, condensed as well as displaced in transnational localities. Thus, the celebration of the Virgin of Guadalupe in Rome has a materiality of make-believe;[22] it comprises a return of histories and anxieties around the national and the familial. By exploring this nexus of affect, I wish to develop what Aretxaga and others have discussed as a symptomology of the nation and the problematization of national gendered metaphors.[23] To ground my exploration, I examine different settings of the celebration of the Virgin of Guadalupe in Rome, which took place from the mid–2000s to Benedict XVI's celebration in St. Peter's Square in 2011.

La Virgen "Danzante"

In this section I compare the celebrations of La Virgen Danzante (the "dancing" Virgin) Sunday, 10 December 2006, and Sunday, 8 December 2004, at the Church of Nostra Signora di Coromoto, Italy. The annual mass for the celebration of the Virgin of Guadalupe in 2006 is presided over by the Salesian priest Pascual Chávez Villanueva.[24] In the first ten rows and at the altar, priests are dressed in ceremonial white tunics wearing different cassocks, some of which differentiate the priests' origins in Mexico. Chávez is the only one wearing a tunic with the Virgin embroidered on the front. A large reproduction of the Virgin on a banner is standing on one side of the altar. After the mass the banner will be carried in procession from the church to the Mexican Pontifical College, two kilometers away in Monteverde. Visually there is a marked contrast between the priests, dressed in white in the front and at the altar, and the public, among whom many Mexican sisters are present, wearing somber colors and longer plain skirts and veils. As Lucy, a member of a female congregation dedicated to the Sacred Heart, explained to me once in Rome, her superiors recommended that she wear the veil, which she did not wear in Mexico. She longs for the freedom of dress she was allowed back there, but she also recognizes that wearing the veil here allows her not to be confused with lay Latin American migrants in Rome. There are fashions to follow in the clergy too.[25]

Chávez's sermon opens with a dedication to the 475 years' celebration of the "hechos de Guadalupe" (in the sense of the apparition of the Guadalupe). In his words the Virgin is *misionera y alejada* (missionary and faraway). The events of her apparition and subsequent recognition as a Virgin are stories of missions and margins, of "a presence full of *ternura* [caring]" and of that which "gives dignity to sons of God in Latin America." Her celebration, Chávez continues, helps all of us "deepen our faith and make the nation" (as in creating a sense of belonging to the nation). The story he tells is also about remembering that she is a pregnant Virgin "a symbol of the battle for life." and, since her celebration falls during Advent, she is also "a historical presence of salvation . . . who gives us dignity in front of the eyes of God in Latin America." Chávez continues, "Faith is important in public life. . . . Faith has to have a strong social dimension as *citizens and Christians are the same person*, this is the mestizo Christianity [*cristianismo mestizo*]" (my emphasis).

It is important to recall here that a little more than a week before Chávez's sermon, on 1 December 2006, Felipe Calderón was sworn in as the new president of Mexico in a very turbulent and contested inauguration—at midnight, in the middle of a tense atmosphere in the Mexican House of Commons, where deputies had seized the speaker's platform and blocked the doors of the chamber. Calderón, a fervent Roman Catholic, originally from the state of Jalisco, was the candidate of the pro-Catholic PAN party (Partido Acción Nacional), and the contestation raged around electoral forgery and the specter of a parallel presidency by the runner-up Manuel Lopéz Obrador. Lopéz Obrador was the candidate of the PRD party (Partido de la Revolución Democrática), the left-wing contestant in the election and a former mayor of Mexico City. In the aftermath of the election and the recounting of the votes, he founded a movement, the Coalition for the Good of All, that mobilized demonstrations and set up camps in the capital's main square of the Zócalo even after the Federal Electoral Tribunal declared Calderón the winner. Lopéz Obrador himself had performed a mock swearing-in ceremony a week earlier.

At the time, the Mexican press described the atmosphere of the moment as one of extreme social agitation and ungovernability.[26] The inauguration ceremony was cut short and performed, unusually, at midnight, and the presidential speech was recorded in the private presidential residence after Calderón made a short, private visit to the Basilica of the Virgin of Guadalupe. Subsequently, there was a debate over whether vote rigging or a forgery of the judicial recount had taken place, although the consensus now is that this may have not been the case. Yet the lack of clarity in the aftermath of the election seemed due both to the idiosyncrasies of the electoral system[27] and to the mistrust and resentment of the state-run control for potential rigging of the election that seemed biased in favor of the PAN candidate.[28]

In the political climate of 2006, violence around the contested Calderón's election in Mexico became a public secret in Rome, a ticklish, spectral subject.[29] The public secret is the actually failing idea that the nation, or patria, is "for all." A week after the election, on another continent, this failure to pacify a nation beyond the new president and a Catholic response to it is palpable between the lines of Father Chávez's sermon in the Church of Nostra Signora di Coromoto: "The problem is not poverty; it is the cultural model that legitimizes poverty. We cannot stay still; the baptized have to evangelize. The Virgin of Guadalupe is a mission. She is for all of us. The mission is not to do things, but it is to be the manifestation of God. It is to be collaborators of the salvation of God."

The Virgin is a mode of being for "all of us." But there is a historical ambiguity about being for "all of us" Mexicans. To say *todos somos Guadalupanos* (we are all Guadelupians) is to name an important tension with regard not only to the phenomenon of the Virgin of Guadalupe but also to the formation and the reproduction of the Mexican state, which has an anticlerical history at its foundation and yet is devoted to this female figure.

At the end of the mass, after following the standard of the Virgin out of the church, we head up to the Mexican College. It is dark and humid; a drizzle is descending on us. Priests have quickly changed clothes. The procession starts to disperse. This year's procession is somber in comparison with the procession of 2004. There are no people dancing as we sing the rosary and songs dedicated to the Virgin. We pass a major street-crossing full of Christmas shoppers. Some stop to look at this crowd of pilgrims, some in a distracted way, others with interest. A group of youngsters on scooters, bothered by the length of the procession (by now we are around three hundred people), honk their horns and bully some of the priests who are blocking traffic. There is some tension in the air. I later asked Valerio, the Italian husband of the Mexican president of the CCM (Comunidad Católica Mexicana), whether this was a common reaction that they encountered in other contexts in Rome. He pointed out that at the celebrations of the Dias de los Muertos organized by the CCM some Italians had tried to take away pieces of the altar (when in the church) to take home, so that coordinator members always have to watch out. He added that Italians do not understand what Mexican celebrations are about; they do not understand the spirit, and they see them as folkloric. So, for him, the local youths' response to our procession through the street resonates with a sense of belittling of Mexican traditions. However, to what extent this is a local response that indicates treating Mexican Catholic religiosity or of Catholic religiosity in general as folklore is an ethnographic question to explore further.

Following along with the procession, on the other side of the street, Iris, a Mexican woman, focused on the calmness of the mood of the procession: "Look, Valentina, the Virgin of Guadalupe is cultural, also here in Rome; it is for lay and religious people together; it is for the nation [*patria*]. You see we are all here with the Virgin of Guadalupe. The Virgin of Guadalupe is for all of us."

Once we get to the college, we pass in front of a sculpture of a large map of Mexico, which is supported on the back of a statue of a forward-looking Christ. The sculpture celebrates the fall of the Cristero martyrs, with the place of their martyrdom highlighted by worn-out red bulbs. A ghostly presence of the Cristero War is welcoming us in our procession.

Inside the college, a large 1950s bulding on a beautiful hill in Monteverde, the walls are covered with tapestries hanging from the ceiling. Repeatedly inscribed in woven cubical letters is *fe y patria* (faith and nation). As in previous years, an all-male costume band inspired by twelfth- to fifteenth-century university traditions from Spain, the orchestra Estudiantina de Guanajuato, is playing. Padre Lucio, a member of the college is dressed in mariachi clothes and goes on to sing solo for a long while, after the Romatitlán group—a Roman-based mariachi and folkloric dance troupe, whose two leaders are a Sicilian and a *chilango* from Mexico City, has performed. The public is by now mingled; there are not only the Mexican diocesan priests of the Mexican Pontifical College, but also other Mexicans from different congregations and religious missionary orders, as well as many lay people. While we watch these songs and dances the public is mingling in the corridors that face the cloister where the performance takes place. Some are joking that padre Lucio is so good that he should not have been a priest but should have pursued a career as a mariachi singer. The mood is by now cheerful. I am sitting not far from a Mexican woman who works in one of the two Mexican embassies in Rome.[30] She is passionately telling Iris that they "will not pass." I step into their conversation and ask who will not pass: "The envoys [of the new Calderón government] just visited the embassy a few weeks ago, and they asked, Why is there not a Virgin of Guadalupe [here]? But the Mexican state is not *that*, and we are not going to change. . . . They were cross and arrogant; we *should not let them [pass]*, but it's difficult" (my emphasis).

The "that" is a perceived threat of interference by the Catholic Church in a domain of the Mexican state seen as secular. We should position this response within tensions in Mexico about a "taking over" of the public sphere of the state by Catholic, conservative forces. Vicente Fox, president from 2000 to 2006, had an ambiguous relationship with the Catholic Church hierarchy, expressing his personal Catholic devotion and using religious symbolism for his own political campaigns but also dismissing criticisms from the Catholic hierarchy concerning, for instance, his marrying a second time.[31] Felipe Calderón Hinojosa, president from 2006 to 2012, had a stronger connection with the Catholic hierarchy.[32]

Without taking up an openly pro-clerical agenda, Calderón had nevertheless promoted a religious politics that facilitated the Catholic Church within a rubric of religious freedom of expression. This involved not reprimanding the Catholic hierarchy's intervention in the public sphere while the church's hierarchy was attacking the secularism of the Mexican state. Moreover, Calderón had been allegedly linked to the ultraconservative secret Catholic society called El Yunque.[33] Hence, the Mexican woman's anxiety is rooted in a felt attack on the laicity of the state or, from another perspective, of an overt push of religiosity into public space. Different registers of history emerge through the nexus of affect of the Virgin of Guadalupe in Rome. Those registers claim different lay and religious roots for the Mexican nation-state.

Racially embodied tensions also emerge in the history of this procession for the Guadalupana in Rome, which was established in the mid-1990s. In retrospect, the celebration of the same procession in 2004 in Rome foregrounded and minimized similar, but also different, narratives. In that procession one group of priests who had trained for a few months had dressed up as *Matachines* and *Danzantes* (dancers dressed up in particular indigenous clothes, partly reminiscent of the medieval European conflicts between Moors and Christians). They performed as a group in two lines dancing rhythmically up to the hill. They wore white robes embroidered with indigenous colorful motifs and conch shells tied around their calves to keep the rhythm of the dance. Drums, maracas, and guitars followed the procession, and many in the procession tried to follow the priests' steps. All of the eight diocesan priests dancing had learned the dance in the previous two months, rehearsing at the college. According to Father Geremia, a member of this group and a leading Mexican student in the college, those who danced were all from the northeast of the republic, where these dances had not in fact originated. The priests from the south were not inclined to dance as Matachines and to wear indigenous clothes in Rome as, in his words, "Those dances are too close to home." Subtle racial and class distinctions thus reappear in the Mexican Pontifical College. Wealthier priests from the north (especially Nuevo León) are often able to pay for *pachangas* (parties) in the college, and some may want to learn to dance, whereas more indigenous-looking priests from the south mainly come from poorer dioceses and families with scarcer resources. These are the ones who do not dance. For many in the latter group, in Geremia's view, priesthood and being sent to study in Rome is a form of upward mobility, an opportunity to distance themselves from their indigenous roots.

Once the procession of the Virgin of Guadalupe from the Church of Nostra Signora del Coromoto arrives at the Mexican College and we are inside the building, in the large cloister that is decorated with traditional Mexican paper cuttings, nuns serve tostadas, beans, and chicken in tomato sauce with a nice warm fruit punch. The catering has been prepared by around fifteen nuns of a Mexican order dedicated to the Sacred Heart, who live on the premises but in a gated compound. They cater to the daily needs of more than 150 diocesan priests together with the help of a smaller group of men from a Mexican order who care for the gardens and the switchboard. The place of the female religious order within the male diocesan college is one of dedicated but also problematic "servitude," and there is some discontent among younger nuns over not being able to properly advance their studies while in Rome, because of the amount of work to be done.

In conversation with me, Martha, originally from Monterrey in the north of the republic and the head of the CCM in Rome, emphasizes that you would never see diocesan priests dressing in indigenous clothes in Mexico, while the college priests are asked to come to this celebration *de collarin*, wearing the white, stiff collar that, with a black suit, clearly marks out a diocesan priest from laypeople. Inside the college, the celebration is officially opened by the spiritual head and counselor of the college, who, dressed with the indigenous *huipil* (traditional embroidered shirt), opens his brief acknowledgments with "I am the spiritual guide of this community, *también si no se parece* [even if it does not look like it]." Everyone laughs. Indigeneity again appears as an ambiguous marker.

Within the specific conjuncture of Rome in 2004, the affective nexus of the Virgin is generated in part through a transnational mimesis and a (mis)recognition of Mexican indigeneity. The fact that in the same celebration two years later references to Mexican indigeneity in the forms of performance or display of elements of indigenous people's heritage disappeared completely from the public performance, both in the procession and in the subsequent fiesta at the college (where these elements partly reappeared in the 2007 celebration),[34] is interesting. It suggests that at a different historical conjuncture, the nexus of affect generated out of an apparently very similar celebration had shifted in significant ways. When asked why there were no danzantes in 2006, a group of college priests whom I queried appeared not to know, but once we continued our conversation two mentioned that the rector thought it was not appropriate for that year.

What had changed? In comparison with previous and later celebrations, the 2006 celebration of the Virgin of Guadalupe points to a nexus of affect that required a performance of a nation emptied of its own indigeneity. This indigeneity, embodied in a performance of indigenous dances, has shifted from being portrayed as an innocent, mythical cultural heritage that is treated as folkloric and proudly national to one that must be played down. It is played down when it may evoke contemporary sociopolitical formations and counternarratives of power involving both indigenous and nonindigenous peoples.[35]

Indigeneity as a discourse of appropriation and belonging around the Virgin of Guadalupe in recent Mexican history is a complex and multilayered phenomenon. We cannot assume a monolithic Catholicism in Mexico or a strict overlapping of the spiritual imaginary around the Virgin and the imaginary of institutional Catholicism. For instance, the Virgin of Guadalupe was evoked by the revolutionary EZLN (the Zapatista National Liberation Army) as part of their collective imaginary.[36] And the PRD coalition headed by Manuel Lopéz Obrador also referred to the Guadalupana while demonstrating in the central Zócalo of Mexico City and demanding a recount of the presidential electoral votes. Needless to say, on that occasion the Mexican Catholic Church hierarchy headed by the conservative Cardinal Norberto Rivera expressed its profound discomfort with the (alleged) manipulation of this image.

The Virgin of Guadalupe as the Virgen Morena (brown Virgin) has also been a key figure in the Teología Indígena (Indigenous Theology), a movement within the Catholic church that, developing out of the implementation of Vatican II in Latin America and liberation theology, has advocated for the revelation and incarnation of the Gospel in indigenous cultures, granting to indigenous spiritual practices a renewed capacity for revelation of religious truth and an important role in interfaith dialogue.[37] Nonetheless, the Teología Indígena has also been a contentious subject between pro-indigenous clergy and the Mexican and Vatican clerical hierarchy, not least concerning its potential to embrace a social (and political) effort for indigenous people's liberation and autonomy and the fostering of an autochthonous church.[38] However, some appropriations of the Teología Indígena, as part of a theology of *inculturación* and a contextual theology, can be read as reproducing neocolonial missionary impulses of assimilation to the Catholic Church rather than as representing a dialogical process of grassroots theological and liturgical formation.[39]

Hence in 2006, in the midst of a struggle in Mexico about the secularization of the state and the religiosity of public life, the nexus of affect that was mobilized in the Mexican College was about a mestizo Christianity (*Cristianismo Mestizo*), a Catholic citizenship ("for all of us") based on the phantom of a unified nation emptied of aspects of its own complex indigeneity. The phantom of national unity was and still is treading the corridors of the Mexican College.

La *"Virgen Cristera"* and the Legionaries

On Tuesday, 12 December 2006, the mass for the celebration of the Virgin of Guadalupe had just ended in the Church of the Virgin of Guadalupe in the Aurelia. This relatively new church is the mother church dedicated to the order of the Legionaries of Christ in Rome. On this day the mass is celebrated by a bishop from northern Italy and some senior priests of the Legionaries of Christ. It is attended by Italian parishioners and members of the Regnum Christi, a lay movement promoted by the Legionaries of Christ. The mass is accompanied by a soprano who is dressed up for the performance. No more than one hundred people are gathered for this Tuesday afternoon celebration, but afterwards a small group of Italians listen to an explanation of the Virgin of Guadalupe delivered in a Spanish accent by a Legionaries of Christ priest. The man is smartly attired in his priestly clothes and fashionable glasses, with well-cut blond hair. He talks in an amicable and soft-spoken tone to this group that seems to not know much about the Virgin, although it will emerge later that a few Italians have traveled to Mexico, where they have experienced the power of the Virgin as "love at first sight," in the words of a well-dressed middle-aged woman.

This priest from the Legionaries of Christ tells the story of the apparition of the Virgin to Juan Diego, and then he explains that she was a support to the fighters of the Cristero War. He narrates some of the encounters of the Legionaries of Christ founder with the Guadalupe, the response that the Mexican people had to the Cristero calls for resistance against the modern Mexican state, and the way in which the founder saw the Virgin of Guadalupe as central to that moment of church history. He also dwells at length on the mystery of the Virgin, much to the interest of the attentive audience. On the walls of the church there is an exhibition about the unresolved scientific mysteries that the Virgin de Guadalupe poses to scientists. Among other things, the priest mentions the image of the retina in the Virgin's eyes and the inexplicable endurance throughout the centuries of the simple cloth on which the image of the Virgin appeared and which is now housed in the Basilica of the Guadalupe. However, the Legionaries of Christ are not the first to have observed the scientific inexplicability of the Virgin of Guadalupe. But for the Legionaries, she is also the *defensora de la vida* (defender of life), an advocate of another sort (a reference to the culture of life). Father Fidel who was for forty years the priest in charge of this church, said that the Virgin "helps people very much. She gives life, which is why the pro-life movements are very devoted to her. She wears two bracelets, which in the Nahuatl culture means she is pregnant, and she is telling us all, Mexican and not, to fight for life with faith, charity and hope. This is what she is."

But back to the church that day. We follow the priest to the vestry where other priests from the Legionaries of Christ are gathering. The iconic feminine image which is presented in the public side of the church is replaced by a series of pictures on the foundation of this particular church: the laying of the first stone, which was brought from the hill of Tepeyac, close to Mexico City, where she appeared, and the blessing by Pius XII in 1955.[40] In another room, there is the picture of the first beatified man of the Cristiada, now Saint Toribio Romo from the Altos of Jalisco, who has also become the popular patron saint of undocumented migrants.[41] We are then invited to sign up for a program called the Virgin of Guadalupe *Peregrina* (female pilgrim). This is basically a rotation among a network of families that will each have a "traveling" statue of the Virgin in their house in Rome for part of the week and will recite the rosary to her. Similar types of home visits of the *Virgen itinerante* are also found in the central and northern parts of Mexico and in Texas.

A man from the group asks the reason for the rotation. In the words of the Legionary priest, "She comes alive when passed from one household to another. . . . She makes the household stronger"; she helps the families "rejoice in praying together in their home." Then the small crowd engages the priest on the point that society is in crisis and that the sharing of the Virgin's presence in one's own household is good. The Spanish priest replies that we are in difficult times, remembering once again the bravery with which the Mexican people defended the faith when it was under attack in the Cristero War.[42] This represents a second evocation of a powerful, sedimented, and transnational history in the same afternoon. So let me turn now to this sedimented history.

As I introduced briefly in chapter 3, the Cristero War remains a complex and difficult part of twentieth-century Mexican history, staging a confrontation between lay and religious forces in matters of Catholic religious cults in the public sphere. Recent readings of this historical period and of some of the Catholic processions that took place at the time capture the fears different actors had about a "forced" secularization of the Mexican state. Important readings of this period illustrate some of the ways in which women became the key in subverting a sacrificial and passive economy of Catholic sanctity: from a passive submission to a perceived attack on the Catholic faith to an active and reactive (and therefore partly violent, as in taking up arms) response to such an attack. Women were not only passively resisting the encroaching of the state on the Catholic clergy; they were central actors in raising up a resistant defense to perceived (secular) enemies of the faith. Describing the aftermath of the killing of Juan Tirado in Mexico (a member of the LNDLR[43] who murdered the Mexican president Alvaro Obregón in 1928), Matthew Butler writes:

> Indeed, women acted as celebrants [at the burial] and sacred orators as well as political-religious agitators, and did so without class distinctions. This social leveling and feminization created an aggressive mood, furthermore, culminating in actual violence: the smashing of the *comisaría* door, the assaulting of [male] state agents. These female socio-religious interlocutors exceeded women's prescribed roles within the Church, yet probably, they saw themselves not as usurpers but as embodiments of a "true," "virile" Catholicism, whose defense could not be left to others. Defense justified any secondary transgressions, even if the subtext of this credo was that enemies of the faith could be killed. As the true faith's custodians, women were not spiritual rebels but Lady Macbeths urging Catholics to screw their courage to the sticking-place and fight an unclean state in the streets.[44]

Female Catholics could then call for more of a "virile" Catholicism, in moments of perceived danger for the Catholic Church. However, Matthew Butler argues that the ways in which the cult of the Guadalupana emerged *after* the Cristero War in Mexico as a symbolically and pedagogically unifying cult had a price. That was the death of the hope for a sociologically embodied and enacted Kingdom of the Cristo Rey, where the national public could militantly sustain and perform its Catholic fervor. I cannot emphasize enough how important this historical and religious conjunction was. The emergence and consolidation of the Guadalupana cult meant that the Cristo Rey and its secular-religious battlefield were "demobbed and dethroned" and "put off for better times."[45] The haunting forces of these better times are uncannily present in contemporary Rome. They are present in the celebration of the Virgin of Guadalupe and in the rhetoric and impulses that foster the transnational rise of the order of the Legionaries of Christ.

In the intimacy of the church vestry of the Legionaries of Christ, in the Via Aurelia, the performance of the circulation of the Virgin and her devotional presence, with an accent on its "inexplicable" scientific reality and its connections to the Virgen Peregrina, evokes another symptomatic lack of unity. The fantasy of and the desire for a unified Catholic family household make up the nexus of affect that the performance of the Virgin presents in this Legionaries of Christ scenario in Rome. But the Guadalupana devotion is also composed of forces associated with the Cristo Rey, as Butler suggests. This is an undisclosed desire for a call to arms to defend a traditional Roman Catholic Church perceived under attack. In this context the Virgin could be seen as a female force that called for resistance in the name of Catholic truth.

Hence, through the perspective of the Legionaries of Christ in Rome, the Guadalupana becomes a powerful nexus that links, among other things, the divine feminine with its historically and ambiguous potential for "right" violence in defense of the Roman Catholic Church, which is, of course, not to say that the Legionaries of Christ and their vision, which other Catholics may also share, demand a "call to arms" and a call for female violence. However, as Butler's reading suggest, a renarrativization of the Cristero War is also about an evocation of a (female) mass violence that at a particular historical conjuncture successfully scuttled a perceived fanaticization against Catholicism.[46] In the context of the 2006 celebrations, this ambiguous lens is the product of a real and potentially violent border within the Mexican nation—an internal confrontation between the secular and religious roots of the nation-state. It is this internal border, with its gendered, historical, and racialized registers that is transnationally resignified and evoked in Rome and which is both reenacted and silenced through the Virgin of the Guadalupe. That border "is a compromised formation in both the political and the Freudian senses, as a symptom in the body of the nation that contains an excess of signification."[47] In this sense, the Virgin becomes a nexus of affect that evokes and mobilizes this border, which enables, just as it also negates, the unity of the nation.[48] This is another element in a Catholic puzzle of the Atlantic return: an excess of signification around affects of the nation.

Guadalupe Spectacles

On the 4 July 2009, I had the opportunity to be part of a television program about the Virgin of Guadalupe. A call went out via the CCM website to gather at the Basilica of St. Nicola in Carcere behind the Teatro Marcello church, where the oldest representation of the Virgin of Guadalupe in Rome is in a dimly lit lateral nave. I arrive there at around four in the afternoon, and there were already some women and a full TV troupe. They will be recording for an RAI 1 Sunday program *A Sua Immagine*, as part of a series that was exploring different sanctuaries in Europe and the Americas. To cut costs and engage with the Guadalupe, they are seeking locals to show the devotion she receives among Mexicans. One woman from this local parish insists that Mexicans come here on the dawn of 12 December at 6 A.M. to sing the *mañanitas* (birthday song) and then share *tamales* and *atole* (typical Mexican food made out of corn and cooked in corn or plantain leaves, and a hot, thick drink prepared with corn or starch). I know she is right because I was there once myself in 2008, but some of the CCM women have never heard of this event, which is definitely small in scale.

We are now a group of around fifteen women and an ex-seminarian with his Peruvian fiancée; they are to be married soon. There is Violeta, who has been in Italy for eighteen years, married to an Italian and then divorced, and now living with a Kung Fu instructor and acupuncturist. She was born in Tala, Jalisco, raised in LA and now works (underpaid) for a Montessori school as an English/Spanish teacher in Rome. She has two sons. Two Mexican women from the Focolare group[49] are there too. Clara, who arrived from Mexico City a few months ago, is also here; she is divorced and looking for a job. She did not want to appear or be interviewed, half-jokingly saying that "she is wanted [by the law]"—she has overstayed her visa, and, at that time, this was a criminal act in Italy. Clearly she does not want to give her name to Martha, who is writing up a list to give to the TV presenter, the flamboyant B.

We rehearse the questions off air: "Is the Virgin of Guadalupe important for you?" and "Why?" None of us is relaxed around the microphone; some of the answers are roundabout: "The Guadalupe is important for all Mexico. . . . You feel received [*acojida*] by her. . . . She is with you always. . . . She does not let you down." I myself mumble a sort of answer, emphasizing that the image of the Virgin is not only Mexican but also global. By then the painting of the Guadalupe has been moved to an opposite nave, and strong TV lights have been turned on. We still have a long while to wait before they begin shooting, and some of the women start to get fidgety. We have already spent a few hours preparing for the recording. B. has reassured us beforehand that she knows that the cult of the Guadalupe is on the rise in Italy and in the migrant population. Nonetheless, she keeps asking why women come to the celebration on the 12 December so early in the morning and then go to work in other people's houses. She does not seem to get that this particular group of women do not come for the early celebration at this church on the 12 December, nor are they in their majority working as *badanti* in Italian families. Only two of our group work as hourly maids although they are married to Italians. Ada is one, and differently from the majority of other women there she is of indigenous origin from the Mayan region of Yucatán.

When B. moves away to the other side of the church, Ada turns and elaborates that she was paid five hundred fifty euros to work in a house caring for two young children from 9 A.M. to 6 P.M., and then the father asked her to do more household chores. Though she needed the money, she asked advice of the other women about whether she should leave that job—it sounds as if she had decided to leave. In Mexico, "They mistreat indigenous people because they talk an indigenous language, but here, I sense we face racism too." Women like her are not tall and slender as the beautiful B., but Ada is more graceful on this occasion, as I will explain below.

While B. mentions that we must wait a little longer for the shooting to begin, a loud thunder is heard through the walls of the basilica. The sky looks particularly dark through the antique and poorly maintained glass window of the little side chapel dome we are now sitting in. While we are waiting, B. is standing at the altar, and the Virgin of the Guadalupe is next to her. We are sitting on the church benches at the feet of the Guadalupe and the TV presenter. Drops of rain begin to percolate through a hole in the dome of this side chapel. One woman stands up quickly to go and find something to clear the water and to check that it is not dripping on the

Guadalupe. The TV presenter begins to joke while we are waiting. She is standing close to the Guadalupe's portrait. She mimics a Hawaiian hula dance while we are rehearsing the song of the Guadalupana; in a way she is mocking the song. I look at Martha—this is not really proper, and we share glances among the group with a sort of grimace. The TV presenter, a glamorous-looking young Italian woman, who should probably know more than we do about sanctuaries and Marian devotions, continues to not get it; she continues mocking the Guadalupan song with her dance at the altar. Something discomfiting is taking place.

The summer storm is over, and so is the shooting. I leave with Violeta, and we walk toward Largo Argentina. While we are walking, she is the first to mention that the television presenter was off-putting. Violeta then reflects that she was so happy when she discovered, during her mother's visit the previous year, that there was a Guadalupe in that church, and that she knows why Italians like B. do not get it. They think she is an image, but she is not: "They do not get it, she *te baña con su calor* [she washes you with her warmth]. . . . In her presence, she is there on your skin, she is in your body, she is not a touristic image. Her presence makes you shiver with sweat."

She is a presence, not an image, Violeta keeps repeating. I share Violeta's anger about the insensitivity of the TV presenter, which was so clear to those of us sitting on the benches. B.R. was bluntly considering the Virgin as folklore; she understood it as one of the many expressions of the "new immigrant communities" in Italy. She was not aware of the affective force that this Virgin carries, although she has also been working for Vatican broadcasting for a while, and clips of the interviews were to be shown in the program *A Sua Immagine* on 26 July. Undoubtedly the awkwardness of this afternoon will be purged from the final product, but this folklorization in the presentation of the Guadalupe probably will not be.

But devotion to the Virgin of Guadalupe is definitely on the rise in Rome. In December 2011, a major event for the Guadalupe was celebrated in Rome. This was an official mass to the Virgin of Guadalupe in Saint Peter's Square celebrated in Spanish and Latin by Benedict XVI for the bicentenary celebration of independence throughout the Latin American continent. In front of official dignitaries from Latin American embassies and cardinals such as Norberto Rivera, Benedict XVI reiterated the church's commitment to the Virgin of Guadalupe. Before announcing in the same sermon a new apostolic visit to Mexico and Cuba in spring 2012, Benedict XVI explained:

At this time, as various parts of Latin America are commemorating the bicentenary of their Independence, the process of integration in this beloved continent is progressing, while at the same time it is playing a new role on the world scene. In these circumstances it is important that its diverse people can safeguard the rich treasure of faith and their historical-cultural dynamism, always being the defenders of human life from conception to natural end and promoters of peace; they must likewise care for the family in this genuine nature and mission, at the same time intensifying a vast grass-roots educational campaign that correctly prepares individuals and makes them aware of their capacities in such a way that they can face their destiny with responsibility and dignity.[50]

The pope goes on to mention the Virgin, confirming the *afán apostolico* (apostolic eagerness) of the New Evangelization that John Paul II introduced on the occasion of the commemoration of the five hundred years of the evangelization of the Americas. Benedict XVI endorsed John Paul II's vision and reiterated that the Virgin is a testimony of this conversion, the roots for a new hope of evangelization for the Holy See. Iris, who works at the Mexican Embassy to the Holy See refers to that mass as *muy emocionante* (very touching), especially since it was a *misa criolla* (lit., a creole mass, a mass musically written in 1964 with the use of Andean instruments by the Argentinian musician Ariel Ramírez in celebration of the Second Vatican Council) within St. Peter's. The sounds of the *charangas* and the *tambores* within St. Peter's Church alone made the experience unique. The return of the mission in this official setting evokes a power of the Virgin in Rome that is on the performative side *criollo*, but at its core the mass is celebrated in the old ritual that Pope Benedict has been championing, the old Latin missal. Latin and criollo are performed side by side in powerful, but still subtly hierarchical, ways.

Transnational Marian Celebrations and Affective Histories

It is clear that the migration of the Virgin of Guadalupe through different political, transnational, and religious terrains in Rome shows a series of desires, losses, and anxieties about the strength of the Roman Catholic Church and different national projects. Her celebration unveils the affective and effective social force of transnational histories, even as devotion to her is misread and misrepresented as a folkloric sentiment. In this respect, the Virgin does not resonate at the symbolic heart of the Vatican and the Roman Catholic Church—as it does in some cases in the United States—with a desire for the empowerment of marginal subjects, especially in relation to migration. Yet it is impossible to deny that she resonates through the history of the relation between the Roman Catholic Church and the Mexican nation-state. This is also a history of martyrdom and violence, linked to anxieties around the secularization of society and the hope for a Catholic religiosity intimately married to public, national, and intimate spheres.

I have argued that to understand this nexus of affect we need to pay attention to symptoms that recur about a loss of unity of the nation—related to repression and renarrativization of religious histories within a modern Mexican nation. This nexus of affect points to a desire for a project of Catholic citizenship as the basis for the unity of both the Mexican nation and the Catholic family, both of which have been, and still are, contested. Read in this context, the Virgin of Guadalupe is not just a symbol, where a signified connects to a historically changing signifier, but also a field of forces. The space of fantasy, the social imaginary, and Catholic rhetorical and discursive practices become a field of forces and affect mobilized by and through the Virgin of Guadalupe. This field exposes a phantomatic unity of the family and the Mexican nation.[51]

If we approach it in these terms, then, any specific mobilization of the Virgin of Guadalupe cannot be understood only as a set of Catholic pedagogical practices but also as an ambiguous excess of signification. Thus we need to pay attention to the circulation of affect and the related social energies that are condensed and dispersed in religious, and in this case transnational, performances. As I have shown, this condensation and dispersal of these social energies exposes remainders of, for instance, the birth of a nation, as forces and histories that are never fully articulated, but that are nevertheless present in the form of anxieties, traces, desires, and symptomatic presences. Thus, a rethinking of affective religious histories is at play in migrant itineraries, and the way these circulate as fields of forces contributes to a broader understanding of Marian cults and to a refining of our tools for analysis toward a more robust anthropology of Catholicism.

I hope it is clear by now that I use a political reading of histories that intersects migrant terrains and itineraries. In this, I use "itinerary" in a different way from the way Thomas Tweed uses the term. His view of religion as a "confluence of organic-cultural flows that intensify joy and confront suffering by drawing on human and superhuman forces to make homes and cross boundaries"[52] is problematic exactly because it tends to evacuate the situatedness and political force of these same religious practices. Although he also draws on the work of de Certeau, he draws on the line of "flows" and free circulation, whereas I focus on aspects of de Certeau's work that speak to the politics of alterity and the misrecognition of official histories that render invisible nonofficial ones.[53]

The conservative aspects of the celebration of the Virgin in Rome—for example, as a defense of a church seen under attack—contribute to enhancing values that constitute Catholic humanitas within the New Evangelization. In other words, in this way of being Catholic, one is loyal to the pope and to traditional Catholic beliefs about family, reproduction, and the primary role of the clergy. So Latin American transnational devotions in Rome not only decenter but also recenter the Roman Catholic Church.

All of this suggests pragmatic ways forward for studies of the relation between transnational religion and the religious practices of transnational migrants. First, we must attend closely to the role of states, which regulate movement and religious expressions and influence the magnitude and character of migrants' transnational religious practices. And so we should consider the ways in which "ordinary individuals live their everyday religious life across borders," and we should "explore the ways in which these activities influence their continued sending and receiving-country membership."[54] Second, we must focus on what I have termed a religious nexus of affects, which are closely intertwined with a symptomatic expression of the state and its unequal formations. Some transnational Marian studies have captured parts of this complexity, especially through an analytical lens of performance, emplacement, and labor, and some have rightly emphasized that, even in local celebrations, a translocal set of social and cultural practices is at play.[55]

Marian devotions in particular cannot fit easily into a modern view of the subject as a singular and individual domain.[56] Religious histories and national religious images are not always shared as a "common" identity,[57] but affectively they are revitalized or repressed at particular local conjunctures, while their effects and forces may be distributed across space and places differently, and they may shape multiple forms of subjecthood. So if Marian religious devotions are about the presence of the divine, the relationship between humans and the supernatural, and thus about "lived" religion, they should also be studied as a constellation of fragments that reemerge in histories that have been partially forgotten or have been abjected and peripheralized. The complexity of transnational Marian devotions and their political forces compels us to engage with these multiple analytical frames.

6.   *Enwalled*

Translocality, Intimacies, and Gendered Subjectivity

> The treatment of enclosure and confinement serves to refract
> aspects of imperial discourse about race, civilization, and place.
> —Dalia Kandiyoti, *Migrant Sites:*
> *America, Place, and Diaspora Literatures*

> You don't put things up on the wall.
> —Rosalinda, Ecuadorian migrant, Rome

In this final chapter, I explore intimate affective domains that emerge in the experiences of gendered migration. I analyze these in their continuity between religious and secular domains. As in the preceding chapters in this book, migration opens up questions of gendered affectivity and its relation to space, labor, histories, marriage, and memories. Here, however, I want to reexamine these questions through the figure—real and metaphorical—of walls, which I examine in connection with the conceptualization of migration and borders.[1]

My project in this chapter extends work I began in chapter 3, through the use of genealogies and histories, where genealogy "seeks to re-establish the various systems of subjection: not the anticipatory power of meaning, but the hazardous play of dominations,"[2] and where history is not a genealogy of origins, a metaphysical closure, but a dynamic of "intensity, lapses, extended periods of feverish agitation, fainting spells."[3] Paying attention, in a de Certeaunian mode, to the destabilizing work of details[4] as dynamics of affective intensity, I wish to counterbalance readings of transnational migration that are driven toward spelling out (sociological) categories that are too neatly conclusive.[5]

It is through affective qualities attached to figures of walls and skins, in both lay and religious migrants' lives, that parallel forms of becoming inter-

sect and are continuously remapped. Walls and skins are fields of potentiality as well as closure; this becomes acutely true in the paradoxical
reproduction of colonialism. The aspirations, dreams, tensions, closures,
and disappointments that stick to these dividing surfaces give shape to complex fields of affective forces that cannot be neatly confined to the Catholic
Church's concept of a culture of life as the base of migrants' experience.
When I discussed the Vatican's current positions on migration and its
understanding of transnational migration in the light of "humanity,"
"civilization," and the culture of life in chapter 1, I argued that these positions effectively erase the complexity and the gendered politics of migrant
intersubjectivity and the affective spaces I am presenting here.

This chapter continues this work by focusing on three differently situated groups of migrant women and their respective relations to walls.
These relations extend through differential spaces of intimacies produced
by specific relations between enclosure and translocality. To better understand migrant itineraries, a focus on biopolitical citizenship needs to be
combined with a focus on gendered affective labor. My interest here is in
fact with the affects that circulate between walls in the process of the
transformation of shared intimacies through the work of love, service/
care, and material/immaterial labor. Throughout this exercise, I wish to
bring up a tension between place and barriers/boundaries, and to tease out
some of the heterologies that manifest at that intersection.[6] Following this
vein, I hope to capture some of the traces of affect that make migrants
"endure also a future that never became present."[7]

Enwalled: Mixed Marriages

DECEMBER 2004

Lorinda's two-bedroom house is simple. It belongs to her brother-in-law,
and he will soon, in August, return to live here. She and Emilio, her
husband, pay six hundred euros a month for the place, although the price
for a flat like this in the San Giovanni area is around one thousand euros.
Housing is expensive in Rome. The walls are pure white, and she does not
like white walls: "They are cold." In a new house, she would love colorful
walls like those in Mexico, but her husband is horrified at the idea. She is
twenty-nine and married to a man who is more than twenty years her
senior; they have a child, Giacomo, who is three. She met her husband at
Termini Station, when she was sleeping there while visiting Rome from
Madrid, where she had a government grant to study for a master's degree

in politics and communication. Lorinda would have loved to go back to work for her beloved PRI (Institutional Revolutionary Party) in Coahuila (Monclova), north of Mexico City, but now she has to be distant from two of her loves: her mother and party politics.

She is very careful about cleanliness. She mops while I am sipping my coffee. I ask if I can help, but she refuses the offer; it's a gift to her, she says, that I am there, chatting, in the house. Her husband points out that she should do the mopping later. She jokes with him that Italian men marry Mexican women because they think they are more *sumisas* (submissive). Maybe. Her husband leaves for work. Although he is retired from the Italian railway company, he is now a waiter in the Roman catering business. This is very professional waitering, done as in the old times. He still pays regular alimony to his first wife and helps out with his two children, who are now grown up.

Lorinda's lower-middle-class in-laws are obsessed with cleanliness— "*todo en la casa es super-limpio, tienen miedo al polvo*" (all in the house is super-clean, they fear dust). With children it is the same: "*no jalan a los niños*" (they do not allow the kids to move around and about); the children have to dig their hands in the earth, "*son animalitos selvajes, que sientan la tierra, que sienta la vida, pero con los italianos no, no es así*" (like little wild animals, they should feel the earth, the life, but for the Italians no, it is not so). For Lorinda, the Italian mother is *chioccia* (henlike): "They suffocate their children, as it is always a no for this, because you could get a cold, no for that as you are going to get a stomachache."

Her in-laws are also obsessed with talking about money—or, better, with talking about the lack of it. That obsession is matched by consistent expenses on the care of the body. Her sister-in-law spends over three hundred euros a month on hairdressers and beauty parlors. It's kind of baffling—on this we both completely agree. Maybe, I think, if she was coming from the neighborhood of Lomas de Polanco in Mexico City she would not notice this, but if that were so, we would not be sitting down in this flat, in this part of Rome.[8] Some members of the family own the flats where they live and have managed to buy or contribute to one for their children. One of her sisters-in-law is now a housewife, but was a nurse a long time ago and has retired with a baby pension—one of the recent labor scandals of Italy.[9] The other sister-in-law is also a housewife, but, in Lorinda's words, no books, cinema, or culture is of any attraction to this class of women. For Lorinda, it's hard to find her place in this fishpond.[10]

Lorinda wishes she could find work, but every time she calls up an agency for a job she is turned down: "It is my accent; as soon as they hear that I am a foreigner, they do not want me." And she does not have the support of her husband on this—he does not help out with the care of the child, nor does he understand or support her aspirations. Lorinda thinks this is because he is afraid that she is more than a pinch better prepared and educated than he is. The battle is a long one.

There are two types of Italian women for Lorinda. One is the ignorant: "They do not know anything; they are gossips and *metiches* [invasive, nosy]." The other kind is educated, knows a lot, reads a lot, and treats you well: "When one arrives in Europe, one thinks that everybody is educated here, but this is not true; you do not expect to encounter such ignorant people." Some of these people think that, as foreigners, they marry for money, but Lorinda married for love. And still, Mexican women have approached Lorinda, both in Rome and in Mexico, about how they could "marry a good man" here.

BACK IN MEXICO, 2006–7

Lorinda tells me about the past year: She is now back in Mexico with her child, after a painful falling out with her husband over his relationship with her in-laws. The marriage is over. However, a few months later, her husband goes to live in Mexico, too. It did not take long for him to change his mind, but it is tough. She has started to work for PRI again, and she is, once again, starting from the bottom—she has lost ground by being away, but the ground is more easily regained than it would be in Italy. In Rome, she missed a richer social life, her outings to chain restaurants such as Sanborns or Vips with her female friends in Monclova.

Emilio is at home a lot in Monclova, and it is scorching hot. No more of the long, pleasant, wandering walks they used to take together in Rome. And in the winter, it is still boiling. They try an Italian catering venture. They are both hard-working and generous people—too generous—and the top-notch parmesan they buy here is too expensive. The red in their accounts balloons. Despite their love for *mamacita,* who speaks to Emilio in Span-Italian, it is time to move back to Rome. Once they are there again they have to buy new furniture to resettle. No savings left.

LORINDA AND THE SUBURBS, NOVEMBER 2007

I visit them in their temporary flat in Rome. It takes a long time to get there from the terminal metro station of Rebibbia. It is another half an hour—and traffic is heavy. The bus to get there is infrequent, so Emilio drives us. Even before we arrive, I sense that Lorinda's wandering spirit feels really trapped in this flat. Trapping is part of an affective map. With this I refer to a sense of dependence on their partners that women like Lorinda experience in immigration to Rome, where reasonably paid employment for mothers like her is difficult to find.

The block is rather isolated and run down. The building company promised a set of stores on the ground floor of this suburban block of flats that were never built. In place of the promised stores are huge concrete holes, partly covered in graffiti and with half-built door frames with no glass—one of the many symptoms of a process of the ruination of the suburbs.[11] Lorinda complains that it is cold and damp here. The flat is tiny, and they had to divide the sitting room with a partition to create a separate space for their child to sleep. The flat belongs to another one of Emilio's brothers, who will need it again soon. As in the previous apartment, they cannot put anything on the walls. Lorinda also feels that Emilio's niece, who is expecting a child and lives next door, visits too often. Emilio's niece has been diagnosed with multiple sclerosis, and Lorinda thinks her parents have given them this temporary flat because it is far away and so, somehow, they can keep an eye on a pregnant woman whose health is uncertain.

They prepare me a wonderful, elaborate meal while we talk about losing weight—Lorinda has put on more than a few pounds, and it has exacerbated a problem with her knees and hip joints. She still wants to find a job, and Emilio's words seem to have mellowed. She is now enrolled in a local program and spends two mornings a week working to pass the exam of *terza media* (middle school). Going back to school is more than a first step. Lorinda cannot wait to leave this flat.

Beyond the Suffering Mother

MAY 2008

We manage to meet one last time at Termini Station for a long coffee on the day before I return to Toronto. We talk about the fact that the working situation has not improved for migrant women, although it is the same for Italians, too. I know she has been attending a few gatherings of the Comunidad Católica Mexicana but with some reservations. We dialogue about the class and racial divides that permeate the Comunidad Católica Mexicana, as she sees they were performed on the Sunday of the Día de las

Madres. She remarks that "algunas mujeres llegaron con su piél, pero después se relajaron y devinieron mas aprochables [some women arrive here guarded (lit., with their skin), but then they relax and become more approachable]."[12]

Emilio has turned 180 degrees and supports her much more. She comes to a full realization that she will never make a living here from her interest in "reading up" and *periodismo* (journalism), but will have to do something more practical, such as opening a small food business—she loves cooking. Food and nation occupy our conversation. She talks about Mexican delicacies and the sacrality of the nation, while Italians have the first but not the second—why do they not sing hymns at school? I am wondering why she is pointing this out now.

There has been a major falling-out within the family. Her husband does not talk to his sister anymore. They were eating at the old mother's house on a Sunday, and she came out with a racial remark, but more vehement than ever, that immigrants should go back home and should not dirty Italian soil. Lorinda could not stand it anymore. She recalls getting up from the table, as an immigrant too: "*El unico que tengo es mi dignidad y tu en fruente de mi no puede decir esto!* [The only thing I have is my dignity, and you cannot say this to my face]." The walls trembled with more heated exchanges. Emilio was furious with his sister; that would not have happened a few years ago. Things have changed. The tensions with the in-laws have never been so high. Lorinda also mentioned that when Emilio fell ill with the Legionnaires' disease, a form of pneumonia, a year after he returned from Mexico for the first time in 2002, they insisted that he must have contracted it in Mexico. She is still scarred by the unfounded remark; you forgive but do not forget. Those marks engrave the veins of mixed marriages.

LORINDA'S NEW FLAT, NOVEMBER 2008

Emilio still does not speak to his sister, and the walls are now a bright patchy orange—signs of an emerging independence, recognition, and the vitality of life. To an untrained eye, these walls look unfinished, but they are painted using a typically Mexican technique called the *esponjado*. You dip a sponge in the paint and then press it onto the wall in seemingly unfinished but regular strokes. It looks very bright, and I think how unique it must be in this area of Rome, imagining the interiors of the many apartments in the unending rows of blocks that can be seen from the open window of this top flat overlooking Arco Travertino. This is actually the flat of Emilio's ex-wife; more precisely, it is the apartment that Emilio and his ex-wife once shared and that was left to her when they separated. They pay only 750 euros a month. Lorinda loves her walls. Now she would not exchange them for anything in the world. Well, maybe for a little more household help. Her life back in Mexico would have been more middle-class, but definitely anchored to very long hours of work and less time spent with her son. Her orange walls are bittersweet.

The sweetness. Emilio is now supportive of her looking for a job. She is actually setting up a business to home-deliver handmade piñatas around the city. It has become a rather popular addendum to kids' birthday celebrations in town. By setting up a web page and doing some market research, she hopes eventually to open a space for children's events. The bitterness. She loves to be out and about, to eat in the *calle* (street), and sometimes to eat kebabs around the corner. But if her husband is off work, no way. As a traditional popular Roman, he wants his meal ready at home—why eat out, what for? Better at home. She knows she will not see eye to eye with him about this. But, maybe, the orange is bright enough.

ON THE BUS TO PARIOLI, MAY 2009

Lorinda and I are on a bus on the way to the upper part of Parioli to deliver a piñata. The piñata, which is stuffed inside a gray rubbish bin and strung with metallic wire, is rather bulky and heavy. It takes us over an hour on the bus, asking directions. We see a hefty Latino woman getting off the bus; her midriff is bare. Lorinda does not wear clothes that bare her midriff; women who are actually Mexican here do not do that, she insists. This is what distinguishes them from the other Latina women here. A piñata wrapped up and a belly exposed. "*Somos mujeres decentes y con estilo* [we are decent women and with style]." Lorinda also got a *piel y no se relaja*—she has a thick skin and does not let herself be taken off guard.

A new phase of life: Lorinda has applied to a program for immigrant women launched by an organization called Risorsa Donna, a World Bank program. The program, DIPA (Donne Immigrate: Percorso per un Autonomia), has, since 2004, promoted the integration of pilot groups of skilled, immigrant businesswomen into the Roman labor market.[13] It is clear to Lorinda that the only way to make it here is to exploit her practical, creative capacities: "*el trabajos de mis manos, no mis estudios y experiencia en la política* [the work of my hands, not my studies or political experiences]." She is really happy with this program and sad that so few migrants know about it. She is the only Mexican there. In a series of meetings, they have assessed her capacities and she has been offered a three-month course to learn about budgeting, legal, and managerial skills to assist her to open a small business here in Rome. The dream of the kids' party space seems closer. And if that does not work, her husband is trying to get a license to open a bar in a nice villa close to where they live, while she has put down her name as a substitute teacher of Spanish for secondary schools. Plans A, B, and C. She is settled now—in her plans.

Her mother-in-law is now in love with her. Lorinda takes Giacomo, her son, to see Emilio's mother once a week in the house she shares with her older daughter and husband, who are living with the old woman in order to leave their other flat to the daughter who has (still mild) MS. The eighty-eight-year-old woman cannot stand the situation, but the house is technically owned by her daughter. Now Lorinda is not the only one to have the experience of being an outcast in her own home. Even if it is not a wonderful intergenerational bond of solidarity, the much improved relationship is a source of relief and a laugh for Lorinda. How things have turned around.

When I tell Lorinda that I want to write about her and her walls, she quickly and fondly remembers a movie with Salma Hayek, *Fools Rush In*, a 1997 romantic comedy. The main WASP character Alex (Matthew Perry) comes back home to find that his once beige flat in suburban Las Vegas has been painted in bright tints by his Chicana girlfriend (Salma Hayek) and her family, who have recently moved in. Changes of colors tint spaces of differential intimacies.

Mexican transnational marriages, at least in the United States, have shown that there is an increase in the impulse to be compassionate and sharing. Documented as an effect of having assimilated aspects of "modern" subjectivity, such as increased independence, marriages become sites for renewed female bargaining agency.[14] Mixed marriages can be brightly colored and contain the kernels of conflicts. Those are conflicts around what Sara Ahmed calls the *narcissistic love* of a nation that celebrates diversity as part of a (forced) unity—the love of the nation is a unitary ideal.[15] Lorinda's case shows the partial (in the sense of temporary) failure to resettle and highlights not only that Italianness is problematic but that Mexicanness is too. Two countries renowned for their emigrants feed the love of their nations out of a failure to retain some of their citizens. They may celebrate this centripetal national tendency in poetic forms, but there is still a failure at stake.[16] However, migration processes are also potentially creative affective spaces, where national ideals are not only broken down but are actually cut, pasted, and reassembled.[17]

Lorinda's story contains some aspects of a tension between enclosure and translocality in the transnational migrant process. On one hand, there are translocal imaginaries and places of memory, the bright walls and the trips to Sanborns with friends. On the other, these tensions contain traces of a colonial power, the transformative forms of historically racialized and class stereotypes that (still) mark forms of exclusion in the everyday life of migrants. Lorinda's story tells that one's own paint on a home's wall may fade or one may not be allowed to paint the walls in the first place, as otherness, "being different," may painfully stick to the skin of migrants within the intimacy of family meals. Yet there is transformation.

Lorinda's itinerary points to tensions between a space/life of transformation (the potentials of a life in Rome rather than her home city of Monclova) and the aliveness of translocal images of coloniality (her racialized encounters within intimate spaces of Italian families), where class distinctions, race, and gender divisions are subtly inscribed. A migrant spatial reality emerging at Rome's peripheries that has fallen out of the Italian dream of prosperity is marked by regulatory ex-closures. There may be no regular bus service to take you back home, and the dwellings there are dumpy and often overpriced. But if there is space for colorful walls, that space can be conquered, willfully and day by day, in a dynamic negotiation internal to the intimacy of the family and kinship relations. It is at the intersection of intimate and public that the battle for labor and gender recognition for married Mexican women in Italy is being fought.

Whenever possible, Lorinda attended the celebration of the Virgin of Guadalupe at the Church of Nostra Signora di Coromoto, although she is critical of some of the clerical postures, and especially of the Legionaries of Christ (she used to work for the PRI press agency in her town of Monclova, so her anticlerical attitude is no surprise.) The nation is not only symptomatically present in the celebration of the Virgin of Guadalupe, but it is lived here through particular ethical intersubjective positionings ("we respect the older people in Mexico") that are colored through a *no dejarse* (do not give in) struggle for a space of visibility in Italian culture and society. The tensions in Lorinda's household are as much about a transformation of shared intimacy as they are about class repositioning and the gendered language that has to first be fostered and then mastered in these negotiations.

These tensions are also about intertwining Catholicism into her migrant itinerary. While hanging together in Rome in May 2011, Lorinda shared new histories about her growing involvement with the life of the local

Catholic parish, which allowed her to meet more Italians and widen her social network. It also allowed her to negotiate some aspects of gender positioning beyond the immigrant Catholic image of the *mujer sufrida* (suffering woman) championed by the MLA (Latin American Mission).

Her reality resonates with that of other Mexican women who have married Italian men in Rome, and their communalities emerge not so much from being "authentically Mexican"—there are too many class and racial divisions and forms of distinction for a collective authenticity—but from a sense of the communal vulnerability they share. They are affected by, rather than merely subjected to, the movement of migration in terms of "a common experience of displacement and fractured reality";[18] there isn't a unitary experience of intimacy and belonging.[19] In this respect, the affective fields of intimacy have more "forms, fits, materialities,"[20] and, I would add, colors on the walls, than a normative, Catholic semantic of migrant intimacy and its culture of migrant recognition allow for. Mixed marriages thus become a revealing staging ground where an affective multiplication of intimacies and differences confronts a liberal and Catholic dream of equality. When migration is the cradle of the culture of life for the Catholic hierarchy, a Catholic reading of the culture of life can turn into a hegemonic force attempting, but never succeeding, to achieve an ideal and to resolve the never-ending differences.[21]

Enwalled: Badanti

JULY 2009

We are walking toward the back entrance of the Coliseum metro station with a group of around ten Peruvian women and men, *compañeros de la Iglesia*, giggling and chatting. We have just left a local park where a number of Latin Americans meet on Sundays to play volleyball and soccer and to eat inexpensive homestyle food. Parks are the cradle of "freedom" and contention in the transformation of Roman urban space. They chart a fine, and often embattled, line between a Rome as *Capi Mundi* and *Kaputt Mundi* (leader of the world and the end of the world)—the visible limits of a sophisticated episteme of integration (*integrazione*).

Now in her early forties, Magdalena has been in Italy on and off since 2002. She explains to me that you can be lucky in a house, have your bathroom, too, but there are *nonitas* (an endearing Spanish-Italian word for grandmothers) who do not want you to use the bathtub. Your bedroom might actually be a storage room. Even worse, your bed might be a fold-out couch in the sitting room. The friends walking with us are enjoying *la libertad*. They peek, dash, and creep out of the houses where they live during the long part of the week. Living-in is not a joke. A woman has arrived late at Mass today because the nonita always asks her something when she is at the point of leaving. Sometimes they ask for coffee when you are well into your afternoon break. The dictates of the rhythm of older people has a real hold on the daily and sleeping routines of live-in caregivers.[22] These interuptions make temporal boundaries even more porous than spatial ones.

A nail or a tack on the wall is a boundary trespassed. You may have to leave the house soon, so you had better be ready. Under these conditions of precariousness, holes are signs of possession. Magdalena had worked for a family in Parioli for over two years. The patrons were both screenwriters and helped her file her residency papers in the 2007 *sanatoria*[23]—they were *gente muy buena* (very good people). Two years later, Magdalena is still waiting for her *permesso di soggiorno*. The father of the two that Magdalena cares for is a bit absent-minded, and when *la signora* was away for work Magdalena has to be doubly vigilant—in her words, he is a third child to care for. A friend replaced her when she needed to go back to Peru. Replacement is a must among migrants who are maids, child caregivers, or *badanti*, but it is a murky business, always risky, for the employers might not like your replacement, or they might like them too much. There was no more work with her employers when Magdalena returned from Peru; the replacement got the permanent job. Magdalena is still sad about it.

Magdalena is a devoted Catholic, and she has been coming to the Latin American Mission since she came across it in 2004. For her, the house walls are *protección, alegría, sufrimiento* (protection, joy, suffering). They become the materialities of the burden of another person's household: "At times you feel you are carrying these walls and your head is bursting with headache because of all the problems one has, but you call on Him, who is always with us, and the walls are less heavy, and sometime, if you are happy, they share your joy."

When Magdalena arrived in Rome in 2002, she did not want to go out. She lived in the barrio close to St. Peter's, and she recalls that an older man living nearby kept following her while she was out on little shopping trips for *la signora*. Another man stopped her while she was going to church: "I suffered from *nervios*[24] for a week, a strong headache from the fear; I thought that the man was going to kill me, and I could not speak with anybody about it." The parish of Santa Maria della Luce has been her family ever since, where she gets recharged. Hence the Scalabrinian order plays a role in maintaining one form of porosity of other walls, or in women's peeking through the windows. The walls of the church are still damp, but there is now sun outside.

I have known Magdalena for a few years now. We have walked to the city center, many times enjoying ice cream. Now our relationship has changed: We sit down at a café in Santa Maria in Trastevere—not at McDonald's.[25] I first met her when she said she was used to always having a *maleta* (suitcase) ready to go to leave her place of work. As a badante, or a live-in caregiver, she is constantly on the go—the nonitos may become too aggressive or make unwanted sexual advances; the older couple can turn despotic over the organization of your work time and ask you to wear polished white maid dresses (in their posh houses) with hair tied back and no makeup. This is a disciplining of the female body that positions a few young migrants on one side, and the more educated on the other find it painful to reconcile in the mirror. It is not easy to come in and out of new skins; skins are pride, boundaries, and memories.

The maleta, though, can be the hope for a new skin. These are the words of Alma, a well-educated Peruvian woman who arrived in 2006 to support her two children through university in Lima. She has moved through many different families, sometimes to the bewilderment of her friend in the mission; it is a long story about one of the too many elderly and frail nonitos dead in her care. Or maybe it is because of what she should not have seen in the posh flat of a couple living in Piazza Flaminio, where she was employed for two months—many dinner parties at home, cocaine in the woman's suit that was to be taken to the drycleaners, a missing diamond watch (she spent a few days frantically trying to find it, finally finding it in another suit). When the lady of the house fell into a depression because she was no longer in her accustomed inner circle, Alma decided to leave. These migrant women may have been the unwilling witnesses to the everyday acting out of a beauty-and-the-beast social imaginary of the Italian Berlusconi era.[26]

Magdalena has now taken up a second job for a year to pay for her upcoming visit to Peru; she starts at two on Saturday and is finished at eight in the evening on Sunday—she is living *puertas afueras* (living out). Now she shares a flat with a cousin in the suburbs along the Via Flaminia; however, it takes hours to get back from the center of Rome. The flat where she currently works is large; *la signora*, in her forties, and her husband, the owner of a hotel chain, have another five-and-a-half-days-a-week maid and need Magdalena's help when the other is off. And *la signora* is always worried that something is out of place in the flat, and tells Magdalena time and time again about closing the downstairs entrance door to the building well.

Double shifts, double commitments. Magdalena is also paying a mortgage, three hundred and seventy euros a month for five years for a plot of land in a suburb of Lima. She wants to build her dream there, a small pharmacy for her daughter. This is also an investment plan, and a future option to generate rent money. Her daughter, in her mid-twenties, has come twice to work in Italy, but now is back in Peru and has started a family. This is also a change for Magdalena. Since I met her, she has become more managerial in her migrant strategies. She is not drained anymore by her hopeless ex-husband. Good, I think, she is settled now—in her heart.

To decorate a room is like staking out territory and a politics of visibility.[27] A focus on maintaining the borders of homely spaces (in the sense of feeling at home) is a way to balance an otherwise overwhelming condition of spatial and temporal precariousness. Walls are walls: They cannot be moved. They can be knocked down, but it takes work, and it takes more work to build them up again. Walls are literal signs and the excess of signification of situated politics of home and away, where home is both an exclusionary space and a space of mutual recognition.[28] I am intrigued with how Latin American caregivers not only perform a labor of love, but how existing imaginative geographies and inscribed temporalities together create walls that "affective claims and relations simply do not cross."[29] I am interested in walls and bounded intimacies as affective fields of object-subject relations, which index not only forms of invisible servitudes but also transformative potential.

The productiveness of migrant women is a transnationally produced fantasy. If Latin American female migrants in Rome are hired for the particular self they carry (good with children, Catholically devoted to elder care, clean), in fact, they are hired for what they can become in the eyes of their employers.[30] Some mold themselves better than others—some stay longer, some leave. The evangelization and the socialization that takes place in the Latin American Mission inscribes these women in multiple ways. On one hand, they become better subjects of enduring suffering; on the other hand, the mission provides forms of sharing and negotiating work that otherwise would be difficult for individual migrants to achieve.

An unintentional side effect of Scalabrinian evangelization is that the church is providing migrant women a network for sharing information that makes them more savvy in how to negotiate with their employers by using tactics such as silence, misinformation, and "lying." "Lying" plays an important role in migrants' lives and cuts across gender divisions. Maria, from Ecuador, has come to the MLA saying she has just arrived and, quite anxiously, that she has no place to go for the night. After a short interview with her, the Italian nun who is helping at the front desk of the MLA that day anxiously calls Catalina, the housekeeper, but Catalina is not in. She really needs advice on what to do with this poor woman in need. A place is found for Maria for the night, and a potential employer for the following day as well, but when Catalina has a talk with the woman a few days later; it is clear to Catalina that the woman has been in Rome for much longer than she said, that she was not in as desperate a need as she portrayed, and it also came out that Maria actually had a sister living in Rome. She concealed much information from the nun working at the desk. As Catalina puts it:

> Italian people, and even the religious nuns and seminarists working here at the MLA, do not know how to read us migrants. You should never take a word for granted, but you should look at a whole series of things, how the person talks, how she is dressed, who she knows, what she cooks, her cellular phone. . . . We know how to read those signs among ourselves.

However, "lying," or concealing, has a different moral valence for these migrants than it has for the priests working with them. If concealing information or misrepresenting is an ordinary act in the everyday life of some of these men and women, for the priests it is a moral flaw in the character of the Latin American migrants. But migrant "lies" and concealments are somehow forms of enwalling, of enclosing what may be difficult to guard. Read in parallel to an intimate sphere, where physical intimacy and privacy are often hard to set up for these migrants, concealments play a role of guarding, and a certain power of separation.

In a long conversation I had with Padre Alfonso, the Italian Scalabrinian *Capillano* (chaplain) of MLA, who had lived for long time in Argentina, he says:

> The pastoral of the migrants here is a centered on problem resolution. . . . The pastoral with the Brazilians is especially with the youth, with the Spanish-speaking, it is more a female pastoral; the feminine figure is at the center. They are adventurers, not in that sense [meaning sexually],

but they do it for improvement [*riscattarsi*], for their children, their families, they try . . . . But for the Latina women there is no youth; they pass too quickly from puberty to wanting to have kids and a partner; they do not live the stage of doing things together with friends, of having fun, since they think their mother had a kid at sixteen so they can at eighteen. . . . But the real problem is the ambiguity [*ambiguità*]; hence you tell them something, to tell this or that to their [prospective] employer, and they say, yes, yes, but when they arrive they say something else; they say they do not want to work as a live-in maid, but they want to work for hourly wages; so it is difficult. On the top of this, they sell work, and they do not tell us. If they have more than one [job], they give it to another woman for a price. . . . However, women are courageous, more than men, but they suffer from solitude which is affective, moral, and spiritual [*solitudine che e' affettiva, morale e spirituale*]; they have a circumstantial faith. They live with a fragility of affects, and they also give their bodies for money.

If domestic workers, and especially live-in workers experience a disjunction between home and family,[31] then boundary-making has a profound effect on subjectivity and the art of concealment. Spatial and narrative boundaries intertwine here: If you cannot put a nail up, then you can attempt to control through "lying." While making up temporal narratives, one may well be trying to counterbalance spatial forms of being subjected and navigate those vulnerabilities. From this perspective, "lying" can be about faith too. A protection of one's own intimate space, secret and sacred, is maintained within a community of fellow migrants by shared secrecy and codes: Faith and concealing may have more in common than we think.

However, these tactics are not the only forms of ambiguity lived by domestic workers, nor are they mere reactions to spatial restrictions. Space and its appropriation show a migrant's ambivalence toward transiency and the temporality of relations,[32] an ambiguity in the continuity of one's own personal narrative. Hence the lack, to a lesser or greater extent, of this continuity is not an exception, but rather it is constitutive of the ambiguous everyday matrix of subject formations for Latin American migrants attending the Catholic Mission in Rome.

Enwalled: Mexican Nuns

These are thick walls. My mobile phone does not pick up a signal. It is cool and damp even though we are already in May. On the wall of my room and in other parts of the convent there is a representation of the cross of the Apostolate, which is a nineteenth-century version of the Sacred Heart. Adela explains that it is an upright cross, a living cross that comes from the heart. It has thorns and smaller crosses over it; these are the sins of the priests, and nuns pray for them, dedicate their life to them. I am living in the Roman home of a nineteenth-century Mexican female order, with six wonderful women between thick walls of a sixteenth-century palace. This is now the home of the male Mexican order of the M.E.S., which hosts the Mexican female order of O.J.S. formed in 1924 and officially founded in 1937 by a French Father F.J.R. to assist the M.E.S.[33]

The female order to which these women belong has been in this house in Rome for twenty-five years, but the house has a much longer religious history. St. Paul is said to have lived around the corner in this neighborhood of La Regola, and in 1834 this palace came into the hands of the Order of Minime of St. Francis of Paola. However, because that order lost vocations, the house was sold to a male Mexican order, which was then escaping from religious persecution in Mexico during the Cristero War. With the help of an Irish sponsor, T.F., the founding father of this order, bought and secured this house as the refuge in Rome for the order in 1926. This house is, then, yet another Mexican presence in Rome born out of traces of the Cristiada.

Many chores need to be done during the day, particularly taking care of the bodies and souls of male priests who reside on the upper floors of the house. We always eat in the basement, with no natural light, watched over by two huge china vases, and a bust of the founder in storage in this dining area. The air is stifling—nearly gluey. We are underground, a few yards away from a very busy tourist street that leads to the Campo de Fiori, where a painful historical mistake of the church is catching the often distracted gaze of tourists—a statue of Giordano Bruno, a Dominican friar and astronomer burned at stake by the Inquisition in 1600. And we share a massive wall with a tucked-away little square where another less spectacular, but nevertheless painful, chapter related to the history of the church is memorialized. In 1604, the Monte di Pietà was a pawnshop, built by the Franciscans and Pope Clement VIII. It stands today as a reminder of a history in which Jews were condemned to "immoral" economies by the Catholic Church. A thickness of affective traces leaks in through the sometime porous, sometimes too thick walls and eats with us at the dining table covered with a plastic cloth arranged with natural and plastic flowers—aesthetic sensibilities of a life in a Mexican pueblo.[34]

Each day we need to prepare food for over thirty people. I start to bring down one of the many cases of food left weekly by the deliveryman on the ground floor. Rosa Maria, a nun from Monterrey, gently approaches and whispers that I shouldn't do that chore. I am puzzled, but as a good anthropologist I bring the crate back to where I found it. Still puzzled, I rinse the salad. Rosa giggles and with her northerner accent says, "If we do it, the padres get used to it and that's it; they pretend they become used to us doing it." Here we are: tactics of gendered labor relations in practice. Mexican nuns and Latin American *badanti*: With veils or without, they all need to set up as well as trespass boundaries.

This gendered negotiation is a public secret among the clergy, and it is often portrayed to outsiders in terms of female heroism. Padre Hector, an intelligent and informed Mexican diocesan priest from Orizaba, in Veracruz, says,

> The women are the strong hands in Mexico and so they are here. The religious sisters here live off their rents, but women here in Italy do not go into religious orders, so the orders receive new blood from Mexico. For example, the order of the A.P.—they now have six Mexican nuns in Ischia, two in Castellamare, and some in the convent at the headquarters in Rome. Or the same for the order of S.S.M.A. in Chioggia. Now they have vocations in Chioggia who are running the convent, who are from Veracruz! The Italian nuns are very old. This *el pago de la evangelización* [payback of evangelization], these nuns come back with the gospel. The more middle-class nuns in Mexico go to orders that are expert in education, but the others from more working-class [backgrounds] often end up here, to take care of the older Italian sisters. They are heroic nuns.

But where there is heroism there is often strife. The evening before I leave the convent, Madre Consuelo, the superior of the house, shares what has been burdening her. She closes the door. They are at war. War is permeating these walls, not only dampness. It's a historic war. They call it negotiation of labor between diocesans and religious orders and between gendered religious orders. They are at war with the padres of the house. She would like to negotiate a new and better three-year contract with them, but her superior in Mexico "doesn't want to hear [about it]." Her superior does not know the real prices of *zapatos* (shoes) in Rome, and Mother Consuelo has to juggle with the bookkeeping—not to go into the red.

So Consuelo has told the nuns to take their time in doing the chores, to not iron too fast, to leave the mess the fathers may leave on display for longer, and to take time to study and eat more leisurely together. These are fallen words still for some of the nuns—for Consuelo is clear that doing too much weakens their collective labor position, and creates too much of a wrong love: "The fathers may give you more and more to do, but it is *hasta aqui* [up to here]." I love the wit in her eyes and the spirit of her voice. There is not only Sor Juana de la Cruz, but there have been scores of nuns taking on that battle in Rome from all corners of the world. The walls bounce memories back, even in a tucked-away basement. And there is wrong love, too:

El amor de cuando te pisotean, te aplastan y tu sigues serviendole, mas y mas también cuando pudieran hacerlo ellos mismos, y no dices nada, pero esto no es amor. [The love of when they step on you, they squash you and you carry on serving them, more and more even when they could do it themselves, without saying anything, but this is not love.]

Tensions of intimacy and servitude, in the past phrased as tensions between choir and servant nuns, has a long history from the time of the early modern monastic female communities.[35] The products of a post-Tridentine Roman Catholic discourse, such tensions are still a signature of religious labor and love.[36] The roots of servile love in the present day have multiple historical registers. In this case, not so much about a subjection to a mastery of personal care of upper-class nuns, servitude exposes a language of rights rather than duties. Duties immolate female work and sanctify it. That others have a right to use what is the property of a person as a labor-object is not sanctification, however, but a *tontería* (stupidity) for Madre Consuelo.

The line between amor and tontería is a fine one. And there is right love—the affective labor of praying. This order of O.J.S. is dedicated to the support of priests; it was founded in Mexico in the mid-nineteenth century with the specific aim of helping priests on their long road of priestly vocation. In Madre Consuelo's words,

What we do is strong. A nun has to love many who are in need, and sometimes this is very demanding. The priests take a long time in their formation, more than nine years, and after that we carry on following them so that they will be strong in their sacerdotal life, and we have to carry many of them. . . . This is another type of love; it is a vocation of the heart [*esto es otro tipo de amor, es una vocación del corazón*]. If you get married, you have only one family, but we, you do not know how many we have. And those who do not know us think we are lonely between these walls [*entre estas paredes*]. [She laughs.] Those poor people—they do not know we have so many [*y no saben que tenemos a tantos*].

The nuns then imagine their own migrant itineraries in terms of other forms of ambiguity, quite distinct from the heroic sacrifice explicit in Father Hector's words, and over different boundaries of family and intimacies. They speak also of religious families that do not work, and of intimacies that are shared, but at times also resisted.

But nuns do not only pray for priests, they also pray for *el amor de mi vida, que nunca fué* (for the love of my life that never was). These are the words of Adela. She grew up in a little village in the state of Jalisco, on the road to Colima. Dirt poor and the eldest of seven children, she fell in love at fourteen, and the bond was very strong. One day he told her to come and live with him, regardless of what her parents would say. That was a form of marriage proposal, in the pueblo's code. She recounts how she was set to do it, but then while stepping out with him at sunset with her heart beating and about to leave, her mother came down the road, unexpectedly, with a shawl on her head. The chance was lost; she never left with him.

Then he went to the States to try his fortune. When he returned to the village a year later, she had, in the meantime, heard the call and applied to enter the convent. A few years later, she was about to take the first perennial vows and had gone back to the village after a long while away. She asked his family if she could see him for the last time before marrying Christ—she knew he was married now with two children. "What, don't you know?" his sister said in a quiet voice; he had died in a car accident the week before.

Adela says she knew then that consecrated life was her true call, her true love; that death had strengthened her deed. But she has been praying for him since—every day of her life, she says. Nuns are, of course, not immune to earthly love. Loves left behind, loves met in prayers every day with an Archimedean precision; loves of distant lands and homely hearts. *Pero no son tontas* (but they are not stupid). With another nun, Ricarda, I discuss what the intimate root of love is and whether a missed earthly love is the root of *el amor en que te pisotean* (the love in which they walk over you). She replies that the root of that love is fear, it is like a "fear of your parents" when one was living in the pueblo. But out of that fear can also be born the opportunity of a vocation. Love is not that simple, and sometime you need to *cortar raices* (cut roots).

Consecrated life is also a land of discovery and *maletas* (suitcases). Some of the nuns' female friends, from the time they were growing up together in the villages, have married but gone backward. Those friends hoped for a better life, in bigger urban centers, with an education, and some found themselves tied down by difficult husbands, many children, and in *ranchitos*. Not the life of seeing different parts of the world that these nuns, in their way, live. This is a real option for women who have grown up in humble, rural, and semi-urban parts of Mexico. It is a vocation, and to them it is a liberation from the flimsy dream of a secular marriage. Although Mexican nuns are from relatively humble origins, their male diocesan counterparts in Rome often are not. Some of these men are *escogidos de sus diócesis* (chosen in their dioceses), and the most brilliant are the renewing blood of the "Club de Roma"—the crème de la crème of the Mexican church in Rome. If Mexican nuns of different orders mainly come to Rome to care for the priests or for older (often Italian) nuns, priests and seminarists come to care for their vocation, education, and career—gendered divisions of religious labor.

Nuns also have learned to wear *el hábito* earlier on their journey, though they may have shed some tears in the acquisition of such habits when they entered the order—tears of frustration. You have to learn to wear el hábito, Madre Consuelo repeats. It is all white, with a light cotton crinoline underneath, a tunic on the top, and then another tunic on top of that, open on the sides and kept together by two laced ribbons on each side. Their veil is black with white trim, and kept in place with some wiring that they pass underneath the trim. The heavy dress garment, with a collar that wraps around part of the neck, is the same in winter and summer. It's demanding to keep the hábito white and spotless. The nuns now are relieved, since the general of the order has recently allowed them to wear a gray dress when they travel or go on visits. However, their everyday life is married to this handmade, deceptively simple garment. Matilda explains that you need to learn to wear it and move accordingly. You learn to stir the food at some distance, to wash your hands so that you do not wet the sleeves. Consuelo, who entered the convent when she was fourteen and is now thirty-six, remembers that she used to wear short sleeves before entering, and liked flowered patterns.

If you stain it, you quickly rinse it—skills learned for a never-ending reproduction of an earthly grace. The white dress is also a source of pride. Of another order of nuns they know, who wear gray, they say,

It is easier for them to get around, and appear to be in order, you do not see the dirt on their dress, but if you get close to them you pick up sometimes the smell of fried cooking. It is a labor [*tienes que batallar*] to keep our dress clean and suffer the heat [*aguantar el calor*] in the summer, but we do not smell of cooking [as other nuns in gray or black clothes may].

The control of bodily smells and fluids is an acquired technique of a gendered body. Smell is an index of grace, too, although, historically, it was not always so.[37]

Hence in this place, walls and boundaries of gendered affective labor point to material details of everyday and heroic wars. Walls, religious habits, the circulation of odors become the material and affective struggles of servitude and the production of love(s) that stick to migrant women. If affects circulate between bodies and signs/objects, they also stick to the surface of certain religious bodies.[38] Their articulation involves histories of gendered labor too, of absence of recognition, of abjection of histories,[39] when reread in some clerics' perspectives as forms of "heroism."

In previous chapters, I have explored the transnational reproduction of the Mexican Catholic Church in Rome through traces of the affective reemergence of a history of the Cristiada and a church under attack, so to speak. In this chapter, I have shown ways in which (lay) immigrant female bodies—with a particular attention to the subject of skin(s) and walls—are racialized not only vis-à-vis a hosting Italian society but also in subtle ways within their same Catholic, migrant community. And I also have emphasized a reproductive gendered labor that nuns perform and a form of Mexicanness they embody.

These Mexican nuns pray for the well-being and vocation of the priests, for their strength in carrying on in the path, but with their affective labor and prayers they are also supporting a tumbling, national Mexico as well as the reproduction of the Roman Catholic metropolitan center. Although religious vocations of Italians are dying out, this transnational labor constitutes the reminder of a process of ruination of the traditional Roman Catholic core.

This female affective labor has different aspects. Praying is a conscious "respiration of the soul,"[40] but it is also the transnational reproduction of Mexicanness in Rome. This essentially affective labor of reproduction takes the form of, among others things, a hope to turn away evil spirits from Mexico, which had been attacked as the cradle of an outbreak of swine flu.[41] Affective labor is also a regimentation of the body as a technology of the self that is shaped by the gaze of other orders' stylistic choices (Rome has its religious Fifth Avenues after all). Moreover, the contractual labor negotiations that take place within the O.S.C. order (at least between the Roman house and the mother house in Mexico City) and between it and the male order of the M.E.S. that hosts them require an immaterial component. What is required of these women is not only the physical handling of the household chores but also daily prayer for the well-being of the male order.

If a study of the transnational reproduction of the Mexican and Latin American Catholic Church and its Latin American missions in Rome demands an anthropological inquiry into the situated unfolding of affective traces of histories, it also requires a refinement in our understanding of gendered subjectivity and the complexity of parallels, continuities, and tensions between fields of religious and lay transnational migration that are too often artificially divided. If the convent's walls defend those sisters from some of the riddles and racialization of current Italian and Roman policies on migrant citizenship, they nonetheless also reflect long histories of affective and immaterial labor that is today, perhaps more than ever, required by a care labor market that has become the common niche for female lay Latin American transnational labor in Rome.

If an ideal form of lay Latin American transnational caring labor is professed by the church missionary discourse as a female "heroic journey" in Rome, it is constantly interrupted by ambiguity, strategies of concealment, and stretching the time taken to carry out tasks between the walls of the convent. If religious transnational female vocations require a constant affective material and immaterial labor for both female and male orders' reproduction at the metropolis, they are also, as Father Hector would have it, heroic journeys. As such, they are marked by subtle wars over the division of labor. With this I refer to everyday modes of living and interaction carried out through delaying, deflecting labor, and animated by wrong and right loves: the *amores tontos* and *de verdad* (stupid love and true love).

By now I hope it has become clear that the labor of love required and often performed by Latin American lay female workers is in continuity and counterposition to that of some Mexican religious nuns in Rome. More than a decade ago, Bridget Anderson noted that domestic work is key to a productive and affective social reproduction, and that transnational migrant care work should be examined via biopolitical registers where intimacy, invisibility, and "intimate anonymity" are painfully woven together.[42] However, as we have also seen, care work can also become the affective platform for renewed and creative forms of subjectivity.[43] More than one story is often at stake.

Labor associated with guilt has made some Latin American migrants in Europe invest and spend little on themselves and focus much on remittances. Reproductive and productive capacities in care work positions are also often kept together by a sense of loyalty, not so much to the employers' family, but to the tradition of mother-care in the Catholic imaginary.[44] Mexican nuns in Rome also perform a labor of love, which is resisted and negotiated in resounding ways by their lay counterparts outside the convent walls. If church networks seem to provide a sense of belonging for lay migrants, especially where Catholicism is a minority religion in their own country,[45] at the geopolitical center of Catholicism, and today more than ever, pedagogies of santification, purification, suffering, and the cultivation of family are complied with as well as challenged by migrants' lives and their devotional rituals.

To conclude, I turn to a final short history, that of a woman who crossed between these imaginaries and labor worlds, which are legally kept apart by a Catholic Church that is still very much a state within a state in Italy, and therefore benefits from a different migrant legal status. This crossing signals an anxiety to be born again and to acquire a "new skin," which, as Lorinda suggested, is still an index of class inscription for Mexican women in Rome, but it is also a potential for transnational gendered explorations and affective openness.

Se Quitó el Hábito: *She Dropped the Habit*

Julia, once a nun living in a convent in Rome, has a warm smile and is good looking. I notice that the thick black eyeliner, drawn to emphasize her beautiful brown eyes, matches her shining, long, raven hair. From Guanajuato and in her later twenties, she had been in Rome for more than four years at the time I visited her at her house in the spring of 2007. She is among the few Mexican women I know who share a home with Italian friends—in her case, a colleague from work and the woman's disabled boyfriend. The flat is simple, on the ground floor of a 1950s-era building in a popular working-class neighborhood of Rome. Her room is tidy, decorated with colorful Mexican textiles, some small pieces of pottery, pictures of her *mamá*, and some makeup lying on one shelf. Julia learned about eyeliner two years ago. One winter back in Irapuato, in Guanajuato, and just after having left the order, her niece helped her choose the right earrings, matching clothes, and new mascara. She recalled crying at that time, since she did not know what to expect to see in the mirror. She still works as hard as she did when she was in the order, which sent her to study catechism and communication at the Gregorian University in Rome. However, a lingering thought to leave the order had become stronger and stronger. So she could not stay any longer, and finally she left.

She recalls that the vitality she had felt on entering the convent at fourteen had vanished by the time she left, leaving a ghostly sense of misunderstanding and a sense of awkwardness, mixed in with a fear of how her older sister, who was still in the order in Guanajuato that Julia had left, might have been intimidated. There is much shame that flows over nuns and priests who decide to leave their order; it is an uphill battle for a while. The strength Julia found to make this shift came in this way:

> My strength is due to the devotion to the Sacred Heart, but not in the manner of the nuns where I was [who were dedicated to the Family of the Sacred Heart], who kept on telling me don't do this, this is bad, or if you do this, this other will happen. But for me no, the Sacred Heart gave me joy, not fear. It gave me the strength to overcome fear.

And Julia has remained steady as she pushes to have her religious visa changed to a study visa. She is committed to completing her studies in nursing. She has been working in one of the private clinics that underpay irregular immigrant labor in the health sector, but she is happy and has a plan. She is also sending money back home to build a little house in Irapuato. Her Italian friends are caring for her; her flatmates share food brought back from their families in the south of Italy and help her fill out the never-ending papers that, she hopes, will legalize her status.

Julia is witty and bright and has been one of the pillars of the Comunidad Católica Mexicana. She realizes that there are friends there who have been here for longer, but they live behind their little shields. Their Italian is still not good, and even if they are hard-working and admirable, in her mind, they have never taken advantage of the opportunities that life in Italy offers. Here is a very deceptively fine, anxiety-ridden, solid, and exciting wall. It is clear that, for Julia, you are either on one side or on the other.

Two years later, she has earned her diploma, received a *contratto indeterminato* (permanent contract) in a private hospital in the center of Rome, and married Arnulfo, a Mexican man working reception in a hotel, whom she lives with in a tiny one-bedroom flat. The house in Irapuato is nearly finished; the eyeliner is still carefully penciled; and Rome has opportunities.

Epilogue

As one of millions around the world glued to their screens in the early evening of Wednesday, 13 March 2013, I watched Cardinal Jorge Bergoglio step onto the Vatican balcony facing Saint Peter's Square in his new role as Pope Francis. After a relaxed salutation to the crowd, his first move was to ask the multitude there and around the world for their blessing. In his new white attire, the tall man bent down gently, closed his eyes, and stayed silent. Only after that did he bless the masses. This gesture was historically unprecedented, the media rightly suggested later. While watching, I could not stop thinking of Father Joselito and the impromptu blessing and the laying on of hands that he received from the female migrants in Santa Maria della Luce.

Nor could I forget the awkwardness that some of those women expressed afterward; they worried that they had done something out of place. This awkwardness may or may not melt away in the transformations that this current and new papacy of Francis seems to promise, under the leadership of a man who has been chosen from "the ends of the earth." Hence the moment at the balcony, read by many as representing the humility of the new pope, also tells a larger story of the church as a passionate machine and the renewing apostolic wave of the Catholic Church through the first Jesuit pope, Francis.

One book's end is another book's beginnings. Researching and writing this book over more than a decade have challenged my thinking that the Catholic Church could be defined in terms of clear-cut camps. What appeared instead were multiple often not easy-to-read forces in the church, which Gramsci called, in 1924, *insidiosa e inafferrabile*.[1] Growing up in northern Italy in a household at once Catholic and anticlerical and then

---

Opposite: Virgin of Guadalupe hanging on a wall of a migrant's house

living in a *colonia popular* (low-income barrio) in Guadalajara in the early 1990s near a Jesuit house for seminarians, I have learned to hesitate when tempted by quick conclusions and to query the complexity of Catholicism—and migration. More than ever before, the Catholic Church is a key political subject in matters of mobility and ethics, and the multilayered experience of being Catholic today illuminates the conditions that shape transnational migration worldwide. This applies not only in the forms of practical interventions on migration that the Catholic Church, as an institution, articulates in national and local jurisdictions around the world. It also reflects the ways in which the Catholic ethics of service and refuge, homely and unhomely, shape localized and simultaneously global responses to transnational migration and politics. If I have shown how Catholic humanitas is both a principle and a practice at the heart of the Roman Catholic Church, then I have illustrated how the church fosters a duplicitous, often patronizing, pedagogy toward transnational migration and immigration in Italy—and possibly, I would argue, elsewhere. And by using the word *pedagogy*, I have stressed the role—often framed as a teacher/pupil, parent/offspring one—that the Catholic Church has had in shaping migrants' personhood.

On one hand, the Atlantic Return to the historical and geopolitical heart of the Catholic Church, especially by segments of its Latin American clergy, reignites a passion for Catholicism based on papal directives, the culture of life, truth versus relativism, and the importance of morals in Catholicism. To speak of a Catholic humanitas in this sense is to emphasize a *unitary humanitas*. This position conceives of migration through the prism of a heteronormative family and sexuality within wedlock as well as through a certain nervousness about non-Catholic immigration in Europe. This perspective on being Catholic is part of a long tradition that has married Roman civitas to Catholic liturgy. Championed clearly by Benedict XVI's interventions, and resonating with the orientation he has promoted in the church, this is a powerful and political understanding of Catholicism harbored in the timeless transmission of grace through the liturgy—beyond its transformation through historical encounters. To counterpose this perspective to the forms and the stakes promoted by Vatican Council II exposes the challenging role that migration—as a sign of the times—has played in this most recent and ongoing chapter of the church's history. In sum, one way of thinking about the contemporary church through the figure of an Atlantic return entails addressing the challenge that migration and immigration raises not only theologically but as a *political ontology*.

On the other hand, although this return is also apostolic and central to the current Catholic Church's project of the New Evangelization, it is indeed a pedagogical challenge and a challenge for church governmentality. Through the church's ambiguous political and symbolic investments in Latin American migrant imagined communities, migrants become a vessel for new blood in a Europe perceived as having cooled to the Catholic faith. Here transnational Latin American Catholic migration is a vital dynamism that can unify the church in its diversity—a new *afán apostólico* (apostolic eagerness).[2] This is a church perceived as composed of different cultures and modes of being Catholic but within the unified framework of the Catholic liturgy and sacraments. It is an emphasis on the multiple expressions of *humanitas* in a same Catholic Church.

Nonetheless, Catholic Latin American migrants in Rome struggle to be recognized, caught in the politics between diocesan territorial jurisdictions and the praxis of religious orders (Scalabrinians mainly, but Jesuits too). As Archbishop Marchetto remarked, the road to successful implementation of *Erga Migrantes Caritas Christi* at the diocesan level is still a long one. What is at stake in this unfinished project is a distinctly Catholic politics of visibility and the counterbalancing of the weight of gendered and racial histories, which get "stuck to the skin" of migrants. In some instances, these histories cannot be contained, pacified, or even addressed, by a perspective of the church that puts a culture of life at the center of a migrant catechesis. If this culture of life has been deployed theologically as a moral axiom beyond and above histories, it falls short of addressing the ethical encounters between differently gendered and racialized people and the affective and erotic transmissions that haunt the church.

This divergence is still part of a central tension in Catholicism. A debate on the nature of life has a long and dense history within the Catholic Church, one that can be conceived in terms of an ongoing tension between *modus operandi* (as the form of living) and *modus operatum* (the structured form, in the sense here of the given liturgy). The legacy of Benedictine and Franciscan monasticism in the twelfth and thirteenth centuries saw the primacy of a *regula vitae*, where rule and life came together. In these expressions of monasticism—centering the nature of ethics in forms, rhythms, and the temporalities of living rather than in the sphere of action—life had to be applied to the norm and not the norm to life.[3] As Agamben has suggested, this form of monastic living (associated with a radical rejection of property rights and the embrace of the "highest" poverty, as the right of use) was in continuous opposition to the "liturgical paradigm" championed by Pope John XXII[4]—the *opus operatum* of the divine economy, of the Heavenly Church, so to speak.[5] So papal interventions on the importance of liturgy, to which Benedict XVI has contributed, have a long history of framing labor, faith, and property. This is because to favor a modus operatum over a modus operandi is to privilege "the" truth of the Catholic Church, the timelessness of its teaching and the centrality of the pope to the church.

Nonetheless, we can see that contemporary transnational expressions of faith do not fully "fit" into liturgy—as an opus operatum. In fact, as I've argued, lay and religious works create, in very different ways, affective spaces that are in turn racialized and gendered in ways that complicate received notions of Catholic family and love. More than ever in Rome, and among the heavily female and feminized labor force, there is a struggle for recognition of a heterodox model of family. Betrayals within and of the family are central to many migrant itineraries in Rome, so often generated out of a need for erotic attention, touch, and a sense of the familiar; these are often in conflict with the church's axiomatic conceptions of the family. Twenty-first-century migrants are not thirteenth-century monks, of course; but I argue in this book that it important to understand transnational migration and the Catholic Church within this long history of Catholicism and labor. In short, for the Catholic Church this is embedded in a long-time tension between the modus operatum (as the given liturgy) and the modus operandi (as the form of living) of Catholicism.

This is why I have favored migrant *itineraries* rather than a study of migrant *communities*. I have argued in this book that we need to move beyond studying how religious memberships are tied to particular national immigrant groups and associations as well as the waxing and waning of those memberships. Instead, I have explored how a long history of local and national narratives, affects, fantasies, and material devotions orient our understanding of migration as a multilayered articulation of the homely and the unhomely. In this sense, I have sought to apprehend migrant itineraries in terms of Catholicism's problematic intersection of bodies, histories, labor, and devotion. Based on this analysis, I hope migrant itineraries can further our analysis of migration, whether in relation to religion or not, beyond an unhelpful divide between the psychology of agency of migrants and the economic and political contexts of migration.

Carnality is a key theological hinge in Catholicism and in Catholic migrant itineraries. It has been part of a long durée of the afán apostolico: Although central to being Catholic, as the history of Jesus reminds us, carnality has also been feared by the clergy as the site through which earthly emotions might come to rule us (see the Sacred Heart). Being Catholic in migrant itineraries is less about being converted by listening to the word of the Gospel or the conundrum of making the divine present—as is the case in different forms of evangelical Christianity—but more about being *touched* by, being harbored in, and finding the homely (or the unhomely) in the materiality of devotions to, for example, the Virgin of Guadalupe, the Señor de los Milagros, and the Sacred Heart. Carnality encompasses the mystery of the divine nature of Christ's human body, as it is a force that produces and contains affects and attachments between people.

Transnational migration highlights different *almas* (souls) of the church, which overlap and contrast at times. I have traced the way that notions of migrants as sacrificial carriers of the Catholic faith expose the heavy influence and investment of the Roman clergy in the collective identity of migrants. Beyond the obvious problems, the church also often fails to recognize the diversities and tensions within the migrant churches. Groups such as the Comunidad Católica Mexicana, though deeply Catholic, refuse to rehearse the sacrificial and in practice enhance a sense of Catholic as the festive national. And the religious Mexican national also becomes, as I have shown, a terrain of political contention in Rome.

Pontifical, diocesan, and religious orders' responses to migration and immigration are often more critical of each other than it appears at a first glance, especially in relation to the church's position vis-à-vis changing state legislation on migration in Italy—immigration policy that still privileges jus sanguinis over jus soli. A part of the church, which is close to a sensibility of Catholic humanitas as Roman civitas, tends to align with those who champion aspects of anti-immigration and legislation that criminalizes immigration. Interestingly enough, this soul of the church, given concrete form in figures such as Cardinal Angelo Sodano, has also been immersed in the less then legal financial economy of the IOR (Instituto per le Opere Religiose), the Vatican financial institution. This book mentions this aspect of Vatican involvement in parallel economies only in passing; another whole book would be needed to address that issue.

Against the background of a Catholic Church that emphasizes the sanctification of the migrant on a suffering journey, gendered migrant stories are often about betrayal. Many histories of women associated with the MLA who have left Peru, Ecuador, and other Latin America countries point to an affective betrayal. Migrant itineraries unfold on a note of betrayal of love and families and nations, nations that struggle to contain the fantasies of possibilities for (new) labor and gendered life.

Thus, fieldwork that engages the realm of religion and migration needs to go beyond what Robert Orsi has called the "meaning-making subject."[6] Orsi suggests a study of a tragic religious subject that emerges in a space of in-between, where different ways of being Catholic should be understood as responding to psychological and physical sufferings.[7] Instead of this approach, I have tried to model a study of being Catholic that steps away from the psychological domain of suffering to examine the laboring of faith in which affects get stuck to particular bodies and forms of labor in specific spaces, situations, and narratives. This work shows that people flourish or live diminished lives depending on the affects to which they get attached.[8] In other words, there is a politics of unequal circulation of affects that a study of the intersection of Catholicism and migration should bring to light.

Betrayal, Adam Phillips reminds us, is an impossibility of return, a forced field of transformation of intimacies.[9] Betrayal and desfase—as an unacknowledged disappointment with the experience of migration, which is manifested through a sense of suspension instead of living in the here and now—interrupt neat narratives of transnational migration that portray linear accumulation and the maternal sacrificial effort for the staying-behind families. Affective impasses such as desfase emerge at the conjuncture of particular economies of caring labor, ideas of migration as sacrifice, and the disruptions to national fantasies of accumulation through transnational migration. If desfase and betrayal are part of transnational migrant itineraries, then a pedagogy of the church that emphasizes the nuclear, heterosexual family and family reunification struggles on two fronts. One struggle is for the church to embrace spaces and degrees of abjection; the other is that the church ought to enhance the potential for the emergence of a renewed, gendered female subjectivity that can, and should, be expressed in the process of migration. This is an ongoing process, and we have yet to see how the papacy of Pope Francis will affect this recalibration of the Catholic Church, within and without.

One path of resistance to some of the church pedagogies on migration is to claim citizenship in growing pluricultural Roman and Italian society. Transnational returns of Mexican histories to Rome, especially those condensed in the figure of the Virgin of Guadalupe, show some of the wounds as well as the potential affective transformations of a national psyche. They reawaken early twentieth-century church-state conflicts and interrupt current church pedagogies that long for a pan–Latin American Catholic community and read the migrant's path as ultimately a universal one.

A rhetoric of the suffering migrant and a common Catholic humanitas often struggle with rooted and at times divisive national impulses. Paradoxically, migrant pedagogies of the Catholic Church foster, yet ultimately fail to contain, the affect of the nation(s). To paraphrase Márquez's words from the beginning of this book, the lingering drives and unfinished histories of Catholicism are still very much here. The limbs of Marquez's character, Margarito, are both animated by and entangled in these histories, and so too are the migrant itineraries that are so essential for the reproduction of flexible labor in Europe and of the Catholic Church as a passionate, apostolic machine.

Notes

Introduction: Catholic Humanitas

1. El Santísimo is the adoration of the body of Christ in the Eucharist, which is normally housed physically within a sacred niche in the altar of the church and kept in a precious urn. No particular historical event is associated with the emergence of this adoration, but the institution of the Corpus Domini, and the beginning of its calendrical celebration in 1264 is considered to be the time that this adoration became central to Catholic faith in monasteries and convents across Europe. The adoration of the body of Christ is different from the veneration of the relics of saints.

2. See Statement by Archbishop Silvano M. Tomasi to the 22nd Session of the Human Rights Council for the Application by the Holy See for Membership in the International Migration Organization. 5 December 2011. See http://www.zenit.org/article-33963?l=english, accessed 1 March 2013.

3. See Tsing 2005.

4. The fieldwork for this book took place in multiple yearly field trips of up to two months each between 2004 and 2011—and shorter follow-ups in 2012 and 2013. Fieldwork periods often coincided with major Marian and other Catholic festivities. Although the Latin American Mission is hosted in seventeen different parishes in Rome dedicated to different nation-states, I focused my research on five churches: Santa Maria in Trastevere, Santa Maria degli Angeli, Santa Lucia, Santa Maria in Via, and Oratorio del Caravita. I also attended celebrations, such as the annual celebration of the Festa dei Popoli or Day of the Migrants in San Giovanni in Laterano, and the Days of the Dead and the Day of the Mexican Independence organized specifically by the Comunidad Católica Mexicana. In 2004–7, I also closely followed the radio program "Hola mi Gente," during which time the program was relocated from the Gregorian University to the premises of Vatican Radio. I made extensive use of ARSI, the Secret Archives of the Company of Jesus in Rome and the Pontifical Vatican Library. I spent time with migrants in their homes and lived in a Mexican convent for more than a month. Throughout this work, I enjoyed Sunday ice-cream strolls with (migrant) friends in Piazza Risorgimento, hanging around in Piazza Mancini, and following migrants in often lengthy trips on urban public transport.

5. This is, of course, the vector of my own mobility that brings into this book's analysis other dimensions of desire and longing. Disappointments and

betrayal, as I engage them in this book, are also part of the migrant itineraries I have come to navigate and have been informed by.

6. See De Certeau 1984, 174.

7. I use here the term *public secret* to evoke Taussig's usage, which indicates the violent nature of the tension between logical possibilities of enunciation and the possibilities of enunciation by defacement and negation (Taussig 1999, 50).

8. *Badanti* from the root *badare*, meaning to look after, is a now a constitutionally recognized labor figure in Italy connected to the care of children, the elderly, and the sick.

9. For an informed feminist perspective on this in medieval times, as well as in particular relation to U.S. debates, see Castelli 2004, 2005, 2007.

10. Catholic pedagogies also evoke a particular field of Augustinian theology that sees the horizon of "walking together" as an inner path. *Christus docens* is the object of that orientation, not so much as a model to be imitated, but as an internal source of perennial revelation.

11. I refer here in particular to the work of Lauren Berlant 2011, and to some of its anthropological engagements, see, e.g., Muehlebach 2011, 2013.

12. The concept of living blood is used here to address a form of relationship among soul, faith, and movements. Blood has been read within a Christian medieval analysis as compassion and repentance, especially regarding the blood of Christ as an ambiguous vessel of divine justice and judgment (Duffy 2005, 108). Anthropological analyses of the notion of blood have been focused on practices of relationality, descent, and nationalism, but also its complex role in different forms of vitalism and flows: "The uniquely animated properties of blood are associated with the properties of flow and movement that connote vitality" (Carsten 2011, 29). I read this concept of living blood here as opening up the interfaces between the historical conjuncture of the New Evangelization, the desire for a revivification of local churches, migrant brotherhoods, and the mystery of the blood of Christ. See the evocation of blood, brotherhood, and diaspora in Paul VI's *Lumen Gentium:* "In them the faithful are gathered together by the preaching of the Gospel of Christ, and the mystery of the Lord's Supper is celebrated, that by the food and blood of the Lord's body the whole brotherhood may be joined together. In any community of the altar, under the sacred ministry of the bishop, there is exhibited a symbol of that charity and unity of the mystical Body, without which there can be no salvation. In these communities, though frequently small and poor, or living in the Diaspora, Christ is present, and in virtue of His presence there is brought together one, holy, catholic and apostolic Church. For the partaking of the body and blood of Christ does nothing other than make us be transformed into that which we consume." Finally for an illuminating work on blood and its reverberations in Christianity see Anidjar 2014.

13. This is also a phrase much loved by Mons. Josemaría Escrivá de Balaguer (who also wrote a book with the same title), the founding father of the Spanish Catholic movement Opus Dei.

14. See Goldberg and Quayson 2002.

15. Mignolo 2011, 179.

16. Napolitano and Norget 2011.

17. I refer here to the rich debate on the anthropology of Christianity both in its missionary global sites and in its historical Dutch and Central European centers of power. See, among others, the work by Joel Robbins, Matthew Engelke, Webb Keane, Ruth Marshall, Kevin O'Neill, Girish Daswani, and Simon Coleman.

18. Napolitano and Norget 2011, 252.

19. Cannell 2006, 7.

20. Povinelli 2006, 16.

21. For a discussion on the relation between the Holy Trinity and economics see Agamben 2013.

22. On this and evangelical congregations in the United States, see Harding 1987, 2000.

23. I refer here too at the relations of the body, flesh, migration, and place making in the work by Sayad (2004). Sayad is particularly interested in the suffering that emerges in ways in which migrant bodies are permeated and become the knots of colonial histories.

24. For a debate on this in modern Zimbabwe see Engelke 2007, 27.

25. De Certeau 1986, 4.

26. Pandolfo 2007.

27. See Holmes 2000.

28. Muehlebach 2009, 498.

29. Schmitt 1996, 7.

30. Ibid., 8.

31. See Brennan 2004.

32. Berlant 2011.

33. Berlant 2008, 6. Specifically, I am interested in the historical sensorium, as Berlant puts it, but with a partly different take on affective histories than her analysis. I explore in this book the present as an affective symptom of the past, but I also explore Berlant's sense of affect as a generative crisis of the present. So if a visceral possibility for another present(s) can never be fully encompassed in neatly shared and fully understood narratives/events, I nonetheless acknowledge, more than Berlant would, a "weight of the past" into an affective present and future that can or cannot be.

34. See Navaro-Yashin 2012.

35. See Bynum 2005.

36. Ex-centric anthropologies have developed important insights into the relation between anthropology and Catholicism; see, for example, the work of Ernesto de Martino and his work on the Italian south, and if not ex-centric, but definitely in a minority, the Oxford school of Catholic anthropology, for example, the work of Mary Douglas and Julian Pitt-Rivers (Fardon 1999). See also Mayblin, Napolitano, and Norget 2016.

37. See Orsi. 1985, 2005; Tweed 1997.

38. See Tweed 1997 and 2006; Galvez 2010; Orsi 1996.

39. See Stepick, Rey, and Mahler 2009 on Catholicism and immigration in Miami, Florida. Within a North American debate I find more compelling and analytically inspiring approaches such as the one by Alicia Schmidt Camacho (2008). Reflecting on the importance of ex-votos and saints' protection for Mexicans in the southern United States, she explores how migrants occupy a place and no place at once (2008, 311) and how that is central to what she calls "migrant melancholia."

40. See Hondagneu-Sotelo 2008, 8.

41. Orsi 2007.

42. On the unsettling politics of the gendering of humanitarianism, see Ticktin 2011.

43. See in particular the work of feminist medieval historians of Christianity such as Caroline Walker Bynum, Amy Hollywood, Rachel Fulton, Elizabeth Castelli, and Bettina Bildhauer.

44. See Ginzburg 1972; De Certeau 2000. The engagement with Ginzburg and de Certeau is a genealogy that pays particular attention to the relation between religious history and spatial and juridical politics. A plurality of histories can create a type of space where the performance of religious devotions shows a vitality of pasts into a present—for an excellent example see Palumbo 2004, on the "War of Saints" in rural Sicily.

45. *Imitatio Christi* is a very powerful configuration of mimetic processes around the figure of Christ and his perfection, and the nature of divine incarnation. Thomas à Kempis has been considered the author of the manuscript, titled *Imitatio Christi*, published anonymously in 1418. The book is divided into four parts and develops admonitions and consolations about the nature of spiritual life and devotions. It has had a great impact well beyond the time in which it was published.

46. I discuss this in chapter 2, but for now I wish to point out that this is a term coined by John Paul II and particularly inspired by missionization in, and from Latin America, and taken up by Benedict XVI as a central point of action for the church. Benedict XVI established a New Pontifical Council for the Promotion of the New Evangelization in September 2010 and held a major synod of bishops in October 2012 on this theme in Rome.

1. Migrant Terrains in Italy and Rome

1. The mayorship of Ignazio Marino (from the Democratic Party), mayor since 12 June 2013, is not analyzed here.

2. Policies implemented by the fourth Berlusconi government have been very detrimental to existing and renewed budgets for local authorities. The abolishment of the IRPEF (Imposta sul Reddito delle Persone Fisiche), for instance, a municipal tax on the first house ownership has de facto curtailed one

of the most important local forms of tax revenue without introducing any particular new federal support. Hence even right-wing city mayors, including Alemanno, have openly complained about the lack of funding for implementing vital local authorities services.

3. The Lega Nord, or Northern League, is an Italian "neo-nativist" party created in 1991 in northern Italy to promote forms of federalism (fiscal, administrative, and cultural) and (de facto) anti-immigration policies (especially when Roberto Maroni, one of its leaders, was minster of Internal Affairs between 2008 and 2011). Against broad notions of national belonging, the Northern League has maintained a strong focus on local activism and concerns, and it was rather successful in defending and fostering local entrepreneurial interests in a changing global economy (Baldini and Cento Bull 2010). However, since 2013 the Northern League has lost ground to a new movement called Movimento 5 Stelle, led by an ex-comedian named Beppe Grillo; Movimento 5 Stelle champions a politics against the state and established political forms of representations. I cannot go into details here about how this political constituencies has shifted across these two parties, but both share anti-state and localist impulses.

4. I need to emphasize again that this book takes into account a period before the end of the fourth Berlusconi's government in 2011 and the establishment of a new "technical" government led by the economist Mario Monti. Strong countervoices have begun to emerge against this Decreto Sicurezza within Monti's government as well in later PD governments led by Enrico Letta and Matteo Renzi, but this is within a period that I do not analyze in this book.

5. In 2008, criminal acts carried out by migrants diminished by 7.6 percent and in the Lazio Region by 15.3 percent during the previous two years even though the overall migrant population increased by 15 percent (CARITAS/Migrantes 2009).

6. Piazza Mancini is in the north-center of Rome close to Ponte Milvio and a large bus and tram terminal, which makes it a very good meeting place for migrants who often do not own their means of transport, but depend on public transportation.

7. For an analysis of the Scalabrinian order, see chapter 4.

8. This is a type of police in Italy dealing with local public safety and security.

9. Later in 2007, Madisson Godoy became consigliere aggiunto for the American continent in the municipality of Rome. Consigliere aggiunto is one of five administrative posts to represent broadly five different migrant communities, related to the five different world constituencies in the municipality of Rome. These councillors take part in the work of the municipal council, but have no right to vote. Their institutionalization was seen also as a potential step toward the right for legal, resident migrants to vote in municipal elections in Italy, a shift in legislation that has not happened yet.

10. I refer here to a very important book, *Cuore* (1886), by Edmondo de Amicis, which is a classic in the formation of the new Italian national identity

after unification (1860). The book celebrates, in a rather paternalistic way, Catholic values of honesty, obedience, and the newly imagined role of labor in overcoming class differences at play in the utopic formation of the new Italian national consciousness. In the book, migration from the south of Italy to the Americas begins to unsettle the picture and threatens to undermine the core of these national and gendered values. Needless to say, there are important resonances here with the twenty-first-century setting of migration to Italy and the utopic ethical landscape of shared values across migrant and citizen divides.

11. I refer here to Sara Ahmed's notion of affective cultural politics of emotions, which I read very much as an interpretation of affective politics (Ahmed 2004), and Jaqueline Rose's notion of resistance of the mind to fruitful inquiry within too easy affective politics of (Jewish) national hate and love (Rose 2007). I particularly find fruitful Ahmed's understanding of affect as shaping people's body and skin.

12. Bouchard 2010, 105.

13. Ibid., 108. A range of sociologists have written in insightful ways about the process of othering and migration in Italy. Among those whose work I would highlight, see Dal Lago 2004 on migrant representations in the media and denial of personhood, and Ambrosini 2007, 2008, 2013.

14. See Gramsci 1967, 84.

15. In the words of Pius XI:

> Now there are three necessary societies, distinct from one another and yet harmoniously combined by God, into which man is born: two, namely the family and civil society, belong to the natural order; the third, the Church, to the supernatural order. In the first place comes the family, instituted directly by God for its peculiar purpose, the generation and formation of offspring; for this reason it has priority of nature and therefore of rights over civil society. Nevertheless, the family is an imperfect society, since it has not in itself all the means for its own complete development; whereas civil society is a perfect society, having in itself all the means for its peculiar end, which is the temporal well-being of the community; and so, in this respect, that is, in view of the common good, it has pre-eminence over the family, which finds its own suitable temporal perfection precisely in civil society. The third society, into which man is born when through Baptism he reaches the divine life of grace, is the Church; a society of the supernatural order and of universal extent; a perfect society, because it has in itself all the means required for its own end, which is the eternal salvation of mankind; hence it is supreme in its own domain. (Encyclical *Divini Illius Magistri,* 1939)

16. See Brandi and Todisco 2006.

17. Since 2000, CARITAS and the "Observatory of Migrations," a Catholic NGO, have produced a yearly Dossier Statistico sulle Migrazioni, and since 2004 also a Report on Migrations specifically on Rome.

18. See Conti and Strozza 2006, 39. Dossier Caritas 2010 reported the following numbers for legal migrant residents in Italy: Peruvians—87,000; Ecuadorians—85,000. Mexicans are demographically a much smaller community: In 2010 the legal number of residents was more than 3,500, but there is a significant number of unrecorded migrants who have not legalized their status yet via Italy's cumbersome procedures, or who are entering on a tourist Visa and overstaying. As such, the CCM (Comunidad Católica Mexicana) leaders' estimate of Mexican migrants in Italy is closer to 6,000, with the majority living in Rome and in the northern province of Milan. In 2013 the population of Peruvians had reached 110,000, of which more than 60 percent was female; the number of documented Mexicans on Italian soil was more than 5,700, and in the Roman province around 2,500. Moreover, the majority of women attending the MLA are in their thirties or older, and they have come to Italy mainly on their own, following relatives, friends, or acquaintances. Many have dependents in their place of origin, although the group of the Hermandad del Señor los Milagros, which is an increasingly active part of the MLA, shows an older immigration trend and a more nuclear family–oriented migrant demography.

19. See Bodo and Bodo 2005, 29.

20. See http://www.romamultietnica.it/.

21. This is a pejorative word in Italian to indicate migrants coming from outside the EU and from the global South.

22. Another initiative introduced by Veltroni's government and then undercut and only briefly revivified in 2011 by the Alemanno's municipal council was the Rete Provinciale delle Comunitá Straniere, with the aim of creating social networks and liaisons across the province between local migrants and Italian institutions; see http://www.migranews.it/rete.htm.

23. See Bodo and Bodo 2005, 52.

24. The case of the Roma people stands out during the Alemanno's government. For instance, in one case among many, in April 2011 a fire broke out in a camp, which stirred a significant municipal response to evacuate many of the inner city camps, and this in turn created debate about what to do with the Roma population and where they should live. It also prompted an outcry from human rights organizations.

25. There is a vast literature on female transnational migration and the labor of love that goes into raising a family in the country of arrival at the expense of the country of origin. Here I am building on this literature to discuss the particular angle of the subjectivity fostered by the Catholic Church. See early work by Finch and Groves 1983; Hondagneu-Sotelo 1994, 2001, 2008; and England 2010. See also the work on Italy by Quiroza 1991; Andall 2000; Fullin and Vercelloni 2009; and Fullin 2010.

26. See the work of Queirolo Palmas 2004; Torre and Queirolo Palmas 2005; Ambrosini and Queirolo Palmas 2005.

27. See Boccagni and Piperno 2010, CARITAS/Migrantes 2009. Although sociologically very informative, this literature only minimally engages with the

idiosyncrasies and the abjections of migrant itineraries and asks different types of questions than those I ask here.

28. See Grilli and Mugnaini 2009. *Badanti* is both a legally defined and a commonly used word to name those who work as caretakers of the elderly and people in need.

29. CARITAS is a confederation of Catholic organizations present in more than 200 countries that organizes relief, social justice work, and humanitarian intervention. It is directly connected to the Holy See for the promotion of Catholic forms of humanitarian intervention.

30. CARITAS/Migrantes 2009, 190, my translation.

31. See http://www.comune.roma.it/wps/portal/pcr?contentId=NEW268270&jp_pagecode=newsview.wp&ahew=contentId:jp_pagecode.

32. Ibid.

33. Ibid.

34. The head of this observatory is Massimo Introvigne, an Italian sociologist and a good friend of Silvio Berlusconi's; he is also connected to the MP, Alfredo Mantovano, whom I discuss in chapter 3 in relation to his support of the Legionaries of Christ. Both Mantovano and Introvigne have launched a (Catholic) campaign to support "the family"; see http://www.siallafamiglia.it/.

35. Balibar 2010, 315.

36. See Sayad 1975, 1993.

37. See two abstracts of his public interventions:

> Lastly it will be appropriate to ensure that nobody forgets that Catholicism, although not anymore "the official religion of the State," is still nonetheless the "historic religion" of the Italian nation, on top of being the principal source of its identity and the key inspiration to most of its authentic greatness [*grandezze*]. Therefore, it is out of place to assimilate this to other religious or cultural forms, to which, yes, we have to guarantee full freedom to be and to operate, without though the implication that this creates a fashioning of an unnatural leveling, or even an annihilation of the highest values of our civilization. (Biffi 2000, my translation)

In another public speech the same year:

> A consistent admission of foreigners to our peninsula is acceptable and can be beneficial, but only if we take care seriously to defend the character of one's own nation [*fisionomia della propria nazione*]. Italy is not a deserted or semi-inhabited moor, without history, without live and vital traditions, without an unmistakable cultural and spiritual character, to be populated without a rule, as if there was not a heritage of humanism and civilization that does not have to be lost. (Biffi 2000; my translation)

Interestingly, despite the open transgression of political boundaries, at the time no Italian political party really opposed or criticized Biffi's request for this selective policy on migration (Romano 2005, 140–41).

38. In the words of Cardinal Martini of Milan in 2000 at the annual vigil devoted to St. Ambrogio, the patron of the city of Milan:

> From here some points of contrast could emerge with our civil code. Therefore, on this front we need today particular attention. Marriage and the family are the heart of civilization; this is the most intimate nucleus of a culture and of a tradition that are all one with our collective identity. The necessary and friendly openness to pluralism of cultures and family models has to live with the attention to the custody of universal principles and values—inheritance of our Western and European tradition. Only the use of this particular attention, within the multicultural society that will be more than ever our own, can help us and protect us from syncretic relativism, on the one side, and the drawbacks of an ethical state, on the other. (Martini 2000, my translation)

39. Migrantes is a foundation based in Rome created by the CEI (Conferenza Episcopale Italiana) in 1987 as a service and support for pastoral care for "human mobility," not only of immigrants in Italy but of migrant Italians abroad. Via IDOS, a research center on migration, the CEI is also involved in the publishing the annual *Dossier Statistico sull'Immigrazione*.

40. Cody 2011, 47.

41. See Jenkins 2007.

42. See Marchetto 2005; Sodi 2007.

43. I am referring here to the hermeneutic of discontinuity in the interpretation of Vatican II by the Bologna School, championed in particular by the late Italian historian Giuseppe Alberigo (see Alberigo 1999).

44. John Paul II, *Laborem Exercens,* 1981.

45. For a great analysis of the Romanization of some strands of the Catholic Church in the United States and the demonization of liberals and Jews in the nineteenth century and the early twentieth century, see D'Agostino 2004.

46. Edwards 2012, 23.

47. Ibid., 40.

2. The "Culture of Life" and Migrant Pedagogies

1. As I mentioned in the introduction, this chapter and book engage with material up to Benedict XVI's resignation of the papacy in 2013. I will address only a few shifts emerging after the election of Pope Francis, which happened at the time the book was already in press.

2. *Exsul Familia* is an encyclical written by Pope Pius XII in 1952, which in a World War II climate opened the Catholic Church to a reflection on migration,

especially through the experience of Italian emigration at the turn of the twentieth century. This encyclical pivots on the role that the church played in caring for migrants through Catholic hospitals, dioceses, and hospices, as well as how the strengthening of the family becomes the privileged model in helping migrants in host societies.

3. The term *governmentality* refers to the work of Michel Foucault on ways in which power works through and in turn constitutes institutions directed toward the right conduct of the population and with the goal of the well-being of the population. But in contrast to Foucault, I use the term less with the emphasis on rationality of conduct that is explicit in his work, and more as way of naming the system of passionate conduct that the church engenders, especially in the context of a parish such as the Latin American Mission, which relies so heavily on a pedagogical practice of promulgating the "good" for the transnational migrants. For an informed discussion on govermentality and its articulation in ethnographic explorations, see T. Li 2007. For a critique of passionate rather than cold forms of governmentalities and bureaucracies, see Navaro-Yashin 2012.

4. The Comunità di Sant'Egidio is a lay movement founded in 1968 by Andrea Ricciardi. It currently has more than 60,000 members in 73 countries with headquarters in Trastevere. The core of this movement includes the transmission of the gospel, a focus on prayer, attention to the poor, and ecumenical dialogue within the Catholic Church. Politically, the movement was close to John Paul II and to the government of the premier Mario Monti (2011–13), during which time the same Ricciardi was nominated minister for International Cooperation.

5. The PRI is the Revolutionary Institutional Party that ruled Mexico from the postrevolutionary time from 1929 (as the National Revolutionary Party) to 2001, when Vicente Fox became the first candidate of an opposition party (in his case the PAN, Party of National Action) to win the presidential election. In 2006, Fox's successor Felipe Calderón Hinojosa won (a rather contested) election; see chapter 4. However, in the July 2012 elections the PRI candidate Enrique Peña Nieto won and marked a return of the PRI to power.

6. *Las Marias* in Mexico City are the women street sellers of indigenous origin, first studied by Lourdes Arizpe (1975).

7. Since the Mexico City mayorship of Andrés Manuel López Obrador (2000–2005) and Marcelo Ebrard (2006–12)—both members of the liberal party (PRD)—Mexico City has promoted some important juridical changes, often in open contrast to both the national government and the Roman Catholic Church in Mexico. The most contested case has been the legislation of same-sex unions, which was ratified by the municipal government of Mexico City in 2010.

8. Tomasi and Rosoli 1997, 309.

9. Ibid., 278.

10. Rosoli 1989.

11. Tomasi and Rosoli 1997, 68; my translation from the Italian.

12. Graziano Battistella is an Italian Scalabrinian priest, a former director of the SIMI- Scalabrinian Institute for Migration Studies in Rome, who then became the director of the Scalabrini Migration Centre in Quezon City, Philippines. This was a personal communication.

13. Scalabriniani 2005, 293; my translation from the Italian.

14. Ibid., 323.

15. See Battistella 2006.

16. F.L., the Jesuit priest who for a while was the spiritual head of the CCM.

17. The Pontifical Mexican College is the official residence for diocesan priests coming from Mexico to Rome in order to study in one of the city's religious universities. It hosts the yearly celebration of the Virgin of Guadalupe that I discuss in chapter 5.

18. Speech given on 30 September 2000; http://chiesa.espresso.repubblica.it/articolo/7283, my translation.

19. Forza Nuova has been analyzed as a renewed defense of national subaltern working classes in Italy at a time of challenges due to globalization (Caiani 2011).

20. See for Alleanza Cattolica http://www.alleanzacattolica.org and Totustuus Network http://www.totustuus.it/index.php; for Il Timone see http://www.iltimone.org/.

21. John Paul II 2003.

22. In the words of Benedict XVI (2009): "Human freedom is authentic only when it responds to the fascination of technology with decisions that are the fruit of moral responsibility."

23. Garza Medina 2008, 17.

24. Garelli 2006, 68.

25. By scriptural economy I refer to de Certeau's understanding of the tension between textuality and experience. When what takes shape as an account, written text, or in this case (Catholic) pedagogical orientation toward immigration is transmitted away from its own phenomenological and contextual space of production, then there is a violence done to the richness of an experience (what de Certeau calls orality) in an act of written translation. Acts of writing can be part of a violent economy of disavowal and poaching, because they select details away from the multitude of the experience itself.

26. This is one aspect of a long, complex, and ongoing debate among Italian intellectuals (including Eugenio Scalfari, the founder of the liberal newspaper *La Repubblica*, or Giuliano Ferrara, a conservative politician and intellectual founder of a much smaller newpaper, *Il Foglio*) and *vaticanisti* (journalists that specialize on covering Vatican news, such as, for instance, Sandro Magister, Matteo Mattiuzzi, Giuseppe di Leo, Andrea Tornielli) on the role of the Catholic Church and the pope's interventions not only on everyday Italian politics, but worldwide.

27. See Zagrebelsky 2008; Remotti 2008, 161, 257.

28. Conceptually, we could say that Sameness is then destabilized by migrant heterologies—"altered feminine discourse" emerging in reaction and at the margins of a given scriptural economy. Heterologies, as de Certeau teaches us, are the inconsistency between emplaced and embodied lives and their representations; they linger at the edges of what is recognized and spoken—they are a thorn in the side of hermeneutic closure (1986, 165).

29. Asad 1996, 267.

30. Keane 1997a.

31. Bartolomé de Las Casas (1474–1566) was a missionary and a colonial chaplain, but he was also a social activist, a writer, and a speaker, and his thinking built on the neo-Thomism of his Salamancan confreres. He went to Española in 1502 as a colonial adventurer, participated in various expeditions, and received an *encomienda*, land with indentured Indians. Perhaps the first person ordained in the Americas, he became a priest about 1512 and took part as chaplain in the conquest of Cuba. Having first resisted the critical preaching of the Dominicans, he was converted on the feast of the Assumption, 1514, and soon announced he was setting free the Indians and working to end the encomienda system. See Lavalle 2009 for a recent critical reflection on Las Casas; see Von Vacano (2012) for an interesting reading of the long history of Latin American philosophical responses to the idea of humanity in the writings of Bartolomé de Las Casas.

32. O'Meara 1992, 573.

33. Cornish 1996, 112.

34. See Locke [1764] 1946; Squadrito 1979.

35. Pope John XXII entered a theological dispute with the Franciscan order over the relation between the correct interpretation of the gospel and the exercise of poverty. It was William of Ockham who, in defending the Franciscans in 1328, first began to define a notion of humans possessing natural rights: "The right that the Franciscans had renounced, he argued, was every kind of worldly right, every right to sue in court, or to own property. But there was also a natural right to use external things that was common to all men and that was derived from nature, not from any human statute; and no one could renounce this right since it was necessary to maintain life. By virtue of this right, Ockham argued, the friars could use justly without having any right derived from human law. 'The friars do have a right,' he wrote, 'namely a natural right'" (Tierney 2004, 9).

36. Cornish 1996, 112.

37. See the work by Todorov 1984; Greenblatt 1991; Pagden 1982, 1994; Hodgen 1971.

38. See Brah 1996; Brah and Coombes 2000.

39. She also argues, reading through Coronil's work, that embodied hierarchization of cultural differences is a concern of Atlantic (and global) politics, as I definitely argue here too (Silverblatt 2004, 16).

40. I am referring here to the doing "otherwise" (of gender performativity) developed conceptually by Judith Butler (2006), but also to its dimension of

melancholy, in its impossibility to ever being fully (Butler 1997). However, as are her later critics, I am aware that the potentiality of affectively reinscribing gender and subjectivity is always orchestrated in complex fields of interpellation and at particular conjunctures of political economies, that make often given fantasies of identification still palatable to many, even if clearly detrimental to their emancipatory positions (Berlant 2007).

41. See Pontifical Council for the Pastoral Care of Migrants and Itinerant People 2004.

42. See Cipriani 2004, 449; Hamao 2005.

43. Albahari 2006, 107.

44. Benedict XVI 2006.

45. Pontifical Council for the Pastoral Care of Migrants and Itinerant People 2004.

46. Albahari 2006.

47. In promoting the banning of the death penalty in the UN forum, the Roman Catholic Church is also promoting life as a moral value and as a right that connects humans universally, irrespective of their cultural, racial, and class genealogies. Consequently, this Roman Catholic discourse can easily turn the culture of life into an ethical, universal, anti-abortion stance. For a wonderful and calibrated debate on this and its repercussions in Italian politics see Hanafin 2007.

48. Agamben 2002, 16.

49. Asad 2003, 129.

50. Agamben 2002, 24.

51. See in the words of de Certeau the lingering of the beneath: "Normally, strange things circulate discreetly below our streets. But a crisis will suffice for them to rise up, as if swollen by flooded waters, pushing aside manhole covers, invading the cellars, then spreading through the towns. It always comes as a surprise when the nocturnal erupts into broad daylight. What it reveals is an underground existence, an inner resistance that has never been broken. This lurking force infiltrates the lines of tension within the society it threatens" (de Certeau 2000, 1).

52. Every year since 1991, the Scalabrinians have organized a Day of the Migrant called La Festa dei Popoli on a Sunday in May. This is a celebration in front of San Giovanni in Laterano with an array of stalls that sell food and handicrafts or provide information from different countries. The majority of associations that participate in the event (and pay for space rental) are connected to immigrant associations within Rome. Before the festival begins, a solemn mass takes place in the Basilica, then in the afternoon a concert takes place with the display of folkloric national bands. Some of the women in the MLA have complained that the concert starts too late in the afternoon; by that time they have to head back to look after the elderly who are in their care. For three years I helped the CCM to set up its stall and staffed it throughout the day and enjoyed the banter and the laughter with the others.

53. This violence may not be new or limited to new migrants, but in some places in Rome it echoes multiple histories of social alterity. In the Valley of Hell (Valle dell' Inferno), a neighborhood in Rome, which I have written about elsewhere, there was an eruption of violence in the Casa del Popolo, where Latin American squatter families now reside; the violence resonates with histories of anarchic outbursts present in that same place during the fascist regime. A social alterity embodied by anarchists, socialists, and now migrants is condensed in the Casa del Popolo, a building that has become a material trace of different but related histories (Napolitano 2015).

54. See Giordano 2008.

55. Mahmood 2005, 2009, 2012; J. Butler 2009.

56. For a good mapping of these debates in historically Protestant countries, see Cannell 2010; for key (different) positions on the analytical purchase of secularism and postsecularism, see Connolly 1999; and for philosophically nuanced takes on it, see Taylor 2007. For recent critiques and takes on Taylor's position on secularism as a multifaceted historical, affective and embodied process, see Warner, Van Antwerpen, and Calhoun 2010.

57. Jakobsen and Pellegrini 2008, 17.

58. Coleman 2010, 805; Robbins 2010.

59. Jakobsen and Pellegrini 2008, 28.

60. Ratzinger 2000, 165. See also the influence of the twentieth-century Italian German priest and theologian Romano Guardini (1885–1968) and his work on the relation between the Catholic people and the Catholic Church (Guardini 1935) on the thinking of Benedict XVI.

61. Personal written communication; my translation and emphasis.

62. André 2011.

63. Corriere della Sera 2009.

64. Reynolds 2008.

3. *The Legionaries of Christ and the Passionate Machine*

1. Following the allegation of abuses and misconduct of its founder and the collusions he had with Mexican priest members at the head of the order, the order was put through an Apostolic Visit by Benedict XVI from June 2009 to July 2010, which ended with the nomination of a pontifical delegate, the Scalabrinian Velasio de Paolis, to coordinate a revision of the order from within. In 2011, a further apostolic visit was carried out in the Regnum Christi, the movement connected to the order. In January 2011, de Paolis nominated Juan José Arrieta Ibarrechebea and Jesús Villagrasa Lasaga, Spanish Legionary priests—both of whom I met and interviewed in Rome—to enlarge the general council of the Legionary order, which previously constituted a group of Mexican and Italian members closely allied to the order's controversial founder, Maciel. In this chapter, I discuss the transformation of the order up to this election, but no further.

2. This posture pivots around a defense of the pope's teaching and the integrity of traditional Catholic teaching. Moveover *integralism* refers to a belief

that Catholicism is not only a private religion, but that it should play an important political and moral role in the public sphere (Krogt 1992).

3. There are obviously exceptions, see Yeates 2011.

4. Regarding Father Artaud, Michel de Certeau (another Jesuit) wrote, "The same insistence on the 'motion of the heart' and purity of intention is present in the chapter '*Ministeria zelusque animarum utrum langueant vel efflorescent,*' which upholds the primacy of the affectus over the effectus, that is, the priority of an obedience to the inner movements of the spirit over the objective interest presented by social activities" (de Certeau 1992, 246).

5. Consider, for instance, the fate of the Jesuit Achille Gagliardi, the spiritual counselor of the Italian mystic Isabella Berinzaga. Gagliardi developed a brief and clear compendium to reform the Jesuit order along more mystical lines (Schulte van Kessel 1993, 160). He was soon "forgotten."

6. See Bynum 1987; de Certeau 1992; Hollywood 2002.

7. De Certeau 1992, 259.

8. Molina 2008.

9. Barthes 1976, 72.

10. Ibid., 73.

11. However, there was exactly such an inconsistency within the Jesuit order in the way in which Quietism was regarded. Jesuits such as Lois Lallemant and Jean-Joseph Surin were inspirational to Jean-Pierre Caussade (1675–1751), one of the key players of eighteenth-century Quietism, who interestingly wrote about the heart as sacred and as a cradle of inspiration where no language was needed. In his words: "[The purely heart-charged prayer of simple recollection] cuts away the superfluity of our meditations, readings, and vocal prayers to substituted assets, that is to say, attention to the heart, saviour of the heart, peace and rest of the heart, which many people hardly think of" (Caussade, in Choudhury 2009, 167). This connects to the next chapter, where I analyze the affective dimension of the devotional heart via the discursive and visual emergence of the Sacred Heart in the Latin American mission.

12. Choudhury 2009, 1.

13. I wish to thank General Peter-Hans Kolvenbach for granting me special permission to consult material in the Archivium Romanum Societatis Iesu (ARSI), which ordinarily would not have been possible because the documents were too recent.

14. La Bella 2007, 853.

15. Ibid., 854.

16. Ibid., 862.

17. Ibid., 880.

18. Alberigo 2005.

19. John Paul I's letter to the General of the Jesuit, 30 September 1978. My translation from the Italian and my emphasis. A copy of the letter was also in Latin, and both were consulted in the ARSI, the Jesuit archives in Rome.

20. July 15, 1963. My translation from the Spanish and my emphasis.

21. Marcial Maciel was born in 1920, in Cotija de la Paz, a small town located in the state of Michoacán, Mexico.

22. It was through the intercession of Cardinal Canali that, on 25 May 1948, Maciel received Pius XII's endorsement for his congregation. Immediately upon his return to Mexico, he arranged the founding of the congregation for the date of the feast of Saints John and Paul, 29 June. Although more research would need to be carried out in the archives of the Legionaries, which are currently closed to the public, it seems that Maciel received information that there would be a change of heart about his proposed order, and he, together with Bishop Gregorio Araiza, called the Legionaries of Christ officially into being on the evening of 13 June 1948. By the following Monday, 14 June, the bishop of Cuernavaca, Espino y Silva, received a telegram delaying the canonical election of the new order. However, it was too late: The order was already born, although through murky official back channels.

23. I first heard of the "racial" politics of affiliation within the Legionaries of Christ during an interview with Father Juan, a Mexican diocesan priest from Zacatecas, who was studying in Rome for his degree. Father Juan referred to the Legionaries as "the blond ones with impeccable hair cuts"; he said, "There are no *morenos* like me there." In Rome, I often heard comments about the expensive clothing and the impeccable presentation that Legionaries make in public.

24. This should be understood not only within Vatican geopolitics but also as part of a long process of Atlantic "coloniality of being" that promotes forms of liminality of being(s) that operate as enduring and present forms of racial dehumanization (Maldonado-Torres 2007, 257). However, I do not agree with Maldonado-Torres's conflation of decolonization with a "restoration of the gift" economy (260). Anthropologists have analyzed the complexity and pitfalls of such an economy (Coleman 2004), and again we need, through a postsecular analysis, to query these forms of generosity and to debunk some of the underpinnings of "the unconditional." I am reminded here of the debate on Catholic voluntarism and gratuitous giving, which is of decisive importance for particular forms of labor relations and the compensation for a partial lack of national welfare. I think that a way to limit some of the colonial thinking, which Maldonado-Torres engages in, is to ethnographically situate the complexity and the symptomatic returns of the nation within this process.

25. The Legionaries are behind ZENIT, a thriving multilingual Catholic news service on the internet (http://www.zenit.org/), that until recently was coordinated by the Spanish Vatican journalist Jesús Colina. He resigned in 2011 because of the control the Legionaries have over the governing body of the association, and the impossibility, in his view, of initiating genuinely innovative projects, given the extent of the order's oversight and control.

26. "Primary capital to be safeguarded and valued is man, the human person in his or her integrity" (*Caritas in Veritate*, Benedict XVI, 2009). This is part of an important debate on the Catholic Church's position on labor, sociality, and the

common good, which since Leo XIII's encyclical *Rerum Novarum* (1891) have been important in Catholic social thought. The same nature of "freely given" love and labor, as it is promoted by a concept of *gratuitá* (free charitable giving with no reciprocity, seen as a labor-foundation of society) in Benedict XVI's thinking, is actually paradoxically an endorsement of an increased "catholicization of neoliberalism" (see Muehlebach 2013). Legionaries' ideals and practices of *homo relationalis* are very much part of this Catholicization of neoliberalism, rather than a moving away from it.

27. Holmes 2000, 15.

28. Mahmood 2009, 859–60.

29. During the period of the Cristiada, the Catholic Church lost part of its juridical character in Mexico, and the state gained greater control over its internal organization; for example, only Mexicans who were citizens by birth were allowed to become priests. Moreover, priests could no longer exercise the right to vote, participate in political movements, or form any political party. Catholic education was curtailed in state schools, and secular teaching was made paramount. Religious primary and secondary schools went unrecognized by the state, as did degrees granted by religious seminaries. Finally, multifaith freedom was enshrined in the constitution, and religious cults and practices were officially forbidden outside churches. most important, these laws abolished property rights for the church, rendering it illegal for the church to acquire, administer, or possess real estate in the Republic.

30. See Butler 2009.

31. Paradoxically, the beatifications of Cristiada's martyrs in 2000, championed by John Paul II, were of those who had not actively taken up arms during the Cristiada War. Instead, they were the "active pacifists in it" (González Ruiz 2004, 282). Paradoxically again, those Jesuits who had spearheaded some of the violent confrontations of the war have not been beatified, corroborating the idea that the Catholic Church is still inclined to portray its allegedly "neutral" position at the time of that war.

32. Translated from the Spanish by the author.

33. Mantovano 2007.

34. More recently the Università Europea has seen a direct involvement by Roberto Mattei, one of the organizers of the October 2011 conference titled "Institutions and Charisma in the Evangelization of the Americas." An expert in modern history, Mattei is another notable intellectual connected to Alleanza Cattolica, a Catholic conservative association. His other institutional affiliations include the Catholic apologetic journal, *Il Timone,* and the prestigious Italian National Research Council CNR (Consiglio Nazionale delle Ricerche), for which he has served as a subsecretary since 2003. In the 2011 conference, a continuity between the "new evangelization of the Americas" professed by John Paul II and embraced by Benedict XVI, and the evangelization of the sixteenth century was repeatedly made, as a sign of hope for a renewed orthodoxy and integralism of the Catholic Church.

35. New institutes have sprung from this right-wing Italian think tank, including the Centre for the Study of New Religions (CESNUR) and the Institute for the Doctrine and the Social Information (IDIS).

36. 17 November 2005. My translation. http://www.interno.it/mininterno/export/sites/default/it/sezioni/sala_stampa/interview/Interventi/_sottosegretarioxprecedenti/intervista_397.html_1375993311.html.

37. Abraham 1987.

38. See Navaro-Yashin 2012, 17.

39. See Freud 1955; Rashkin 2008, 94–95.

40. See Skrbiš 2005.

41. Cordoba 2006.

42. From a letter by Father Xavier Baeza, rector of the Jesuit College of Comillas, to the General of the Jesuit order (21 January 1949).

43. Father Enrique Carvajal, S.J., in a letter to the General of the Jesuit order (27 September 1950).

44. The following material has been gathered through conversations with diocesan and Legion priests, participant observation of their meetings and celebration of the Comunidad Católica Mexicana, at events of the Regnum Christi, and through the emerging literature on the Legionaries in the printed press. As well, I have used available and later obscured material that has appeared in cyberspace. The last source is, of course, questionable, but I use it here to corroborate aspects that emerged in participant observation.

45. Legionaries of Christ 2009, 41–42.

46. Massumi 1995.

47. Translated from the Spanish by the author.

48. The Regnum Christi is a lay counterpart movement of the Legionaries of Christ in which women can be consecrated to a religious life without taking religious vows. This movement was the subject of an Apostolic Visitation after the demise of the founder of the Legionaries of Christ; the visitation ended and a report on the order was released in 2012.

49. Legionaries of Christ 2009, 134.

50. Translated from the Spanish by the author.

51. Legionaries 2009, 144–76.

52. But also Mexico, Spain, and Chile.

53. In March 2009, the news broke that Maciel had a daughter living in Spain, at the time in her twenties; later it emerged he had also fathered a son of more or less the same age in Mexico.

54. "It seems to me that his [Michelangelo's] method of inquiry is closely related to the technique of psycho-analysis. It, too, is accustomed to divine secret and concealed things from despised and unnoticed features, from the rubbish-heap, as it were, of our observation" (Freud 1989, 530).

55. Agamben 2009 (English edition), 102.

56. Williams 1977.

57. Ahmed 2004.

58. See the work of Massumi 2002, inspired by Deleuze and Guattari. For a discussion of this genealogy of affects, see Gregg and Seigworth 2010. As explained in the introduction, I read these affective terrains from a parallel genealogy that comes also through the work of Freud and Lacan, via Jacqueline Rose, Michel de Certeau, and Carlo Ginzburg.

59. Regnum Christi is one of the lay movements of the Legionaries of Christ. Its aims are baptismal commitment, personal holiness, and apostolic action, all inspired by the charisma received from God through its founder Marcial Maciel. In February 2012, the director of the consecrated women of this group, the Spaniard Malen Oriol, resigned after the completion of an apostolic visit carried out in the movement.

60. John Paul II supported the founder of the Legionaries of Christ against the accusations of pedophilia, which were reviewed by then Cardinal Joseph Ratzinger in his capacity as head of the Congregation for Doctrine of the Faith.

61. Guerrero Chiprés 2004, 88.

62. Ibid., 172.

4. Migrant Hearts

1. Eloisa, with whom I opened this book, is a woman in her early forties, and with no children. She was a teacher with a degree in her country of origin and arrived in Italy in 2003, where she lived as a live-in-maid for a few years in the home of a well-to-do Roman family. I have decided to withhold more biographical information about her for reasons that will become clearer in the text.

2. I refer here to the generative, ground-breaking work of Teresa Brennan on affects as the physiological shifts that accompany judgment: "I am using the term 'transmission of affect' to capture a process that is social in origin but biological and physical in effect. The origin of transmitted affects is social in that these affects do not only arise within a particular person but also come from without. They come via an interaction with other people and an environment. But they have a physiological impact. By the transmission of affect, I mean simply that the emotions or affects of one person, and the enhancing or depressing energies these affects entail, can enter into another" (Brennan 2004, 3). This is why, following Brennan, I consider the relation between skin and affects very important.

3. For critical studies on transnationalism and anthropology of Catholicism see Vásquez and Marquardt 2003; De Theije 2011; Napolitano and Norget 2011.

4. See Orsi 1985, 1996; Tweed 1997; and Lorentzen et al. 2009.

5. De Certeau and Giard 1997, 134, my emphasis.

6. This emerged in an interview with Dr. Franca Cohen, the head of the Assessorato alla Multietnicitá (Council for multi-ethnicity) in Walter Veltroni's municipal government. She articulated her view contrasting the archaeological, artistic, and touristic cultural heritage (*beni culturali*) of Rome with the "lack of

culture" of incoming Latin American migrants, and for that matter of other economic migrants to the city. Interview with the author, October 2005.

7. Fanon 1968, 4. See also McClintock 1995.

8. Mayblin and Course 2014.

9. Freud 1953, 1961.

10. Dalia took care of a string of elderly people with Alzheimer's disease and dementia, and two of them died while in her care.

11. Ryan 2002.

12. I refer here in particular to celebrations I participated in the CCM (Comunidad Católica Mexicana) on the day of the Fiesta Patria in 2004, 2005, and 2007, as well as the Via Crucis being carried out of Santa Maria della Luce by the MLA at Easter in 2006 and 2008.

13. I attended celebrations of the Altar de los Muertos in November 2005 and again in 2009. In 2005, the celebration I attended was hosted in a church near the periphery of Rome and run by a group of Trappist monks; in 2009, at the Oratory of the Caravita, a small Jesuit church close to the main one of St. Ignatius, hosted the celebration. In the first instance, the altar was set up in the hall connected to, but outside of the church itself. In the second instance, it was arranged inside. The Oratorio del Caravita is not normally open to the public for regular masses, so it is not a regular neighborhood church. Thus, unlike the celebration in 2005, there were no problems in having the altar set up "within" the church. Issues of politics and folkloric expressions of Mexican indigeneity in Rome and the Catholic Church emerged clearly in these celebrations; I return to this topic in the following chapter.

14. Morgan 2008, 2009.

15. See the Amy Hollywood reflection on Beatrice of Nazareth's text, about expanding the loving heart and its bursting veins, away from a perspective of enfleshed martyrdom's reflection of the life of Jesus (Hollywood 2002, 263). See also de Certeau's work on the possession of Catholic nuns in Loudon and their incomprehensible excesses of speech (2000).

16. Within Catholicism mystical aspects can also be read as a narrative of spiritual histories of female suffering (and death) with a purpose to inspire, cultivate, and instruct away from "what really happened." In a beautiful study of a mid-sixteenth-century orphanage home for young women (Casa della Pietà) in Florence, Nicholas Terpstra shows how female deaths, critically accounted for in many cases in mystical and near-hagiographic tones, should be reread in terms of the conditions of young female dispossession, abandonment, and illnesses afflicting particular group of women at specific moments of social and economic transformation (Terpstra 2010).

17. I refer here to a historicization of the study of the flesh, praying, and aesthetic and ethical modes of apprehension coming from interesting medievalist perspectives. See Largier 2008, 2010.

18. O'Neill 2010b.

19. Jonas 2000.

20. Harvey 1989.

21. Ibid., 222.
22. Mitchell 2005, 10.
23. Pozzi 1993.
24. Molina 2008.
25. Zambarbieri 1987, 339.
26. Orsi 2005, 111–12.
27. See also chapter 2.
28. Consider also Benedict XVI's meditation on the Sacred Heart as a gift of love, keeping in mind a political economy of free giving in Catholic pedagogies of citizenship, which I have stressed in the introduction, that corroborate rather than undermine a form of moral neoliberalism:

> Starting with this interior attitude, one sees that the gaze fixed upon his side, pierced by the spear, is transformed into silent adoration. Gazing at the Lord's pierced side, from which "blood and water" flowed (cf. John 19:34), helps us to recognize the manifold gifts of grace that derive from it (cf. "Haurietis Aquas," Nos. 34–41) and opens us to all other forms of Christian worship embraced by the devotion to the Heart of Jesus. Faith, understood as a fruit of the experience of God's love, is a grace, a gift of God. Yet human beings will only be able to experience faith as a grace to the extent that they accept it within themselves as a gift on which they seek to live. (Benedict XVI 2006)

29. Benedict XVI 2010.
30. Bataille 1998, 17.
31. Ibid., 23.
32. Bynum 2011a, 35.
33. Ibid., 33.
34. I am referring here in turns to the work of Morgan 1998, 2005 (first), Keane 1997a, 1997b, 2007, 2008, and Engelke 2007 (second), and Taussig 1992, 1997 (third).
35. Bynum 2011a, 32.
36. See Bataille's take on discontinuity and eroticism: "The whole business of eroticism is to strike to the inmost core of the living being, so that the heart stands still. The transition from the normal state to the one of erotic desire presupposes a partial dissolution of the person as he exists in the realm of discontinuity" (1998, 17).
37. Lilli 2001; De Stefano 2001.
38. Menjivar 1999.
39. Paerregaard 2008.
40. Ibid.; Paerregaard 2010.
41. They are El Señor de los Milagros, El Señor de la Justicia, El Señor del Cachuy, La Virgen del Chapy, and the Cruz de Motupe y Santo Madero. All are part of a loose group called El Cabildo de Hermandades Peruanas of Rome. The first two Hermandades are of Penitents, the last three are of Glory.
42. Stevens 1997, 275.

5. The Virgin of Guadalupe: A Nexus of Affects

1. Freud 1993, 274.

2. Symptoms register "past failures to respond to calls for action or even for empathy on behalf of those whose suffering belongs to the form of life of which one is a part. They hold the place of something that is there, that insists in our life, though it has never achieved full ontological consistency" (Santner 2005, 89).

3. Ibid., 107.

4. Wolf 1958.

5. "The Guadalupe Virgin, produced by a sign and a sign herself, was the 'portrait of an idea,' a mental, then figurative representation; the Christian supernatural in the sense of a collection of signs endowed with their own life, capable of regulation and autoregulation. . . . Immaterial image that existed in space and time without apparent intervention, the representation of the Tepeyac Virgin was enough to stupefy and fascinate the baroque gaze" (Gruzinski 2001, 129).

6. Ibid., 220.

7. Brading 2001, 11.

8. Sánchez 1648.

9. Wright-Rios 2004, 57–58.

10. Traslosheros 2002, 113–14.

11. Bantjes 2006, 140.

12. Elizondo 2000, 516.

13. See Elizondo 1997, 28.

14. Matovina 2005, 176–77.

15. Gálvez 2010.

16. Pérez 2007, 267.

17. Anzaldúa 1987.

18. Tweed 1997.

19. By *social imaginary* I refer to the realm of fantasy and desires that emerges out of and often exceeds a given symbolic order,while engaging with particular sociohistorical worlds. See Moore 2007, 60.

20. Napolitano 2002, 9–10.

21. Moore 2007, 14–15.

22. I use the word *materiality* in Navaro-Yashin's sense (2007). Discussing "make-believe" papers in the realm of law and order, she writes: "Material objects of law and governance [are] capable of carrying, containing, or inciting affective energies when transacted or put to use in specific webs of social relations. . . . Documents, then, are phantasmatic objects with affective energies which are experienced as real" (Navaro-Yashin 2007, 81). The Virgin of Guadalupe is not, of course, a document, but it has a materiality that is constantly, transnationally reproduced and ethnographically performed, whose affective energies are experienced as embodied and real.

23. See Aretxaga 1995.

24. Head of the Salesian order from 2002 to 2008.

25. Similar remarks about the diversity of status of religious migrants (as clericals and nuns) as opposed to lay migrants in Rome emerged in discussions with other members of religious congregations in Rome.

26. Garduño, Mendez, and Perez Silva, 2006.

27. Schedler 2007, 94.

28. Álvarez Béjar 2007, 14.

29. Žižek 2000, 238.

30. The two embassies are to Italy and the Holy See.

31. During their 2001 visit to Rome, Vicente Fox and his new wife, Martha Sahagún, were received separately by John Paul II. They both remarried without first obtaining an annulment, which provoked no little disapproval within the Catholic hierarchy.

32. This ambiguity, especially about the relation between Mexico as a secular state and the Catholic Church, was still strongly felt in debates leading up to the 2012 presidential election, and for Benedict XVI's visit to Mexico in March 2012.

33. Alvarado 2007; González Ruiz 2004.

34. I participated in the same procession in 2007. The December 2007 celebration had again a display of indigeneity. Once within the college, some priests performed the Danza de los Abuelitos in costumes typical of the region of Michoáchan in Mexico. The sermon was given by Cardinal Javier Lozano Barragán, and the focus was on Catholic inculturation through the Virgin of Guadalupe. In comparison with previous years, and since Pope Benedict XVI's call for a return to Latin in the mass, more than half of the masses in the Church of the Nostra Signora di Coromoto were sung in Latin chants.

35. Cadena and Starn 2007, 12.

36. The mobile headquarters of the EZLN were named after Guadalupe Tepeyac, and the image and the power of the Virgin of Guadalupe have been called upon by the EZLN as a symbol for the defense of indigenous rights.

37. Norget 2004, 166–69; Judd 2004, 218

38. Judd 2004, 212; Norget, 2004, 167.

39. This was the case of 2001 canonization of Juan Diego in the Basilica of Guadalupe by Pope John Paul II, when "the mise-en-scène of the event reduced the Indian contribution to a spectacle of feathers and drums that was far from 'inculturated evangelization' and even further form the syncretic indigenous theology espoused by certain groups outside the tent of orthodoxy" (Beatty 2006, 329).

40. In 1993, Jesús Posadas Ocampo, archbishop of Guadalajara, was made cardinal. From that point on, this church was assigned to the cardinal of Guadalajara in Rome. After Ocampo's controversial murder at Guadalajara's airport in 1993, the church was assigned to the elected cardinal of Guadalajara Juan Sandoval Iñiguez. It is clear that, at least symbolically, this church is very important in the connection between Guadalajara and Rome.

41. Saint Toribio Romo was born in 1900 in the Altos of Jalisco and was killed in 1927 by *agraristas* in the Cristiada clashes. There is now a temple and a

reliquary dedicated to him in his native village, Santa Ana de Guadalupe, and it has become an important pilgrimage destination.

42. In the words of Marcial Maciel, the founder of the Legionaries of Christ, "There is no direct, demonstrable relation between the religious persecution in Mexico and the Legion of Christ, but my faith tells me that the Legion is in a certain sense the fruit of those martyrs' blood, because blood shed for love of Christ always bears fruit. I do believe that in his wisdom and providence God has wished that blood to bear fruit through the apostolate of the Legion of Christ and Regnum Christi" (Colina 2003, 4).

43. Liga Nacional Defensora de la Libertad Religiosa (National League for the Defense of Religious Liberty) is an organization founded in 1925 in Mexico City to organize against a perceived opposition of the Mexican state at the time toward public practices of religion, and particularly Catholicism. This organization was crucial in the Catholic activism during the Cristero War.

44. M. Butler 2004, 160.

45. Ibid., 163.

46. Bantjes 2006, 151.

47. Aretxaga 2005b, 87.

48. We could also read this as a transnationalization of a national paradox—"the effect and the condition of possibility of Mexican culture's sacral-secular design"—where the *mestiza* Guadalupe, in a Lacanian interpretation, is oscillating between being the Self and Other, a double evocation of what is affirmed as Self and what is negated as Other (Feder 2001, 237).

49. Focolare is one of the fastest-growing lay movements in the Roman Catholic Church. Founded by Chiara Lubich in the late 1940s in Italy but now spreading worldwide, the Focolare group advocates a return to community living as well as direct experience of the message of the gospel, while remaining critical of more intellectual mediations of Catholicism.

50. See Benedict XVI 2011.

51. This interpretation does not, of course, exhaust all the facets of contemporary Guadalupe celebrations in Rome, but it highlights a focus on affect and historical traces that needs ethnographic and anthropological attention.

52. Tweed 2006, 54

53. See de Certeau 1986, 1992.

54. Levitt 2003, 852.

55. See Vásquez and Marquardt 2003; Alicia Galvez 2009; Peña 2011; Tweed 2006.

56. Orsi 2009, 216.

57. Mookherjee 2011.

6. Enwalled: Translocality, Intimacies, and Gendered Subjectivity

1. Important work has been done on the biotechnology of militarized walls and contested borders, and the historical shifts that occurred at the end

of the Cold War that have resulted in an increased militarization of the control of illegal migration (at least on the U.S.–Mexican border), but also an increased affective artistic emergence (Montezemolo, Peralta, and Yépez 2006; Kun and Montezemolo 2012). This research has paid attention to the migrant biopolitics and "ethopolitics" that emerge through the presence of surveillance, militarization, and the spatial politics of borders and the reifications of states of security (Andreas 2006; De Genova 2005; Inda 2006; Rosas 2006). This work is rooted in a Foucauldian way of thinking about modern forms of governmentality and discipline, a conceptualization of migration forging and being forged as a state of exception, and particular forms of ethical cultivation of the subject (De Genova and Peutz 2010). Others studies have fruitfully looked at the threads that animate stories at the border and at the border from multiple but interconnected registers of analysis (see Lugo 2008; Schmidt Camacho 2008). I here write implicitly in conversation with these debates on border studies.

2. Foucault 1984, 83.

3. Ibid., 80.

4. Napolitano and Pratten 2007.

5. For work on religion, migration, and adaptation in the United States, see in particular Portes and Rumbaut 2006; Portes and DeWind 2007; Lorentzen et al. 2009.

6. As I discussed in the introduction, heterologies as "altered feminine discourse" make us reflect on how writing about a migrant Other is fixing and streaming some of the complexity of migrant subject formation.

7. Zambrano [1955] 2008, 229.

8. Lomas de Polanco is one of the most exclusive and posh neighborhoods in Mexico City. Not only Mexican but diasporic elites live in this area.

9. A legal system of anticipated retirements of state employers with at least nineteen and half years of service, so-called "baby pensions" allowed workers to retire early, sometimes when they were still in their forties. This clearly financially unsustainable system was finally scrapped, after repeated amendments, by the Dini centrist government in 1996. However, its financial impact is still felt in present-day state pension provisions.

10. Latin American migrants have difficulties in getting their qualifications recognized. This has been documented both in Italy and in Spain. See Fullin and Reyneri 2011; Ambrosini 2011.

11. Stoler 2008.

12. See chapter 2.

13. From http://www.fondazionerisorsadonna.it.

14. Hirsch 2003, 8–9.

15. See Ahmed 2004; Ahmed and Stacey 2001. Transnational migration stirs not only the unity of a national ideal in Catholic migrant pedagogies but also a fantasy about personhood to be maintained through the process of transnational migration.

16. Consider, for example, the call for the best literary expression on the migratory phenomenon, promoted by the Instituto de los Mexicanos en el Exterior, el Consejo Nacional de Población y el Consejo Nacional para la Cultura y las Artes, and titled "Historias de Migrantes." The call was publicized as well by the Comunidad Católica Mexicana in Rome. For details about the circulated call, see http://www.ime.gob.mx/ime2/images/concursos/2009_historia_migrantes.pdf.

17. Ahmed 2004, 140. For a discussion of the popular understandings of national identity in relation to places and sites, real and imaginary, see Radcliffe and Westwood 1996.

18. Striffler 2007, 685.

19. This also signals the collapse of a singular, unifying national identification.

20. Povinelli 2006, 8.

21. Ibid., 178.

22. Deguili 2007.

23. *Sanatoria* was a national and legally endorsed amnesty for a quota of illegal migrants holding specific jobs and mainly already employed by Italians.

24. *Nervios* is a culturally constructed ailment emerging at particular political conjunctures, much written about in anthropological analysis of Latin America. I recall here the work of Scheper-Hughes (1992) in the case of north east Brazil.

25. McDonald's is where migrants attending the LAM, meet, not only because it is cheap, but because you are allowed to sit as long as you wish without reordering. The pressure put on public spaces for sociability away from Catholic institutions is a challenge especially for, but not only for, live-in migrants in Rome.

26. Italian society is cradled in a long history of Catholic culture that privileges a particular relationship between mother, father, and child, which has been read by some as a myth of omnipotent masculine activity and omnipotent female passivity (Accati 1998, 269). This can be seen as central to a beauty/beast "syndrome" that the media fostered during the Berlusconi era.

27. Pratt 1999, 164.

28. Varley 2008, 58.

29. Pratt 2009, 7.

30. Akalin 2007.

31. Lan 2006.

32. Burikova 2006.

33. I have chosen to withhold the names of all orders and their founders for obvious reasons of confidentiality.

34. Napolitano 2002, 43.

35. Evangelisti 2008.

36. Agamben 2008.

37. This is a case of some mystical apprehension of the embodied world, as in the case of St. Marguerite-Marie Alacoque, which I discussed in chapter 4 (Morgan 2008).

38. Ahmed 2004, 117–18.

39. Ibid., 120.

40. Lester 2005, 205.

41. While I was living in the convent in May 2009, the H1N1 flu outbreak erupted in Mexico. The misinformed international press at the time called it a swine flu epidemic and traced the outbreak to Mexico. Travels to and from Mexico were greatly disrupted, as was, for a while, the image of Mexico as a tourist destination for people in Italy. At the time, the sisters received a special prayer from Norberto Rivera, the cardinal of Mexico City, that was, to my understating, distributed to other Mexican nuns, seminarians, and priests in Rome. This prayer was also recited during the evening prayers that took place in a smaller chapel, and exclusively for the nuns, in another section of the convent. An abridged version/reminder of the prayer was put at the bases of the altars in the major, shared chapel of the convent, which read "Let's pray for Mexico and its governments." It was left there for over a week.

42. Anderson 2000.

43. See Anderson 2000; Pratt 2005, 2009; Gutiérrez Rodríguez 2007.

44. Gregorio Gil and Ramírez Fernández 2000.

45. Raijman, Schammah-Gesser, and Kemp 2003.

Epilogue

1. "Insidious and ungraspable" (Gramsci 1967).

2. Pope Francis has also referred to this apostolic zeal. In his first Apostolic Exhortation, *Evangelii Gaudium* (2013) he describes it as a burning force of joy against growing defeatism and pessimism with the church. In a morning homily, given in May 2013 at Santa Marta, where he normally lives, he also preached apostolic zeal as a form of "healthy madness":

> [It is] not an enthusiasm for power, for possession. It is something that comes from within, that the Lord wants from us: Christian with Apostolic Zeal. And where does this Apostolic Zeal come from? It comes from knowing Jesus Christ. Paul found Jesus Christ, he encountered Jesus Christ, but not with an intellectual, scientific knowledge—which is important, because it helps us—but with that first knowledge, that of the heart, of a personal encounter. (http://en.radiovaticana.va/news/2013/05/16/pope_at_mass:_an_apostolic_nuisance/en1–692628 [accessed 10 February 2013])

3. Agamben 2013, 61.

4. Ibid., xiii. The theological dispute between property as ownership versus the right to use had it apex in the confrontation between the Franciscan order and Pope John XXII between 1316 and 1329.

5. Agamben 2013, 24.

6. Orsi 2005, 170.

7. Ibid., 173.

8. Ahmed 2010, 39.

9. See Phillips 2012.

References

Abraham, Nicolas. 1987. "Notes on the Phantom: A Complement to Freud's Metapsychology." Translated by Nicholas Rand. *Critical Inquiry* 13 (2): 287–92.

Accati, Luisa. 1998. *Il mostro e la bella: Padre e madre nell'educazione Cattolica dei sentimenti*. Milan: Raffaello Cortina Editore.

Agamben, Giorgio. 2002. *L'aperto: L'uomo e l'animale*. Turin: Bollati Boringhieri.

———. 2008. *Signatura rerum: Sul metodo*. Turin: Bollati Boringhieri.[English edition: 2009. *The Signature of All Things: On Method*, translated by Luca D'Isanto with Kevin Attell. New York: Zone Books.]

———. 2013. *The Highest Poverty: Monastic Rules and Form-of-Life*. Stanford, Calif.: Stanford University Press.

Ahmed, Sara. 2004. *The Cultural Politics of Emotion*. Edinburgh: Edinburgh University Press.

———. 2010. "Happy Objects." In *The Affect Theory Reader,* edited by Melissa Gregg and Gregory J. Seigworth, 29–51. Durham, N.C.: Duke University Press.

Ahmed, Sara, and Jackie Stacey. 2001. *Thinking through the Skin*. New York: Routledge.

Akalin, Ayşe. 2007. "Hired as a Caregiver, Demanded as a Housewife: Becoming a Migrant Domestic Worker In Turkey." *European Journal of Women's Studies* 14 (3): 209–25.

Albahari, Maurizio. 2006. "Charitable Borders: Pastoral Power at the Southern Edges of Europe, Italy." PhD diss., Department of Anthropology, University of California Irvine.

Alberigo, Giuseppe. 1999. "Il Concilio Vaticano II e le trasformazioni culturali in Europa." *Cristianesimo Nella Storia* 20 (2): 383–405.

———. 2005. *Breve storia del Concilio Vaticano II: 1959–1965*. Bologna: Il Mulino.

Alvarado, René Ramón. 2007. "Denuncian ONG embestida de la Iglesia católica y el Yunque contra el Estado laico." *La Jornada,* 5 June. http://www.jornada .unam.mx/2007/06/05/index.php?section=politica&article=018n1pol.

Álvarez Béjar, Alejandro. 2007. "Mexico after the Elections: The Crisis of Legitimacy and the Exhaustion of Predatory Neoliberalism." *Monthly Review* 59 (3): 12–25.

Ambrosini, Maurizio. 2007. *Gli immigrati e la religione: Fattore di integrazione o alterità irriducibile*. Palermo: Fondazione Ignazio Buttitta.

————. 2008. *Un'altra globalizzazione: La sfida delle migrazioni transnazionali.* Bologna: Il Mulino.

————. 2013. *Irregular Migration and Invisible Welfare.* Basingstoke, Hampshire: Palgrave Macmillan.

Ambrosini, Marizio, and Luca Queirolo Palmas, eds. 2005. *I Latinos alla scoperta dell'europa: Nuove migrazioni e spazi della cittadinanza.* Milan: F. Angeli.

Andall, Jacqueline. 2000. *Gender, Migration and Domestic Service: The Politics of Black Women in Italy.* Burlington, Vt.: Ashgate.

Anderson, Bridget. 2000. *Doing the Dirty Work?: The Global Politics of Domestic Labour.* New York: Zed Books.

André, Jacques. 2011. "The Analyst at Work: Laura, or the Sexual Borders of Need." *International Journal of Psychoanalysis* 92 (4): 761–71.

Andreas, Peter. 2006. "Politics on Edge: Managing the U.S.–Mexico Border." *Current History* 105 (688): 64–68.

————. 2009. *Border Games: Policing the U.S.-Mexico Divide.* Ithaca, N.Y.: Cornell University Press.

Anidjar, Gil. 2014. *Blood: A Critique of Cristianity.* New York: Columbia University Press.

Anzaldúa, G. 1987. *Borderlands: The New Mestiza = La Frontera.* San Francisco: Aunt Lute Books.

Archer, Margaret. 2009. L'enciclica di Benedetto Provoca la teoria sociale. *Vita e Pensiero* 5:52–56.

Aretxaga, Begoña. 1995. "Dirty Protest: Symbolic Overdetermination and Gender in Northern Ireland Ethnic Violence." *Ethos* 23 (2): 123–48.

————. 2005a. "Maddening States." *Annual Review of Anthropology* 32:393–410.

————. 2005b. *States of Terror: Begoña Aretxaga's Essays.* Edited by Joseba Zulaika. Reno: Center for Basque Studies, University of Nevada.

Arizpe, Lourdes. 1975. *Indigenas en la Ciudad de Mexico: El caso de las "Marias."* Mexico D.F.: SEP/Setentas.

Arrupe, Pedro. 1984. *In Him Alone Is Our Hope: Texts on the Heart of Christ (1965–1983.* Edited by Jerome Aixala. Translated by G. Ganss. St. Louis, Mo.: Institute of Jesuit Sources.

Asad, Talad. 1996. "Comments on Conversion." In *Conversion to Modernities: The Globalization of Christianity,* edited by Peter van der Veer, 263–73. New York: Routledge.

————. 2003. *Formations of the Secular: Christianity, Islam, Modernity.* Stanford, Calif.: Stanford University Press.

Baldini, Gianfranco, and Anna Cento Bull, eds. 2009. *Governing Fear: Italian Politics.* New York: Berghahn Books.

Balibar, Étienne. 2010. "At the Borders of Citizenship: A Democracy in Translation?" *European Journal of Social Theory* 13 (3): 315–22.

Bantjes, Adrian A. 2006. "Saints, Sinners, and State Formation: Local Religion and Cultural Revolution in Mexico." In *The Eagle and the Virgin: 1920–40,* edited by Mary Kay Vaughan and Stephen E. Lewis, 137–56. Durham, N.C.: Duke University Press.

Barthes, Roland. 1976. *Sade, Fourier, Loyola.* New York: Hill and Wang.

Bataille, Georges. 1998. *Eroticism.* New York: Marion Boyars.

Battistella, Graziano. 2006. "Verso politiche migratorie eticamente fondate." Presentation at the Meeting Internazionale delle Migrazioni, Loreto, Italy, 11 July.

Beatty, Andrew. 2006. "The Pope in Mexico: Syncretism in Public Ritual." *American Anthropologist* 108 (2): 324–35.

Benedict XVI. 2006. "Letter of His Holiness Benedict XVI on the Occasion of the 50th Anniversary of the Encyclical 'Haurietis Aquas.'" http://www.vatican.va/holy_father/benedict_xvi/letters/2006/d ocuments/hf_ben-xvi_let_20060515_50-haurietis-aquas_en.html.

———. 2007. Angelus of 14 January, on the Occasion of the World Day of Migrants and Refugees. http://www.vatican.va/holy_father/benedict_xvi/angelus/2007/documents/hf_ben-xvi_ang_20070114_en.html.

———. 2009. *Caritas in Veritate.* http://www.vatican.va/holy_father/benedict_xvi/encyclicals/do cuments/hf_ben-xvi_enc_20090629_caritas-in-veritate_en.html.

———. 2010. "Homily: Solemnity of the Sacred Heart of Jesus." St. Peter's Square, 11 June. http://www.vatican.va/holy_father/benedict_xvi/homilies/2010/documents/hf_ben-xvi_hom_20100611_concl-anno-sac_en.html.

———. 2011. Homily, 12 December. http://www.vatican.va/holy_father/benedict_xvi/homilies/2011/documents/hf_ben-xvi_hom_20111212_america-latina_en.html.

Bennett, Jane. 2004. "The Force of Things: Steps toward an Ecology of Matter." *Political Theory* 32 (3): 347–72.

Berlant, Lauren. 2006. "Cruel Optimism." *Differences* 17 (3): 20–36.

———. 2007. "Nearly Utopian, Nearly Normal: Post-Fordist Affect in *La Promesse* and *Rosetta.*" *Public Culture* 19 (2): 273–301.

———. 2008. "Intuitionists: History and the Affective Event." *American Literary History* 20 (4): 845–60.

———. 2011. *Cruel Optimism.* Durham, N.C.: Duke University Press.

Berry, Jason. 2010. "Money Paved the Way for Maciel's Influence." *National Catholic Reporter,* 6 April.

Berry, Jason, and Gerald Renner. 2010. *Vows of Silence: The Abuse of Power in the Papacy of John Paul II.* Toronto: Free Press.

Biffi, Giacomo. 2000. "La questione dell'immigrazione." Nota pastorale, "La città di San Petronio nel terzo millennio." Bologna. 12 September. http://chiesa.espresso.repubblica.it/articolo/7282.

Bildhauer, Bettina. 2006. *Medieval Blood.* Cardiff: University of Wales Press.

Bodo, Carla, and Simona Bodo. 2005. *Diversità culturale e politiche culturali nell' area metropolitana di Roma.* Roma: Associazione per l'Economia della Cultura. [English edition: Carla Bodo and Simona Bodo. 2006. "Cultural Policies and Cultural Civersity in the Metropolitan Area of Rome." In *Metropolises of Europe: Diversity in Urban Cultural Life,* edited by D. Ilczuk and R. Isar, 134–83. CIRCLE Publication 14, Pro Cultura Foundation, Warsaw.]

Bouchard, Norma. 2010. "Reading the Discourse of Multicultural Italy: Promises and Challenges of Transnational Italy in an Era of Global Migration." *Italian Culture* 28 (2): 104–20.

Brading, David. 2001. *Mexican Phoenix: Our Lady of Guadalupe: Image and Tradition across Five Centuries*. New York: Cambridge University Press.

Brah, Avtar. 1996. *Cartographies of Diaspora: Contesting Identities*. New York: Routledge.

Brah, Avtar, and Annie Coombes. 2000. *Hybridity and Its Discontents: Politics, Science, Culture*. New York: Routledge.

Brandi, Maria Carolina, and Enrico Todisco. 2006. "Stranieri residenti a Roma: Modelli insediativi a confronto." In *Gli immigrati stranieri e la capitale,* edited by Cinzia Conti and Salvatore Strozzi. Milan: Franco Angeli.

Brennan, Teresa. 2004. *The Transmission of Affect*. Ithaca, N.Y.: Cornell University Press.

Burikova, Zuzana. 2006. "The Embarrassment of Co-Presence: Au Pairs and Their Rooms." *Home Cultures* 3 (2): 99–122.

Butler, Judith. 1997. *The Psychic Life of Power: Theories in Subjection*. Stanford, Calif.: Stanford University Press.

———. 2004. *Undoing Gender*. New York: Routledge.

———. 2006. *Precarious Life: The Powers of Mourning and Violence*. London: Verso.

———. 2009. "Sexual Politics, Torture, and Secular Time." In *Intimate Citizenships: Gender, Sexualities, Politics,* edited by Elizabeth H. Oleksy, 17–39. New York: Routledge/Taylor and Francis Group.

Butler, Matthew. 2004. *Popular Piety and Political Identity in Mexico's Cristero Rebellion: Michoachán, 1927–29*. Oxford: Oxford University Press.

Bynum, Caroline Walker. 1987. *Holy Feast and Holy Fast: The Religious Significance of Food to Medieval Women*. Berkeley: University of California Press.

———. 2002. "The Blood of Christ In the Later Middle Ages." *Church History* 71 (4): 685–714.

———. 2005. *Metamorphosis and Identity,*New York: Zone Books

———. 2011a. *Christian Materiality: An Essay on Religion in Late Medieval Europe*. New York: Zone Books.

———. 2011b. Review of *St. Ursula and the Eleven Thousand Virgins of Cologne: Relics, Reliquaries and the Visual Culture of Group Sanctity in Late Medieval Europe,* by Scott B. Montgomery. *Journal of Ecclesiastical History* 62 (4): 812.

Cadena, Marisol de la. 2005. "Are 'Mestizos' Hybrids? The Conceptual Politics of Andean Identities." *Journal of Latin American Studies* 37 (2): 259–84.

———. 2010. "Indigenous Cosmopolitics in the Andes: Conceptual Reflections beyond 'Politics.'" *Cultural Anthropology* 25 (2): 334–70.

Cadena, Marisol de la, and Orin Starn. 2007. *Indigenous Experience Today*. Oxford: Berg.

Caiani, Manuela. 2011. "L'estrema destra in Italia fra passato e presente: Il discorso sulla globalizzazione." *Società/Mutamento/Politica* 2 (3): 133–51.

Cannell, Fenella. 2006. Introduction to *The Anthropology of Christianity,* edited by Fenella Canell, 1–50. Durham, N.C.: Duke University Press.

————. 2010. "The Anthropology of Secularism." *Annual Review of Anthropology* 39:85–100.

CARITAS/Migrantes. 2009. *America Latina-Italia. Vecchi e nuovi migranti.* Rome: IDOS (Dossier Statistico Immigrazione).

Carsten, Janet. 2011. "Substance and Relationality: Blood in Contexts." *Annual Review of Anthropology* 40:19–35.

Castelli, Elizabeth A. 2004. *Martyrdom and Memory: Early Christian Culture Making.* New York: Columbia University Press.

————. 2005. "Praying for the Persecuted Church: U.S. Christian Activism in the Global Arena." *Journal of Human Rights* 4 (3): 321–51.

————. 2007. "Persecution Complexes: Identity Politics and the 'War On Christians.'" *Differences* 18 (3): 152–80.

Castelli, Elizabeth A., and Brent D. Shaw. 2005. "Martyrdom and Memory: Early Christian Culture Making." *American Historical Review* 110 (3): 847–48.

Choudhury, Mita. 2009. "A Betrayal of Trust: The Jesuits and Quietism in Eighteenth-Century France." *Common Knowledge* 15 (2): 164–80.

Cipriani, Roberto. 2004. "Carità e Trasformazioni Sociali." In *La nazione cattolica: Chiesa e società in Italia dal 1958 a oggi*, edited by Marco Impagliazzo, 439–56. Milan: Edizioni Angelo Guerini e Associati.

Climo, Jacob, Mary G. Cattell, and Nayanika Mookherjee. 2006. "Social Memory and History: Anthropological Perspectives." *Journal of the Royal Anthropological Institute* 12 (4): 957–58.

Cody, Francis. 2011. "Publics and Politics." *Annual Review of Anthropology* 40:37–52.

Coleman, Simon. 2004. "The Charismatic Gift." *Journal of the Royal Anthropological Institute* 10 (2): 421–42.

————. 2010. "An Anthropological Apologetics." *South Atlantic Quarterly* 109 (4): 791–810.

Colina, Jesús. 2003. *Marcial Maciel: "Mi Vida es Cristo."* Barcelona: Editorial Planeta.

Connolly, William E. 1999. *Why I Am Not a Secularist.* Minneapolis: University of Minnesota Press.

Conti, Cinzia, and Salvatore Strozza. 2006. *Gli immigrati stranieri e la capitale: Condizioni di vita e atteggiamenti dei Filippini, Marocchini, Peruviani e Romeni a Roma.* Milan: Franco Angeli.

Cordoba, José de. 2006. "Wealthy Kingdom." *Wall Street Journal*, 23 January.

Cornish, Peter. 1996. "Spanish Thomism and the American Indians: Vitoria and Las Casas on the Toleration of Cultural Difference." In *Difference and Dissent: Theories of Toleration in Medieval and Early Modern Europe*, edited by C. J. Nederman and J. C. Laursen, 1–16. Lanham, Md.: Rowman and Littlefield.

Corriere della Sera. 2009. "*Ddl sicurezza, il Vaticano: 'Una legge che porterà dolore.'*" 2 July. http://www.corriere.it/politica/09_luglio_02/santa_sede_no_ddl_45cd6100-66f9-11de-9708-00144f02aabc.shtml.

D'Agostino, Peter R. 2004. *Rome in America: Transnational Catholic Ideology from the Risorgimento to Fascism.* Chapel Hill: University of North Carolina Press.

Dal Lago, Alessandro. 2004. *Non-persone: L'Esclusione dei migranti in una società globale*. Milan: Feltrinelli.

Daswani, Girish. 2013. "On Christianity and Ethics: Rupture as Ethical Practice in Ghanaian Pentecostalism." *American Ethnologist* 40 (3): 467–79.

De Amicis, Edmondo. 1967. *Cuore: Libro per i ragazzi*. Bari: Edizioni Paoline.

De Certeau, Michel. 1986. *Heterologies: Discourse on the Other*. Minneapolis: University of Minnesota Press.

———. 1988. *The Practice of Everyday Life*. Berkeley: University of California Press.

———. 1992. *The Mystic Fable*. Chicago: University of Chicago Press.

———. 2000. *The Possession at Loudun*. Chicago: University of Chicago Press.

De Certeau, Michel, and Luce Giard. 1997. *Culture in the Plural*. Minneapolis: University of Minnesota Press.

De Genova, Nicholas. 2005. *Working the Boundaries: Race, Space, and "Illegality" on Mexican Chicago*. Durham, N.C.: Duke University Press.

De Genova, Nicholas, and N. M. Peutz, eds. 2010. *The Deportation Regime: Sovereignty, Space, and the Freedom of Movement*. Durham, N.C.: Duke University Press.

Deguili, Francesca. 2007. "A Job with No Boundaries: Home Eldercare Work in Italy." *European Journal of Women's Studies* 14 (3): 193–207.

De Mattei, Roberto. 2010. *Il Concilio Vaticano II: Una storia mai scritta*. Turin: Lindau.

De Stefano, F. 2001. "The Maternal Ideal and the Catholic Marian Cult." *Sociologia* 35:83–98.

De Theije, Marjo E. M. 2011. "Local Protest and Transnational Catholicism in Brazil." In *Local Battles, Global Stakes; The Globalization of Local Conflicts and the Localization of Global Interests*, edited by T. Salman and Marjo De Theije, 61–80. Amsterdam: VU Uitgeverij.

Dokecki, Paul R. 2004. *The Clergy Sexual Abuse Crisis: Reform and Renewal in the Catholic Community*. Washington, D.C.: Georgetown University Press.

Duffy, Eamon. 2005. *The Stripping of the Altars: Traditional Religion in England, c.1400–c.1580*. 2nd ed. New Haven, Conn.: Yale University Press.

Edwards, Lisa M. 2011. *Roman Virtues: The Education of Latin American Clergy in Rome, 1858–1962*. New York: Peter Lang.

Elizondo, Virgilio P. 1997. *Guadalupe, Mother of the New Creation*. Maryknoll, N.Y.: Orbis Books.

———. 2000. *The Future Is Mestizo: Life Where Cultures Meet*. Boulder: University Press of Colorado.

Engelke, Matthew E. 2007. *A Problem of Presence: Beyond Scripture in an African Church*. Berkeley: University of California Press.

England, Kim. 2010. Home, Work and the Shifting Geographies of Care. *Ethics, Place and Environment* 13 (2): 131–50.

Espinosa, Alejandro. 2003. *El Legionario*. Miguel Hidalgo, México, D.F.: Grijalbo.

Evangelisti, Silvia. 2008. "To Find God in Work: Unmarried Women's Social Stratification in Early Modern Italian Convents." *European History Quarterly* 38 (3): 398–416.

Fabian, Johannes. 1983. *Time and the Other: How Anthropology Makes Its Object.* New York: Columbia University Press.

Fanon, Frantz. 1968. *The Wretched of the Earth.* New York: Grove Press.

Fardon, Richard. 1999. *Mary Douglas.* London: Routledge.

Feder, Elena. 2001. "Engendering the Nation, Nationalizing the Sacred: Guadalupanism and the Cinematic (Re)Formation of Mexican Consciousness." In *National Identities and Sociopolitical Changes in Latin America,* edited by M. F. Durán-Cogan and A. Gómez-Moriana, 229–68. New York: Routledge.

Finch, Janet, and Dulcie Groves. 1983. *A Labour of Love: Women, Work, and Caring.* Boston: Routledge and K. Paul.

Finchelstein, Federico. 2010. *Transatlantic Fascism.* Durham, N.C.: Duke University Press.

Fondazione Migrantes. 2004. "La comunità cattolica messicana di Roma in fase di decollo." http://www.chiesacattolica.it/documenti/2004/01/00009049_la_comunita_cattolica_messicana_di_roma_i.html.

Foucault, Michel. 1984. "Nietzsche, Genealogy, History." In *The Foucault Reader,* edited by P. Rabinow. New York: Penguin.

Freud, Sigmund. 1953. "A Special Type of Choice of Object Made by Men." In *The Standard Edition of the Complete Psychological Works of Sigmund Freud, Volume XII,* edited by J. Strachey, A. Freud, and A. Richards, 165–75. London: Hogarth Press.

———. 1955. *Moses and Monotheism.* New York: Vintage.

———. 1961. *Beyond the Pleasure Principle.* New York: Liveright.

———. 1989. "The Moses of Michelangelo." In *The Freud Reader,* edited by Peter Gay, 522–38. New York: W. W. Norton.

———. 1993. *On Psychopathology: Inhibitions, Symptoms and Anxiety, and Other Works.* Translated by James Strachey et al. Harmondsworth, Eng.: Penguin Books.

Fullin, Giovanna. 2010. "Immigrazione femminile e lavoro per le famiglie: Esperienze e percezioni di colf e badanti." *Prisma* 2 (2): 34–52.

Fullin, Giovanna, and Valeria Vercelloni. 2009. "Dentro la trappola: Percezioni e immagini del lavoro domestico e di cura nei percorsi delle donne immigrate." *Polis* 22 (3): 427–62.

Fulton, Rachel. 2002. *From Judgment to Passion: Devotion to Christ and the Virgin Mary, 800–1200.* New York: Columbia University Press.

Gachuz–Meza, Luis A. 2002. "Women, Freedom, and God: The Cristero Rebellion and the Work of Women in Small Towns of Los Altos." *Berkeley McNair Research Journal* 10:51–70.

Gálvez, Alicia. 2010. *Guadalupe in New York: Devotion and the Struggle for Citizenship Rights among Mexican Immigrants.* New York: New York University.

Garduño, Roberto, Enrique Mendez, and Ciro Perez Silva. 2006. "Desaseo legal y político al asumir calderón el cargo." *La Jornada*. http://www.jornada .unam.mx/2006/12/02/index.php?section=politica&article=003n1pol.

Garelli, Franco. 2006. *L'italia cattolica nell'epoca del pluralismo*. Bologna: Il Mulino.

Garza Medina, Luis. 2008. *La battaglia per l'anima del mondo: Sfide per il cristiano del ventunesimo secolo*. Rome: Art.

Gillis, Chester. 2003. "American Catholics: Neither Out Far Nor in Deep." In *Religion and Immigration: Christian, Jewish, and Muslim Experiences in the United States*, edited by Yvonne Yazbeck Haddad, Jane I. Smith, and John L. Esposito, 33–51. Walnut Creek, Calif.: Rowman and Littlefield.

Ginzburg, Carlo. 1972. *Folklore, magia, religione*. In *Storia d'italia, vol. 1: I caratteri originali*. Turin: Einaudi.

Giordano, Cristiana. 2008. "Practices of Translation and the Making of Migrant Subjectivities in Contemporary Italy." *American Ethnologist* 35 (4): 588–606.

Goldberg, David Theo, and Ato Quayson. 2002. *Relocating Postcolonialism*. Oxford: Blackwell.

González, Fernando M. 2001. *Matar y morir por cristo rey: Aspectos de la cristiada*. México, D.F.: Universidad Nacional Autónoma De México.

———. 2006. *Marcial Maciel: Los Legionarios de Cristo: Testimonios y documentos Inéditos*. México, D.F.: Tusquets Editores.

———. 2009. *La iglesia del silencio*. Mexico, D.F.: Tusquets.

González Ruiz, Edgar. 2004. *Los otros cristeros y su presencia en puebla*. Puebla, Mexico: Gobierno del Estado de Puebla.

Gramsci, Antonio.1967. *Il vaticano e l'italia*. Edited by E. Fubini. Rome: Editori Riuniti.

Greenblatt, Stephen. 1991. *Marvelous Possessions: The Wonder of the New World*. Chicago: University of Chicago Press.

Gregg, Melissa, and Gregory J. Seigworth. 2010. *The Affect Theory Reader*. Durham, N.C.: Duke University Press.

Gregorio Gil, Carmen, and Angeles Ramírez Fernández. 2000. "¿En españa es diferente . . . ? Mujeres inmigrantes dominicanas y marroquíes." *Revista de Sociología* 60:257–73.

Grilli, Simonetta, and Fabio Mugnaini. 2009. "Badanti on the Edge: Networks beyond Frontiers in Domestic Elderly Care: An Ethnographic Study of Migrant Women Workers and Contemporary Families in Italy." In *Networking across Borders and Frontiers,* edited by J. Barkhoff, and H. Eberhart, 169–94. Berlin: Peter Lang.

Gruzinski, Serge. 2001. *Images at War: Mexico from Columbus to Blade Runner (1492–2019)*. Translated by Heather MacLean. Durham, N.C.: Duke University Press.

Guardini, Romano. 1935. *The Church and the Catholic*. New York: Sheed and Ward.

Guerrero Chiprés, Salvador. 2004. *El círculo del poder y la espiral del silencio: La historia oculta del padre Marcial Maciel y los Legionarios de Cristo*. México, D.F.: Grijalbo.

Guillermoprieto, Alma. 2010. "The Mission of Father Maciel." *New York Review of Books*, 24 June, 57:28.

Gutiérrez, Ramón A. 1991. *When Jesus Came, the Corn Mothers Went Away: Marriage, Sexuality, and Power in New Mexico, 1500–1846*. Stanford, Calif.: Stanford University Press.

Gutiérrez Rodríguez, Encarnación. 2007. "The 'Hidden Side' of the New Economy: On Transnational Migration, Domestic Work, and Unprecedented Intimacy." *Frontiers* 28 (3): 60–83.

Hamao, Stephen Fumio. 2005. *The Instruction Erga Migrantes Caritas Christi: A Response of the Church to the Migration Phenomenon Today*. http://www.vatican.va/roman_curia/pontifical_councils/migrants/pom2005_97/rc_pc_migrants_pom97_sedos-hamao.html.

Hanafin, Patrick. 2007 *Conceiving Life: Reproductive Politics and the Law in Contemporary Italy*. Aldershot, Eng.: Ashgate.

Harding, Susan F. 1987. "Convicted by the Holy Spirit: The Rhetoric of Fundamental Baptist Conversion." *American Ethnologist* 14 (1): 167–81.

———. 2000. *The Book of Jerry Falwell: Fundamentalist Language and Politics*. Princeton, N.J.: Princeton University Press.

Harvey, David. 1989. *The Urban Experience*. Baltimore: Johns Hopkins University Press.

Hirsch, Jennifer S. 2003. *A Courtship after Marriage: Sexuality and Love in Mexican Transnational Families*. Berkeley: University of California Press.

Hodgen, Margaret T. 1971. *Early Anthropology in the Sixteenth and Seventeenth Centuries*. Philadelphia: University of Pennsylvania Press.

Hollywood, Amy M. 2002. *Sensible Ecstasy: Mysticism, Sexual Difference, and the Demands of History*. Chicago: University of Chicago Press.

Holmes, Douglas R. 2000. *Integral Europe: Fast-Capitalism, Multiculturalism, Neofascism*. Princeton, N.J.: Princeton University Press.

Holsinger, Bruce W. 2005. *The Premodern Condition: Medievalism and the Making of Theory*. Chicago: University of Chicago Press.

Hondagneu-Sotelo, P. 1994. *Gendered Transitions: Mexican Experiences of Immigration*. Berkeley: University of California Press.

———. 2001. *Doméstica: Immigrant Workers Cleaning and Caring in the Shadows of Affluence*. Berkeley: University of California Press.

———. 2008. *God's Heart Has No Borders: How Religious Activists Are Working for Immigrant Rights*. Berkeley: University of California Press.

Hughes, Jennifer Scheper. 2010. *Biography of a Mexican Crucifix*. Oxford: Oxford University Press.

Inda, Jonathan Xavier. 2006. *Targeting Immigrants: Government, Technology, and Ethics*. Malden, Mass.: Blackwell.

Jakobsen, J. R., and Ann Pellegrini. 2008. "Times Like These." In *Secularisms*, edited by Janet R. Jakobsen and Ann Pellegrini, 1–38. Durham, N.C.: Duke University Press.

Jenkins, P. 2007. *The Next Christendom: The Coming of Global Christianity*. Rev. and exp. ed. New York: Oxford University Press.

John Paul II. 1979. Third General Conference of the Latin American Episcopate. Puebla, 28 January. http://www.vatican.va/holy_father/john_paul_ii/speeches/1979/january/documents/hf_jp-ii_spe_19790128_messico-puebla-episc-latam_en.html.

———. 1981. Encyclical, *Laborem Exercens,* http://www.vatican.va/holy_father/john_paul_ii/encyclicals/documents/hf_jp-ii_enc_14091981_laborem-exercens_en.html.

———. 2000. Homily, at the Canonization of Twenty-Seven Saints. 21 May. http://www.vatican.va/holy_father/john_paul_ii/homilies/2000/documents/hf_jp-ii_hom_20000521_canonizations_en.html.

———. 2003. For the 90th World Day of Migrants and Refugees Message. http://www.vatican.va/holy_father/john_paul_ii/messages/migration/documents/hf_jp-ii_mes_20031223_world-migration-day-2004_en.html.

Jonas, R. A. 2000. *France and the Cult of the Sacred Heart: An Epic Tale for Modern Times.* Berkeley: University of California Press.

Judd, S. 2004. "Indigenous Theology Movement in Latin America: Encounters of Memory, Resistance and Hope at the Crossroads. In *Resurgent Voices in Latin America: Indigenous Peoples, Political Mobilization, and Religious Change,* edited by E. L. Cleary and T. J. Steigenga, 210–30. New Brunswick, N.J: Rutgers University Press.

Keane, Webb. 1997a. "Religious Language." *Annual Review of Anthropology* 26 (1): 47–71.

———. 1997b. "From Fetishism to Sincerity: On Agency, the Speaking Subject, and Their Historicity in the Context of Religious Conversion." *Comparative Studies in Society and History* 39 (4): 674–93.

———. 2007. *Christian Moderns: Freedom and Fetish in the Mission Encounter.* Berkeley: University of California Press.

———. 2008. "The Evidence of the Senses and the Materiality of Religion." *Journal of the Royal Anthropological Institute* 14 (S1): S110–27.

Krogt van der, Christopher. 1992. "Catholic Fundamentalism or Catholic Integralism?" In *To Strive and Not to Yield: Essays in Honour of Colin Brown,* edited by James Veitch. Wellington: Department of World Religions, University of Victoria.

Kun, Josh, and F. Montezemolo, eds. 2012. *Tijuana Dreaming: Life and Art at the Global Border.* Durham, N.C.: Duke University Press.

La Bella, Gianni. 2007. *Pedro Arrupe: Un uomo per gli altri.* Bologna: Il Mulino.

Lan, Pei-Chia. 2006. *Global Cinderellas: Migrant Domestics and Newly Rich Employers in Taiwan.* Durham, N.C.: Duke University Press.

Largier, Niklaus. 2008. "Praying by Numbers: An Essay on Medieval Aesthetics." *Representations* 104 (1): 73–91.

———. 2010. "The Plasticity of the Soul: Mystical Darkness, Touch, and Aesthetic Experience." *MLN* 125 (3): 536–51.

Latour, Bruno. 1993. *We Have Never Been Modern.* New York: Harvester Wheatsheaf.

Lavalle, Bernard. 2009. *Bartolomé de Las Casas, entre la espada y la cruz*. Madrid: Ariel.

Legionaries of Christ. 2009. Censored Legion of Christ and Regnum Cristi Document Collection. Unpublished documents.

Lester, Rebecca J. 2005. *Jesus in Our Wombs: Embodying Modernity in a Mexican Convent*. Berkeley: University of California Press.

Levitt, Peggy. 2003. "'You Know, Abraham Was Really the First Immigrant': Religion and Transnational Migration." *International Migration Review* 37 (3): 847–73.

Li, Tania. 2007. *The Will to Improve: Governmentality, Development, and the Practice of Politics*. Durham, N.C.: Duke University Press.

Li, Victor. 2002. "The Premodern Condition: Neo-Primitivism in Baudrillard and Lyotard." In *After Postructuralism: Writing the Intellectual History of Theory*, edited by T. Rajan and O. Michael, 88–109. Toronto: University of Toronto Press.

Lilli, Romeo. 2001. "Sister Floriana and the Cenacoli Serafici: An Ethnographic Study in South Lazio." *La Critica Sociologica* 137:100–116.

Locke, John. [1764] 1946. *The Second Treatise of Civil Government: Letter concerning Toleration*. Edited by J. W. Gough. Oxford: Blackwell.

Lomnitz-Adler, Claudio. 2001. *Deep Mexico, Silent Mexico: An Anthropology of Nationalism*. Public Worlds, vol. 9. Minneapolis: University of Minnesota Press.

Lorentzen, Lois Ann, Joaquin Jay Gonzalez, Kevin M. Chun, and Hien Duc Do, eds. 2009. *Religion at the Corner of Bliss and Nirvana*. Durham, N.C.: Duke University Press.

Lugo, Alejandro. 2008. *Fragmented Lives, Assembled Parts: Culture, Capitalism, and Conquest at the U.S.-Mexico Border*. Austin: University of Texas Press.

Mahmood, Saba. 2005. *Politics of Piety: The Islamic Revival and the Feminist Subject*. Princeton, N.J.: Princeton University Press.

———. 2009. "Religious Reason and Secular Affect: An Incommensurable Divide?" *Critical Inquiry* 35 (4): 836.

———. 2012. "Religious Freedom, the Minority Question, and Geopolitics in the Middle East." *Comparative Studies in Society and History* 54 (2): 418–46.

Maldonado-Torres, Nelson. 2007. "On the Coloniality of Being: Contributions to the Development of a Concept." *Cultural Studies* 21 (2–3): 240–70.

Mantovano, Alfredo. 2007. *Immigrazione senza regole*. Rome: Fondazione Magna Carta.

Marchetto, A. 2005. *Il Concilio Ecumenico Vaticano II: Contrappunto per la sua storia*. Vatican City: Libreria Editrice Vaticana.

Marshall, Ruth. 2009. *Political Spiritualities: The Pentecostal Revolution in Nigeria*. Chicago: University of Chicago Press.

Martínez de Velasco, J. 2002. *Los Legionarios de Cristo: El nuevo ejército del papa*. [Madrid]: La Esfera de los Libros.

Martini, Carlo Maria. 2000. "Discorso alla città di Milano alla vigilia di St. Ambrogio, 6 December." http://www.we-are-church.org/it/attual/Martini -Famiglia.html. Last accessed 30 January 2014.

Massumi, Brian. 1995. "The Autonomy of Affect." *Cultural Critique* 31:83–109.

———. 2002. *Parables for the Virtual: Movement, Affect, Sensation.* Durham, N.C.: Duke University Press.

Matovina, Timothy. 2005. *Guadalupe and Her Faithful: Latino Catholics in San Antonio, from Colonial Origins to the Present.* Baltimore: Johns Hopkins University Press.

Mayblin, Maya, and Magnum Course. 2014. "The Other Side of Sacrifice." *Ethnos* 79 (3): 307–19.

Mayblin, Maya, Valentina Napolitano, and Kristin Norget, forthcoming, 2016. *The Anthropology of Catholicism: A Companion Reader.* Berkeley: University of California Press.

McClintock, Anne. 1995. *Imperial Leather: Race, Gender and Sexuality in the Colonial Contest.* New York: Routledge.

Menjivar, Cecilia. 1999. "Religion Institutions and Transnationalism: A Case Study of Catholic and Evangelical Salvadorian Immigrants." *International Journal of Politics, Culture and Society* 12 (4): 589–612.

Meyer, Jean A. 1973. *La cristiada.* México: Siglo Veintiuno Editores.

———. 1976. *The Cristero Rebellion: The Mexican People between Church and State, 1926–1929.* New York: Cambridge University Press.

Miccoli, Giovanni. 2007. *In difesa della fede: La Chiesa di Giovanni Paolo II e Benedetto XVI.* Milan: Rizzoli.

Mignolo, Walter. 2011. "Crossing Gazes and the Silence of the 'Indians': Theodor de Bry and Guamán Poma de Ayala." *Journal of Medieval and Early Modern Studies* 1 (41): 173–223.

Mitchell, W. J. T. 2005. *What Do Pictures Want?: The Lives and Loves of Images.* Chicago: University of Chicago Press.

Molina, J. Michelle. 2008. "Technologies of the Self: The Letters of Eighteenth-Century Mexican Jesuit Spiritual Daughters." *History of Religions* 47 (4): 282–303.

Montezemolo, Fiamma, René Peralta, and Heriberto Yépez. 2006. *Aquí es Tijuana!* London: Black Dog.

Mookherjee, Nannike. 2011. "The Aesthetics of Nations: Anthropological and Historical Approaches." *Journal of the Royal Anthropological Institute* 17 (S1): 1–20.

Moore, Henrietta L. 2007. *The Subject of Anthropology: Gender, Symbolism and Psychoanalysis.* Cambridge: Polity.

Morgan, David. 1998. *Visual Piety: A History and Theory of Popular Religious Images.* Berkeley: University of California Press.

———. 2005. *The Sacred Gaze: Religious Visual Culture in Theory and Practice.* Berkeley: University of California Press.

———. 2008. *The Sacred Heart of Jesus: The Visual Evolution of a Devotion.* Amsterdam: Amsterdam University Press.

————. 2009. "The Look of Sympathy: Religion, Visual Culture, and the Social Life of Feeling." *Material Religion* 5 (2): 131–53.

Muehlebach, Andrea. 2009. "Complexio Oppositorum: Notes on the Left in Neoliberal Italy." *Public Culture* 21 (3): 495–515.

————. 2011. "On Affective Labor in Post-Fordist Italy." *Cultural Anthropology* 26 (1): 59–82.

————. 2013. "The Catholicization of Neoliberalism: On Love and Welfare in Lombardy, Italy." *American Anthropologist* 115 (3): 452–65.

Mutolo, A. 2005. "The Mexican Episcopate during the Religious Conflict in Mexico from 1926 to 1929." *Cuicuilco* 12 (35): 117–36.

Napolitano, Valentina. 2002. *Migration, Mujercitas, and Medicine Men: Living in Urban Mexico*. Berkeley: University of California Press.

————. 2007. "Of Migrant Revelations and Anthropological Awakenings." *Social Anthropology* 15 (1): 71–87.

————. 2015. "Anthropology and Traces." *Anthropological Theory* 15 (1):47–67.

Napolitano, Valentina, and Kristin Norget. 2011. "Economies of Sanctities." *Postscripts: The Journal of Sacred Texts and Contemporary Worlds* 5 (3): 251–64.

Napolitano, Valentina, and David Pratten. 2007. "Michel De Certeau: Ethnography and the Challenge of Plurality." *Social Anthropology* 15 (1): 1–12.

Navaro-Yashin, Yael. 2007. "Make-Believe Papers, Legal Forms and the Counterfeit: Affective Interactions between Documents and People in Britain and Cyprus." *Anthropological Theory* 7 (1): 79–98.

————. 2012. *The Make-Believe Space: Affective Geography in a Postwar Polity*. Durham, N.C.: Duke University Press.

Norget, Kristin. 2004. "'Knowing Where We Enter': Indigenous Theology and the Popular Church in Oaxaca, Mexico." In *Resurgent Voices in Latin America: Indigenous Peoples, Political Mobilization, and Religious Change*, edited by E. L. Cleary and T. J. Steigenga, 154–86. New Brunswick, N.J.: Rutgers University Press.

O'Meara, Thomas F. 1992. "The Dominican School of Salamanca and the Spanish Conquest of America: Some Bibliographic Notes." *Thomist* 56 (4): 555–82.

O'Neill, Kevin L. 2010a. "The Reckless Will: Prison Chaplaincy and the Problem of Mara Salvatrucha." *Public Culture* 22 (1): 67–88.

————. 2010b. "I Want More of You: The Politics of Christian Eroticism in Postwar Guatemala." *Comparative Studies in Society and History* 52 (1): 131–56.

Orsi, Robert A. 1985. *The Madonna of 115th Street: Faith and Community in Italian Harlem, 1880–1950*. New Haven, Conn.: Yale University Press.

————. 1996. *Thank You, St. Jude: Women's Devotion to the Patron Saint of Hopeless Causes*. New Haven, Conn.: Yale University Press.

————. 2005. *Between Heaven and Earth: The Religious Worlds People Make and the Scholars Who Study Them*. Princeton, N.J.: Princeton University Press.

————. 2007. "When 2 + 2 = 5." *American Scholar* 76 (2): 34–43.

————. 2009. "Abundant History: Marian Apparitions as Alternative Modernity." In *Moved by Mary: The Power of Pilgrimage in the Modern World*, edited by A. Hermkens, W. Jansen, and C. Notermans, 215–25. Burlington, Vt.: Ashgate.

Paerregaard, K. 2008. "In the Footsteps of the Lord of Miracles: The Expatriation of Religious Icons in the Peruvian Diaspora." *Journal of Ethnic and Migration Studies* 34 (7): 1073–89.

———. 2010. "The Show Must Go On: The Role of Fiestas in Andean Transnational Migration." *Latin American Perspectives* 37 (5): 50.

Pagden, Anthony. 1982. *The Fall of Natural Man: The American Indian and the Origins of Comparative Ethnology*. New York: Cambridge University Press.

———. 1994. *The Uncertainties of Empire: Essays in Iberian and Ibero-American Intellectual History*. Brookfield, Vt.: Ashgate.

Palumbo, Bernardino. 2004. "'The War of the Saints": Religion, Politics, and the Poetics of Time in a Sicilian Town." *Comparative Studies in Society and History* 46 (1): 4–34.

Pandolfo, Stefania. 2007. "'The Burning': Finitude and the Politico-Theological Imagination of Illegal Migration." *Anthropological Theory* 7 (3): 329–63.

Paul VI. 1964. *Lumen Gentium*. http://www.vatican.va/archive/hist_councils/ii_vatican_council/documents/vat-ii_const_19641121_lumen-gentium_en.html.

Peña, Elaine. A. 2011. *Performing Piety: Making Space Sacred with the Virgin of Guadalupe*. Berkeley: University of California Press.

Pera, Marcello, and J. Ratzinger. 2004. *Senza radici*. Milan: Mondadori.

Pérez, L. E. 2007. *Chicana Art: The Politics of Spiritual and Aesthetic Altarities*. Durham, N.C.: Duke University Press.

Phillips, A. 2012. "Judas' Gift: In Praise of Betrayal." *London Review of Books* 34 (1): 14.

Pius XI. 1939. *Divini Illius Magistri*. http://w2.vatican.va/content/pius-xi/en/encyclicals/documents/hf_p-xi_enc_31121929_divini-illius-magistri.html.

Pius XII. 1952. *Exsul Familia*. http://www.papalencyclicals.net/Pius12/p12exsul.htm.

Pontifical Council for the Pastoral Care of Migrants and Itinerant People. 2004. *Erga Migrantes Caritas Christi*. http://www.vatican.va/roman_curia/pontifical_councils/migrants/documents/rc_pc_migrants_doc_20040514_erga-migrantes-caritas-christi_en. html. Last accessed 15 March 2014.

Portes, A., and Josh DeWind, eds. 2007. *Rethinking Migration: New Theoretical and Empirical Perspectives*. New York: Berghahn Books.

Portes, Alejandro, and Rubén G. Rumbaut. 2006. *Immigrant America: A Portrait*. Berkeley: University of California Press.

Povinelli, Elizabeth. A. 2006. *The Empire of Love: Toward a Theory of Intimacy, Genealogy, and Carnality*. Durham, N.C.: Duke University Press.

Pozzi, Giovanni. 1993. *Sull'orlo del visibile parlare*. Milan: Adelphi.

Pratt, Geraldine. 1999. "Geographies of Identity and Difference: Marking Boundaries." In *Human Geography Today*, edited by D. Massey, J. Allen, and P. Sarre, 151–67. Cambridge: Polity Press.

———. 2005. "Abandoned Women and Spaces of the Exception." *Antipode* 37 (5): 1053–78.

———. 2009. "Circulating Sadness: Witnessing Filipina Mothers' Stories of Family Separation." *Gender, Place and Culture* 16 (1): 3–22.

Pratt, Geraldine, and Caleb Johnston, C. 2007. "Turning Theatre into Law, and Other Spaces of Politics." *Cultural Geographies* 14 (1): 92–113.

Pritchard, Elizabeth A. 2010. "Seriously, What Does 'Taking Religion Seriously' Mean?" *Journal of the American Academy of Religion* 78 (4): 1087–1111.

Quayson Napolitano, V. 2005. "Social Suffering and Embodied States of Male Transnational Migrancy in San Francisco, California." *Identities: Global Studies in Culture and Power* 12 (3): 335–62.

Quayson, Ato. 2012. *The Cambridge History of Postcolonial Literature.* Cambridge: Cambridge University Press.

Queirolo Palmas, Lucas. 2004. "Oltre la doppia assenza: Percezioni di cittadinanza fra gli ecuadoriani di Genova." *Studi Emigrazione* 154:319–40.

Quiroza, Marco E. 1991. "Colf Latino-Americane a Roma." In *Per una società multiculturale*, edited by Maria Macioti. Naples: Liguori.

Radcliffe, Sarah A., and Sallie Westwood. 1996. *Remaking the Nation.* London: Routledge.

Rahner, Karl, S.J. [1981] 1967. "'Behold This Heart!': Preliminaries to a Theology of Devotion to the Sacred Heart." In *Theological Investigations,* vol. 3. New York: Crossroad.

Raijman, Rebeca, Silvina Schammah-Gesser, and Adriana Kemp. 2003. "International Migration, Domestic Work, and Care Work: Undocumented Latina Migrants in Israel." *Gender and Society* 17 (5): 727–49.

Rashkin, Esther. 2008. *Unspeakable Secrets and the Psychoanalysis of Culture.* Albany: State University of New York Press.

Ratzinger, Joseph. 1990. "Concerning the Notion of Person in Theology." *Communio* 17:439–54.

———. 2000. *The Spirit of the Liturgy.* San Francisco: Ignatius Press.

———. 2007. *Europe Today and Tomorrow: Addressing the Fundamental Issues.* San Francisco: Ignatius Press.

Remotti, Franco. 2008. *Contro natura: Una lettera al papa.* Rome: Laterza.

Reynolds, Thomas E. 2008. *Vulnerable Communion: A Theology of Disability and Hospitality.* Grand Rapids, Mich.: Brazos Press.

Robbins, Joel. 2007. "Causality, Ethics, and the Near Future." *American Ethnologist* 34 (3): 433–36.

———. 2008. "On Alterity and the Sacred in the Age of Globalization. Is the Trans- in Transnational the Trans- in Transcendent?" *Mana* 14 (1): 119–39.

———. 2010. "Anthropology, Pentecostalism, and the New Paul: Conversion, Event, and Social Transformation." *South Atlantic Quarterly* 109 (4): 633.

———. 2011. "Transcendence and the Anthropology of Christianity: Language, Change, and Individualism." *Journal of Finnish Anthropological Society* 37 (2): 5–23.

Romano, Sergio. 2005. *Libera chiesa, libero stato?: Il Vaticano e l'italia da Pio IX a Benedetto XVI.* Milan: Longanesi.

Rosas, Gilberto. 2006. "The Thickening Borderlands: Diffused Exceptionality and 'Immigrant' Social Struggles During the 'War On Terror.'" *Cultural Dynamics* 18 (3): 335–49.

Rose, Jacqueline. 2007. *The Last Resistance.* London: Verso.

Rosoli, Gianfausto, ed. 1989. *Scalabrini tra vecchio e nuovo mondo: Atti del convegno storico internazionale (piacenza, 3–5 dicembre 1987).* Rome: Centro Studi Emigrazione.

Ryan, Louise. 2002. "Sexualising Emigration: Discourses of Irish Female Emigration in the 1930s." *Women's Studies International Forum* 25 (1): 51–66.

Sánchez, Miguel. 1648. *Imagen de la Virgen María, Madre de Dios de Guadalupe milagrosamente aparecida en la Ciudad de México.* Mexico Ciy: Viuda de Bernardo Calderon.

Santner, Eric L. 2005. "Miracles Happen: Benjamin, Rosenzweig, Freud, and the Matter of the Neighbor." In *The Neighbor: Three Inquiries in Political Theology,* edited by S. Žižek, E. L. Santner, and K. Reinhard. Chicago: University of Chicago Press.

Sayad, Abdelmalek. 1975. "Elghorba: Le mécanisme de reproduction de l'émigration." *Actes de la Recherche en Sciences Sociales* 1 (2): 50–66.

———. 1993. "Naturels et Naturalises." *Actes de la Recherche en Sciences Sociales* 99:26–35.

———. 2004. *The Suffering of the Immigrant.* Cambridge: Polity Press.

Scalabrini, Giovanni Battista. 1997. *Scalabrini e le migrazioni moderne: Scritti e carteggi.* Turin: Società Editrice Internazionale.

Scalabriniani, A. C. 2005. *Migrazioni e modelli di pastorale.* Rome: Direzione Generale dei Missionari Scalabriniani.

Schedler, Andreas. 2007. "The Mobilization of Distrust." *Journal of Democracy* 18:88–102.

Scheper-Hughes, Nancy. 1992. *Death without Weeping: The Violence of Everyday Life in Brazil.* Berkeley: University of California Press.

Schmidt Camacho, Alicia. 2008. *Migrant Imaginaries.* New York: New York University Press.

Schmitt, Carl. 1996. *Roman Catholicism and Political Form.* Translated by Georg L. Ulmen. Westport, Conn.: Greenwood Press.

Schulte van Kessel, Elisja S. 1993. "Virgins and Mothers between Heaven and Earth." In *Renaissance and Enlightenment Paradoxes,* edited by Natalie Zemon Davis and Arlette Farge, 132–66. Cambridge, Mass.: Harvard University Press.

Silverblatt, Irene M. 2004. *Modern Inquisitions: Peru and the Colonial Origins of the Civilized World.* Durham, N.C.: Duke University Press.

Skrbiš, Zlatko. 2005. "The Apparitions of the Virgin Mary of Medjugorje: The Convergence of Croatian Nationalism and Her Apparitions." *Nations and Nationalism* 11 (3): 443–61.

Sodi, Manlio. 2007. *Ubi petrus ibi ecclesia: Sui sentieri del Concilio Vaticano II.* Rome: Libreria Ateneo Salesiano.

Squadrito, Kathleen M. 1979. "Locke's View of Dominion." *Environmental Ethics* 1 (3): 255–65.

Stepick, Alex, Terry Rey, and Sarah J. Mahler, eds. 2009. *Churches and Charity in the Immigrant City: Religion, Immigration, and Civic Engagement in Miami.* New Brunswick, N.J.: Rutgers University Press.

Stevens, Scott Manning. 1997. "Sacred Heart and Secular Brain." In *The Body in Parts*, edited by H. David and C. Mazzio, 263–82. New York: Routledge.

Stoler, Ann L. 2008. "Imperial Debris: Reflections on Ruins and Ruination." *Cultural Anthropology* 23 (2): 191–219.

Striffler, Steve. 2007. "Neither Here Nor There: Mexican Immigrant Workers and the Search for Home." *American Ethnologist* 34 (4): 674–88.

Taussig, Michael T. 1992. *The Nervous System.* New York: Routledge.

———. 1997. *The Magic of the State.* New York: Routledge.

———. 1999. *Defacement: Public Secrecy and the Labor of the Negative.* Stanford, Calif.: Stanford University Press.

Taylor, Charles. 2007. *A Secular Age.* Cambridge, Mass.: Belknap Press of Harvard University Press.

Terpstra, Nicholas. 2010. *Lost Girls: Sex and Death in Renaissance Florence.* Baltimore: Johns Hopkins University Press.

Ticktin, Miriam I. 2011. *Casualties of Care: Immigration and the Politics of Humanitarianism in France.* Berkeley: University of California Press.

Tierney, Brian. 2004. "The Idea of Natural Rights: Origins and Persistence." *Northwestern Journal of International Human Rights* 2 (1): 1–12.

Todorov, Tzvetan. 1984. *The Conquest of America: The Question of the Other.* New York: Harper and Row.

Tomasi, Silvano M. 2011. Statement for the Application by the Holy See for Membership in the International Migration Organization. 5 December 2011. http://www.vatican.va/roman_curia/secretariat_state/2011/docu ments/rc_seg-st_20111205_membership-iom_en.html.

Tomasi, Silvano, and Gianfausto Rosoli, eds.1997. *Scalabrini e le migrazioni moderne: Scritti e carteggi.* Turin: Società Editrice Internazionale.

Torre, Andrea T., and Luca Queirolo Palmas, eds. 2005. *Il fantasma delle bande: Genova e i latinos.* Genoa: Fratelli Frilli Editori.

Torres Robles, Alfonso. 2001. *La prodigiosa aventura de los Legionarios de Cristo.* Madrid: Foca.

Traslosheros, Jorge E. 2002. "Señora de la historia, Madra Mestiza, Reina de México: La coronación de la Virgen de Guadalupe y su actualizacíon como mito fundacional de la patria, 1895." *Signos Historicós* 7:105–47.

Tsing, Anna. 2005. *Friction: An Ethnography of Global Connection.* Princeton, N.J.: Princeton University Press.

Tweed, Thomas A. 1997. *Our Lady of the Exile: Diasporic Religion at a Cuban Catholic Shrine in Miami.* New York: Oxford University Press.

———. 2006. *Crossing and Dwelling: A Theory of Religion.* Cambridge, Mass.: Harvard University Press.

Varley, Ann. 2008. "A Place Like This? Stories of Dementia, Home, and the Self." *Environment and Planning D, Society and Space* 26 (1): 47–67.

Vásquez, Manuel A. 2011. *More Than Belief: A Materialist Theory of Religion.* New York: Oxford University Press.

Vásquez, Manuel A., and Marie F. Marquardt. 2000. "Globalizing the Rainbow Madonna: Old Time Religion in the Present Age." *Theory, Culture and Society* 17 (4): 119–43.

———. 2003. *Globalizing the Sacred: Religion across the Americas.* New Brunswick, N.J.: Rutgers University Press.

Vaughan, Mary Kay, and Stephen E. Lewis. 2006. *The Eagle and the Virgin: Nation and Cultural Revolution in Mexico, 1920–1940.* Durham, N.C.: Duke University Press.

Von Vacano, Diego A. 2012. *The Color of Citizenship: Race, Modernity and Latin American/Hispanic Political Thought.* New York: Oxford University Press.

Warner, Michael, Jonathan Van Antwerpen, and Craig J. Calhoun, eds. 2010. *Varieties of Secularism in a Secular Age.* Cambridge, Mass.: Harvard University Press.

Williams, Raymond. 1977. *Marxism and Literature.* Oxford: Oxford University Press.

Wolf, Eric. 1958. "The Virgin of Guadalupe: A Mexican National Symbol." *Journal of American Folklore* 71 (279): 34–39.

Wright-Rios, Edward N. 2004. "Indian Saints and Nation-States: Ignacio Manuel Altamirano's Landscapes and Legends." *Mexican Studies* 20 (1): 47–98.

Yeates, Nicola. 2011. "The Irish Catholic Female Religious and the Transnationalisation of Care: An Historical Perspective." *Irish Journal of Sociology* 19 (2): 77–93.

Zagrebelsky, Gustavo. 2008. *Contro l'etica della verità.* Bari: Laterza.

Zambarbieri, Annibale. 1987. "Per la storia della devozione del sacro cuore in Italia tra '800 e '900." *Rivista della Storia della Chiesa in Italia* 2:361–432.

Zambrano, Maria. [1955] 2008. *L'uomo e il divino.* Rome: Edizioni Lavoro.

Žižek, Slavoj. 2000. *The Ticklish Subject: The Absent Centre of Political Ontology.* London: Verso.

Index

affects, 11; and Atlantic return, 6, 87,
91, 93; and betrayal, 107, 117; and
Berlant, Lauren, 184n11, 185n33,
194n40; and Brennan, Teresa,
201n2; and carnality, 9, 97, 105,
179–80; and Catholic Church, 3,
17, 92; and devotions, 10, 85, 111;
and excess of signification, 143; of
fear and shame, 27; and histories, 2,
13, 54, 70, 91, 94, 98, 117, 125, 128,
145–47; and the homely, 101, 118;
and labour, 29, 39, 100, 151, 167,
170, 171; and Legionaries of Christ,
88–90, 93–94, 142; and migrant
itineraries, 7, 13, 37, 101, 105, 149,
172; and nation, 18, 39, 47, 57, 64,
157; and object–subject relations,
162; and Sacred Heart, 111, 116,
117; and Señor de los Milagros,
124; and sexuality and intimacy,
48, 97, 159, 177; and solitude, 164;
and Spinoza, 12; and subjectivity,
65; and theory of, 11, 12, 131, 179,
185n33, 188n1, 196n50, 197n4,
201n58; and Virgin of Guadalupe,
127, 136–39; and walls, 151, 154,
159, 162, 165, 178. See also betrayal;
desfase
Agamben, Giorgio, 60, 61, 92, 177,
185n21, 195nn48,50, 200n55,
208n36, 209nn3,5
Ahmed, Sara, 25, 157, 188
Alemanno, Gianni, 17, 19–20, 26–28,
30, 36, 40–41, 84, 189n22

anthropology of Catholicism, 8–10,
93, 185n36. See also Critical Catholic Studies
Atlantic return, 2–3, 5, 7, 8, 13, 16, 18,
37, 56, 66, 84, 176; and abjection,
17; affective, 6, 14–15, 66, 91, 98,
143; and Catholic hearts, 125; and
Cristero War, 91; and everyday
life, 151–52, 155, 160, 172–73; and
impossibility of return, 180; and
Legionaries of Christ, 70, 78, 84,
87, 95, 120; and mimesis between
religious orders, 93–94; and new
evangelization, 126; and sameness
and otherness, 53; and Virgin of
Guadalupe, 127–28, 131–32, 146
Augustine, 55

badanti: cases of, 101–3, 115–16, 120;
definition of, 5, 184n8; in Italy, 29,
190, 144; and space, 159–64
Bartolomé de la Casas, 39, 54,
194n31
Benedict XVI (pope): Atlantic return,
7, 70; and *Caritas in Veritate*,
198n26; and Catholic migrant pedagogies, 39, 51, 59, 70, 108, 110; and
Catholicization of neoliberalism,
198–99n26; and civitas (romana),
176; and culture of life, 10–11, 52,
60–61, 125, 193n22; and *Erga
Migrantes Caritas Christi*, 59; and
Guardini, Romano, 196n60; and
Legionaries of Christ, 94–95; and